The Making of the Modern Chinese State

Humphrey Ko

The Making of the Modern Chinese State

Cement, Legal Personality, and Industry

palgrave
macmillan

Humphrey Ko
University China Centre
Oxford, United Kingdom

ISBN 978-981-10-2659-1 ISBN 978-981-10-2660-7 (eBook)
DOI 10.1007/978-981-10-2660-7

Library of Congress Control Number: 2016959015

Printed on acid-free paper

This Palgrave Macmillan imprint is published by Springer Nature
The registered company is Springer Nature Singapore Pte Ltd.
The registered company address is: 152 Beach Road, #22-06/08 Gateway East, Singapore 189721, Singapore

Acknowledgements

My gratitude must go to Rana Mitter at the University of Oxford for his sterling advice in encouraging me to take this research beyond the common ambit of historical studies. I have greatly benefited from his sharp intellectual insights and constructive comments, and I am thankful for his patience in guiding this research to its final conclusion and publication. I also wish to express my special appreciation for the many inspiring discussions with David Faure who initially urged me to embark upon this study of the cement industry, as well as enlightening me on many obscure aspects of Chinese history. Historical research inevitably necessitated the assistance and advice of many people. In this respect, I should like to thank May Bo Ching, Robert Bickers, Weipin Tsai and Chih-yun Chang for their assistance with accessing the archives and materials in China; Tim Wright, Tim Brook, Chloë Starr, Anne Gerritsen, Matthew Johnson, Christopher Munn, Karl Gerth and Dorothy Solinger, for their constructive remarks at various stages; as well as my friends and contemporaries at Oxford and beyond for their the comments, advice and counsel. These include Tim McGuire, Toby Lincoln, Wah Guan Lim and Minling Liang. The invaluable advice from Flemming Christiansen and unremitting guidance from Henrietta Harrison in the initial stages were imperative to the timely completion of this project. Their continuing support and encouragement from afar in Duisburg and Harvard kept me spirited and determined throughout the present study. Furthermore, special thanks must be given to Elisabeth Köll for reading and commenting on an early draft of this book despite the minefields of errors. I am also grateful to Michael West, who generously helped me to identify many mistakes and inconsistencies; and to Amanda Zhang and Beatrice Chu, both of whom lent a helping hand at difficult junctures during the publication stage of this work. Finally, I am forever indebted to the late Professor Philip St John Smart of the Faculty of Law at the University of Hong Kong, who introduced me to the subtle significance of legal personality.

The China Centre Oxford 24 May 2016

Contents

Abbreviations

CCP	Chinese Communist Party
CMC	China Merchants Steam Navigation Company
CPPCC	Chinese People's Political Consultative Conference
GCG	Guangzhou City Government
GCW	Guangdong Cement Works
GDPG	The Guangdong Provincial Government (*Guangdong sheng zhengfu*)
GSME	A General Survey of Municipal Enterprises
GZCA	The Guangzhou City Archives
GZCG	The Guangzhou City Government (*Guangzhou shi zhengfu*)
IE-SASS	Institute of Economics of the Shanghai Academy of Social Science
KMT	The Nationalist Party (*Guomindang*)
NRC	National Resources Commission
PRC	People's Republic of China
ROC	Republic of China
SASS	Shanghai Academy of Social Science
SHAC	Second Historical Archives of China

List of Figures

List of Tables

CHAPTER 1

Introduction: China, Cement and Corporations

A systemic and structural difficulty facing China since the Opium War in the middle of the nineteenth century was the arrival of corporations from the West. Western-type incorporated companies were introduced into the Chinese state in 1904. This progressively gave form to an underlying structure around which history revolved and evolved. The fundamental structural change brought about by the introduction of corporations has so far received very little scholarly attention that concerns China's modern history and its "struggle with the modern world". The imperial state of late Qing China attempted to emulate the industrialisation of Western powers. Yet, as it embarked upon this task it had to grapple with more than the scientific, technical and logistical challenges thrown up by industrialisation. It had to manage the effects caused by corporations, which form the invisible structural backbone of the modern industrialisation process. Initially the empire did not attempt to adopt the corporation, which is a fictitious "legal personality" or "corporate personality". Instead, it attempted to embrace modern industrial and commercial businesses by merely adjusting its ancient imperial system to suit the new modern requirements for industrial ownership and development. Unfortunately, this failed and the empire also failed because both a modern state and a modern corporate law were needed to accommodate the new kind of business entities which sprouted from industrialisation.

This book will tell the story of how the Chinese state struggled with these modern business entities in their incorporated conditions, and

H. Ko, *The Making of the Modern Chinese State*,
DOI 10.1007/978-981-10-2660-7_1

how major political figures such as Sun Yat-sen, Yuan Shikai and Chiang Kai-shek were involved in this process. This book argues for the centrality of the Company Law of 1904, which recognised the corporation as an independent institution and in so doing fundamentally weakened the Chinese state. This is an effort at combining the political history of late Qing and Republican China with business history and legal history. Using the cement industry as a case study, this book focuses on three specific cement companies, which coincidentally were the first three established and functional inside China. They also represent three different types of companies. One was the Qixin Cement Company, which was founded during the Self-Strengthening Movement in North China as an unincorporated imperial firm but was incorporated by Yuan Shikai in 1906. This was a top-down incorporated company. Another was the Guangdong Cement Works, founded in 1906–09 in South China by provincial officials and run by them as a top-down *un*incorporated company. The third was the Shanghai Portland Cement Company, founded by the industrialist Liu Hongsheng in the mid-1920s as a bottom-up incorporated company in East China. This work treats the story of each of these three companies in their contextual background in three parts. The time span goes from the 1880s to the Communist takeover in 1949, and the three parts are examined in a largely chronological order.

This work will show that the enterprises founded during the Self-Strengthening Movement in the late nineteenth century may appear like companies—they issued stocks, for example—but they lacked the legally recognised independent status of modern corporations. As a result, they were subjected to political machinations and had no defensive shelter. The Company Law of 1904 changed the situation entirely. Owing to the fact that it was incorporated, the Qixin company founded by Yuan Shikai was beyond the reach of the Qing court. It thus started an erosion of the empire's political power while enhancing Yuan's own economic power and bringing on the Revolution of 1911. In the Republican era after the collapse of imperial China, the local Guangdong government failed to embrace incorporated industries in the late 1920s and early 1930s. Rather, it relied on the Guangzhou City Government as the corporation to consolidate economic power. Yet, redeploying the pre-modern Qing system of enterprise holding (i.e., *guanban*, *shangban* and *guandu shangban*) did not work in Republican China. This history shows that halting the introduction of Western corporate legal entities in a modernising and industrialising China is unsustainable. Furthermore, corporations flourished in the early Republic, allowing a self-made man like Liu Hongsheng to become wealthy and powerful. But the pendulum began to swing the other way as Chiang Kai-shek took power. By establishing the National Resources Commission around 1932, Chiang began the long process of recapturing economic power at the national level, even as he continued to recognise corporations and legal personality. The Communists, in 1954, went further than Chiang by destroying corporations and corporate personality. In this respect, China in the 1950s went back in time to the situation in the 1880s.

Corporate or *legal personality* (these two terms are used interchangeably) is a Roman invention but it has evolved into the economic and constitutional structures of modern industrial states. Its *commercial* manifestation—the modern business (or commercial) corporation—is the definitive vehicle for industrialisation and its use is almost universal in the modern industrialised world. Its *governmental* manifestation is the constitutional state, which is also the foundation of all modern industrialised countries. This book will show that an indistinct but important approach in unlocking the complexities of modern Chinese history is to understand the struggle for the creation of a modern state that could accommodate the modern industrial and commercial businesses brought by industrialisation. This, however, is defined by the limits that legal personality imposed. The *commercial corporation* and the *constitutional state* both have legal personalities. They are two entities of the same kind and therefore they may complement or conflict with each other. This leads to an important understanding: a stable modern constitutional state is one that *accommodates* the industrial economy by way of legal personality in the form of modern legal corporations. This also means that the "range of choices" available to historical political actors and the "consequences of those choices" were limited by constraints imposed by legal personality.[1] In other words, legal personality defines modern China. This work traces how legal or corporate personality shaped modern China through the lens of a major industrial business: cement. This industry had individual enterprises *incorporated* and *un*incorporated at different times and at different locations, from late Qing to the early People's Republic, all of which interacted in some way with China's power-holders and institutions.

At first glance, cement (an industrial product) and corporations (a legal entity) seem remote from each other. The former is a physical material and the latter is an abstract legal concern. A closer examination, however, will reveal that they have a common origin: both are Roman inventions and, furthermore, both are in fact important building blocks in the modern industrial society in which we live and work.[2] They surround and engulf us: buildings, roads and sewage facilities are built with cement not dissimilar to that used in ancient Roman times two millennia ago. Large modern enterprises and other associations such as railways, banks and universities are organised around large organisations with legally recognised corporate personalities first seen in ancient Rome. It is interesting to note that both cement and legal personality arrived in China around the same time in the late Qing Dynasty, through growing Western contact. So, what kind of effects did these ancient Roman ideas have on an ancient Chinese imperial system? In order to highlight the importance of legal personality in modern Chinese history and further the understanding of this modern idea and its different manifestations, this chapter will first review the history of legal or corporate personality. This will begin by showing how it evolved into different forms in England before it was introduced to China by the British-trained barrister and imperial minister Wu Tingfang when he was involved in the drafting of the first imperial Chinese company law.[3]

What Is a Corporation?

Corporate or Legal personality manifests itself as a corporation. A corporation is a *corporate person* or *legal person*. This is an artificial legal entity created by law and formed through the process of incorporation. A corporation could be constituted by a number of natural persons or other legal entities but it always possesses a separate legal identity from them. As a legal entity the corporation receives legal rights and duties. Some rights always exist for a corporation: the ability to sue and be sued; the right to hold assets independent of the assets of its members; the right to hire agents thus employing staff; the right to a common seal thus bestowing to the corporation the right to sign contracts; and the right to make regulations to govern its internal affairs.

A corporation could have perpetual succession as well as being vested by the law with the capacity to act as an individual in many respects. The type of corporation that is dominant in the modern world is the modern commercial corporation. In addition to legal personality, the modern commercial corporation has other legal characteristics. Firstly, "transferable shares", which means changing of members, will not affect the legal identity or the existence of the corporation; secondly, the capacity for "perpetual succession" despite membership withdrawals; and lastly, "limited liability", which limits the liability of the members for debts or acts of the corporation. The "members" of this kind of modern commercial corporation are the "shareholders". Other forms of corporations do exist and they existed throughout history before the emergence of the modern commercial corporation that has become very common in the contemporary world owing to its ease of formation. Entrepreneurs can easily incorporate companies to facilitate their commercial activities. Moreover, corporations are also formed for social, political, governmental, religious and charitable purposes, giving them legal personality status under law. Legally, any group that has legal personality is referred to as a *corporation*. Historically, integrating the traditional corporation with the joint stock company (an *un*incorporated trading concern) gave birth to the commercial corporation.[4] The practical character and theoretical nature of this abstract Western concept is also very important to the formation of all modern states. In order to comprehend the corporate idea's innate essence and inherent characteristics, it is wise to first understand its developmental history in England under the protection of English common law before this version was introduced into China in 1904.

The corporation is an idea borrowed from Roman law, and corporations existed under the late Roman Republic. They were called "universities" (*Universitates*), and their members were called "associates". They could sue and be sued in a common name. Yet, they were not made by the state and thus unrelated to the state at all. They held property in their own name but the associates had no individual interest. They acted through agents who were chosen by a majority vote and could also adopt by-laws. The property of the university was liable for its debts, but the property of the associates was out of reach and, therefore, achieved limited liability in this way. The corporation is thus different from the associates. There is no record of Roman corporations surviving in England, though it has been contended that the corporate status of the Universities of Oxford and Cambridge had Roman foundations. Their corporate entity is complete but they were not created by any act of the English crown. The modern corporation did not grow out of this Roman foundation but had different origins. Two foundations are attributed to the modern English corporation. One is the institution of the *boroughs* of England. The other was the purely private commercial entity of the *trade guilds*.[5]

Boroughs were towns having citadels or means of common defence. Men joined themselves to a borough for protection against raiders, overlords and ultimately the king himself. It was neither through the benefit of the clergy nor the state that bestowed it with corporate personality. Most boroughs received royal charters in the time of King Henry VI but they were corporations well before that time. Thus, the crown was gathering to itself the governing power of the borough, albeit gradually. This is because in substance the borough was an instrument of government, and it was not easy to separate its existence from that of the state. This royal permission was wanted by the boroughs because they wished to exercise certain state powers. The boroughs thus maintained a corporate character. Yet, they gathered to it *governmental functions*, which in England ultimately became a crown-delegated function. A royal charter thus had two facets to it. Firstly, it was a recognition of an existing corporate entity; secondly, it was *a grant of governmental power*. As for the trade guilds, these represent a parallel corporate development in time but separate development in concept. These also sought and received royal charters in pre-Elizabethan times. Likewise, their corporate character predated their charter. The guild was a *private* association for *private* purposes but, except for a few rare exceptions, demanded no governmental powers.[6]

Columbia University law professor Adolf A. Berle, Jr.,[7] writing in 1928 analysing the nature of corporations one year before the Great Depression caused by sweeping corporate failures, believes that by the time of James II, the policy was to limit ancient corporate rights of the guilds and boroughs. Thus, the boroughs especially were up in arms because "this made the old corporations unsafe and the new ones reflected royal monopolies or exactions". Berle contended that this was at least one of the causes for the revolution of 1688. This is because the general feeling was that their ancient rights and liberties were no longer safe. As such, the old incorporated cities and guilds of England welcomed the enthronement of William and Mary with open arms in this "Glorious" revolution.[8]

How Are Governments and Corporations Related?

By the nineteenth century, this traditional idea of a corporation was integrated with the joint stock company (an *un*incorporated trading concern which can issue shares to investors) to form the modern commercial corporation in the English Companies Act of 1862.[9] Whatever the complexities surrounding this Act's effect in England, it means that the modern English Parliament had agreed to mass production of commercial corporations by simple and low-cost *registration*. At the same time it achieved a balance between commercial efficacy, regulatory necessity, liability incidence and risk control. More fundamentally, however, what the history of the boroughs and guilds shows is that boroughs (public governments) and guilds (private business associations) are fundamentally similar in nature. Understanding this is crucial to understanding the changes that took place in the Chinese state in the twentieth century. Both the state and companies can acquire legal personality and their functions are in fact interchangeable. By nature, they possess the same characteristics under a general law such as the ancient common law of England.[10]

Therefore, it is clear that modern governments and companies are analogous creatures both evolving in Western legal systems. This analogy was first pointed out and explained in 1885 by Albert Venn Dicey[11] at Oxford and simplified for understanding by London School of Economics law professor Laurence C. B. Gower in 1954[12]:

(1) A company, whether statutory, charted or registered will have its basic constitution set out in its statute, charter or memorandum of association, respectively. It is important to note that this constitutional document defines its existence as a corporate entity.
(2) This document which sets out the powers and duties of this legal person is interpreted by the common law and general statute law.
(3) A company has two primary organs, (a) the members in general meeting and (b) the directorate.
(4) In a parliamentary democracy: (a) legislative sovereignty rests with Parliament and (b) administration rest with the executive government (subject to some control by Parliament's power to force a change of government).
(5) A company is similar to a parliamentary democracy, except that a company is not sovereign but has a limited competence only and rule-making authority rests with a general meeting of the members.
(6) The statute, charter or articles will provide for rules constituting a board of directors, corresponding to the executive government of the State. Like the Government, the directors will be answerable to "Parliament" constituted by the general meeting.
(7) In practice they will exercise as much control over the Parliament as that exercises over them just like a Government.
(8) In theory, the general meeting has less power over the directorate than the British Parliament has over the Executive, but more than in the United States of America where there is a complete separation

> of powers. There, the legislature cannot dismiss the Government or curtail its powers.[13]

In the fast-industrialising England of the mid-nineteenth century, the idea of forming corporations was popularised by businesses incorporating by simple registration under the Companies Acts. The age of uncertainty, when incorporation could only be obtained through special statutes or charters such as that of the guilds and boroughs, was over.[14] What is more interesting for China's history is that owing to the fact that China neither had the background general law nor anything similar to Western corporations, the introduction of the Western-type commercial corporations was a process in reverse. First, the corporation was imposed and then the general law slowly developed around it.

Before 1904, China's imperial system did not recognise any form of corporate personality resembling those of the boroughs and guilds in England. The first type of legally enabled corporation recognised by imperial law and indigenous to China was this commercial form of legal personality. This was introduced by the 1904 Chinese Company Law in the form of incorporated limited companies (N.B. in unlimited liability companies, referred to as "unlimited companies", investors as stockholders bear all the risk of the commercial venture. The introduction of limited liability for companies or corporations merely shifts the risk of the venture company from the investors to the creditors). Limited liability also has the effect of strengthening the independent existence of these commercial Chinese corporations. They emulated those created by the English Companies Acts and thus sowed the seeds for permanent change. The introduction of this law in 1904 not only provided China with a bona fide vehicle for commerce, that is, a micro effect,[15] but also, in practice, weakened the state's absolute ability to control industrialisation through imperial industrial monopolies. Incorporated businesses are now protected by this law and enforced by the law courts. Unfortunately for the imperial government this only served to wreck a battered Qing Empire that had already lost a major sea and land war with Japan as well as suffered a destructive invasion by the Eight-Nation Alliance during the Boxer Uprising. The imperial collapse was followed by the arrival of the Republic that brought in the governmental form of legal or corporate personality created by a legal document, this is, the constitutional state. The corporate meaning of the modern state is briefly but concisely captured by the prize-winning author, Australian *jursiprude* and Vice-Chancellor of Melbourne University,

Sir George Whitecross Paton,[16] who explains that "the State has been regarded by some as the greatest corporation known to the law, by others as mere machinery or as one aspect of the legal order". Moreover, "in modern systems the State can be seen as a legal person endowed with such powers as the legal system which supports it provides".[17]

Modern states are created by a general law: the constitution, whether written or unwritten. The new Republic of China created on 1 January 1912 was framed by a rudimentary preliminary written state constitution and then, throughout the unstable warlord period until the formation of the People's Republic of China in 1949, seven subsequent constitutions were written and promulgated in the Republic of China.[18] In the People's Republic, there were also four versions of the Constitution. Therefore, after the imperial collapse in 1911 and the establishment of the Republican state, Chinese company law created Chinese corporations and the Chinese state constitutions created the Chinese state and its governments (national, provincial and municipal). Both these varieties can be said to have legal personality. With this understanding, the scene is now set for further historical investigation of the development of the new Chinese state *vis-à-vis* corporations during the late Qing and Republican periods while China was engaging in industrialisation. This history will be seen through the perspective of the cement industry which, interestingly, was once inextricably connected with the evolution of the modern Chinese state.

What Is a Joint Stock Company?

The Western device that significantly influenced the early industrialisation of China might have logically been incorporated companies and hence the imported ideas of incorporation and legal personality. However, it was not incorporation per se but in fact the birth of the joint stock company (in either the incorporated or unincorporated form) that significantly influenced the early industrialisation of China. Whether a joint stock company is incorporated or not is irrelevant. This is because Western merchants employed these to raise capital in China by issuing and selling shares to the Chinese without regard to the legality of such an action at a time when China had no law to regulate these activities. For example, the shipping company Shanghai Steam Navigation Company which operated in China was not even registered anywhere in the world let alone incorporated. Yet it still operated as a joint stock company and issued shares to finance its operations.[19]

In the British Empire, joint stock companies were basically large unincorporated partnerships which issued shares of stock to raise capital.[20] These were business associations formed by any number of parties that promised to pay the share-bearer a dividend of business profits if this so arose in the course of their various ventures. They were formed and constituted by *private agreements* or *contracts* between the associates or partners. They were not recognised by the law to have a separate entity even when they traded under a common name. Theoretically, in a country with a stable and developed legal environment such as England or the individual states of America in the nineteenth century, each partner or associate would be liable for any loss by the joint stock company and this liability was enforced by the law courts.[21]

In the 1870s, it was the capital-raising ability of these joint stock companies that impressed the influential imperial politician and Governor-General of Zhili province, Viceroy Li Hongzhang. He attempted to emulate these Western joint stock companies in order to raise capital for the arsenals, shipping, mining and other imperial enterprises under his direction.[22] However, it must be emphasised that Li was only interested in the capital-raising method of these Western companies. He showed no inclination for allowing or assisting the establishment of similarly independent indigenous companies in China. For example, Li's shipping firm was established by an imperial edict as a *bureau* only, and, of course, the edict was in Chinese.[23] Its English name "China Merchants Steam Navigation Company" (CMC) was never an official title in the Qing dynasty and probably began its life in English-language newspapers of the time. This name was probably adopted when foreigners began to equate it with other British shipping concerns operating from England and India that were in operation at the time such as Eastern Steam Navigation Co. (since 1848), P. & O. Steam Navigation Co. (since 1840), India General Steam Navigation Co. (since 1844) and Ganges Steam Navigation Co. (since 1845).[24] Thus, unlike Anglo-American companies of the time, the CMC was *not a joint stock company* established by independent partners with a private agreement or contract. More importantly, it was *not a corporation* established under a general law such as Oxford or Cambridge Universities formed under the English common law. Neither was it established by specific statutory legislation such as a Company Act, nor was it created by other prerogative instruments recognised by law such as American state charters or British royal charters.[25]

Did China Have Corporations?

Scholars were often misled by what ***appeared*** to be a kind of joint stock company when the Qing government allowed the establishment of the CMC that imitated Western join stock companies in raising capital by stock issue. Viceroy Li Hongzhang dubbed this scheme *guandu shangban* (official supervision-merchant management). These were plainly not companies as understood in the West and had never been denoted as a *gongsi* (company) under its Chinese name but instead were designated as *ju* (bureau). Thus, these were government "*bureaus* for the recruitment of merchants" (*zhaoshang ju*), and Oxford scholar David Faure pointed out implicitly that the CMC might have derived its name from the "*offices* for the recruitment of merchants" (*zhaoshang chu*) set up by Viceroy Li Hungzhang's mentor Governor-General Zeng Guofan.[26] Suffice to state that, while these bureaus issued stocks to finance their operation, the mere act of issuing stocks on its own ***did not*** transform them into a genuine joint stock company in the Western sense.

The shorthand "*guandu shangban*" was no more than a marketing ploy by Viceroy Li Hongzhang to attract investment funds. The Viceroy was in urgent need after the 1860 war to build a navy but this was at a time when China didn't even have a modern merchant fleet, let alone a military navy.[27] Unlike the previous static arsenals which Li Hongzhang established as government enterprises, a navy would not only involve a large sum of investment, but it also involved dynamic and complex logistical operations.[28] At the time, China only had wooden seagoing junks operated by a few merchants. If the imperial dynasty had any hope of building a navy, then it is more than obvious that a merchant fleet must first have been established to supply the parallel technical and logistical expertise in dealing with large ships. This includes navigation, maintenance, docks, spare parts and fuel, as well as the development of a system of ports. A merchant navy is also important in times of war to transport troops and supplies. In order to solve these problems, Li, after seeing how foreign companies issued and sold stocks in China and how Chinese merchants, especially those in the treaty ports, enthusiastically bought stock, advertised the same in the hope of raising finances for his government's shipping "bureau" on February 1873.[29]

Unlike the genuine private companies, it attracted no interest whatsoever from clear-headed investors. In the end, after more than half a year of unresponsiveness, Li Hongzhang enlisted the Cantonese comprador Tang

Tingshu of the British trading firm Jardines & Co. and rearranged the offer into the so-called *guandu shangban* arrangement devised by Li and launched again in August 1873.[30] Tang brought in capital, investors, ships and skills. Stocks were issued to himself and others who invested. From then on, this government bureau, known widely in English as the "China Merchants' Steam Navigation Company", carried on business under Li's oversight. It can be seen then that this *guandu shangban* was no more than a formula to pitch investment and skills to build a merchant fleet within the structure of the imperial system to assist and complement the desperate effort of navy building. These merchants took investment risks in this odd arrangement and outside observers gained the impression that China had finally adopted a "corporate" form.[31] Far from it: in the absence of any general civil law, this and other *guandu shangban* enterprises were merely imperial government stock-issuing bureaus venturing into business in a time of need. Clearly, this might be a shipping "firm" but to call it a "corporation" without noting the absence of a separate legal personality, which is the most fundamental aspect of a modern corporation, may lead to an incomplete analysis.

Significantly, Li Hongzhang's uncomplicated and elegant shorthand formula is clever and simple. It not only deluded nineteenth-century journalists of his time into believing that the Qing dynasty had embarked upon modern commercial reforms, but also led late twentieth-century scholars to follow the notional construction that he framed. Michigan historian Albert Feuerwerker in his major work *China's Early Industrialization* examined various large Qing dynasty *guandu shangban* enterprises. He believed that the issued "shares" gave away proprietary interest of ownership which cannot be correct: what stockholders bought was not a proprietary ownership right in these "bureaus". This is because these were imperial government branches and they merely bought in it a right to share in profits and took the risk (which is reflected in the market price of the shares) that there would be a return to them.[32] Furthermore, Feuerwerker also constructed his entire analysis by dividing Li Hongzhang's categorisation, not unlike the Qing imperial officials, into *guanban* (official management), *guandu shangban* and *shangban* (merchant management).[33] Thus no attention was given to the most important industrialisation and dynastical power devolution event in two millennia of imperial rule: the legal introduction of Western *corporations* into the imperial system. Incorporated companies, under this simple analytical categorisation framework which Feuerwerker adopted from Li Hongzhang to structure his work, blurred the picture and merely treated the important incorporation process as an uneventful "registration" and any newly incorporated companies as *shangban* merchant management enterprises.[34] There was no appreciation of an incorporated company's fundamental significance as a corporation that acquired legal personality.

Furthermore, unlike Western joint stock companies (incorporated or unincorporated), these *guandu shangban* operations plainly had no *legally recognised independent* status. They were not formed by private parties agreeing a contract and there was no general civil law in China to allow the state to recognise them. Work on the drafting of the Great Qing Civil Code began with the legal reform launched in March 1902 and the final draft was completed in September 1911. This was one month before the revolution broke out, meaning that it was never passed into law. The draft Civil Procedure Law was submitted to the imperial court in 1910 but, likewise, this was never passed into law. Furthermore, the Draft Qing Commercial Code was also submitted to the imperial court in 1909 but suffered the same fate.[35] Nevertheless, these operations were taken to be effective commercial concerns and viewed as such with a correspondingly high expectation of corporate behaviour since the late 1870s. This naturally caused great disappointment and frustration when these bureaus did not behave as expected. An article in the newspaper *Shenbao* in 1887 referring to the *guandu shangban* firms as "*gongsi*" (company) complained that the shareholders' meeting was a farce and that it had absolutely no power:

> There was seemingly a genuine agenda set for discussion in the shareholders' meeting, but in fact the item that was to be discussed had been decided long ago. It was merely a special exercise to let everybody have a quick glimpse of the decided. No one could say no to whatever they had decided to do, and no one could say yes to whatever they had decided not to do.[36]

Albert Feuerwerker's *China's Early Industrialization* focused primarily on the CMC and three other government enterprises. He concluded that bureaucratic capitalism was the main cause of "retarded industrialisation".[37] It is no surprise that later research showed that this leading reasoning seemed somewhat strained as an explanation of the operation of the same firm in its earlier years. University of Queensland scholar Chi-kong Lai who re-evaluated the first 30 years of this "first" *guandu shangban* enterprise concluded that Albert Feuerwerker's depiction of the company as fundamentally flawed by bureaucratism, inefficiency and corruption "does not accord with the objectives of the CMC's founder Li Hongzhang, nor with the record of the company's initial decade of operation from 1873-84". He discovers from more recent sources that flaws only became evident in the *guandu shangban* model from the mid-1880s onward. He believes that the political context in which modern enterprises operated could never be discounted in late Qing China. This was evidenced by the shift in CMC fortunes after 1885. Lai made an important observation which is found to accurately depict the early twentieth-century Chinese companies in the present study that the *company existed within a given political framework*. Thus the historical fortune of the company depended as much on political as on economic circumstances. In short, the CMC foundered not on the rise and fall of the market but on the "unpredictable winds of late nineteenth-century Chinese politics".[38]

Chi-kong Lai's observed conclusion is correct because Li Hongzhang's objective was to jump-start a navy and the CMC was to be formed as a government bureau, thus subjecting it mainly to the "political framework". However, like other scholars, in his article he conceptually followed the nineteenth-century writings by journalists and diplomats in treating the CMC as a "modern corporate form" of organisation and as a "joint stock company". He attempted to explain the paradox surrounding Qing dynasty enterprises by examining "enterprise autonomy" and "managerial autonomy" *vis-à-vis* the government. These were unsurprisingly lacking in the imperial firms and he determined that it was Li Hongzhang's reduced political influence and his declining fiscal options that undermined the "company". Chi-kong Lai, similar to other writers, was at pains to reconcile why "government protection" was needed in the development of these firms, and all were baffled by the fact that the merchants were very disinclined to invest in a home-grown "joint stock company".[39] However, by nature, the CMC was *neither* a corporation *nor* a joint stock company but pretended to be both. Thus it should not be analysed from the perspective of a company formed bottom-up in the legal system as in the case of a genuine competitive joint stock company. This firm and those subsequently formed imperial enterprises were by nature unincorporated government bureaus created top-down for the purpose of going into business deliberately without independence from the imperial bureaucratic structure.[40] The power of these "bureau" firms lies neither with the board of directors nor with the shareholders meeting but with the "*Da Xian* (the Great Charterer)", that is, Li Hongzhang himself. Thus it is not difficult to understand why they were not attractive to street-wise merchant investors. They could easily have invested their money in other independent companies operating in the treaty ports with operations that were genuinely protected by modern law.[41] In sum, China's adoption of corporations and legal personality was initiated with its *commercial form* and only began with the reformist imperial legislation of 1904: the Company Law.[42]

Why Study Cement Corporations?

Early Chinese Cement Corporations are important because the initial development of the cement industry in the early twentieth-century Qing dynasty was enmeshed in imperial politics. This highly politicised industrialisation situation had changed little since the mid-nineteenth century during Li Hongzhang's early attempts at military industrialisation in the 1860s. Even after the Boxer Protocol of 1901, the dynasty's centrally controlled state *industrial* structure remained firmly a part of the *political* structure. Not even the disastrous naval defeat by the Japanese or the utter destruction of Beijing in the Boxer Uprising could fundamentally alter this stagnant imperial order.

After Li Hongzhang's death in 1901, the rising bureaucrat Yuan Shikai was charged with the responsibility to reform the legal system. Empress Cixi made this decision in 1902 following the Boxer events. Legal experts were gathered in Beijing and law professors were employed from Japan to assist in the drafting of new laws. Within a two-year period, a Ministry of Commerce (*shangbu*) was created in 1903 to oversee its implementation and a Company law was promulgated in 1904.[43] However, what is most important is not the publication of legal rules regulating the formation and operation of companies. The crucial point is that the Western corporations were quickly established by senior government ministers and bureaucrats inside the Qing Empire. This fact not only had a major influence on the course of late imperial Chinese history, but also in silently structuring the development of modern China.[44] Consequently, a good understanding of corporations is important because *governments* and *non-governmental associations* alike in the modern world are invariably entities organised with legal personality. Although this study is based on China's political and commercial history of the early twentieth century, the insights gained can contribute significantly towards understanding of the present-day relationships between *governments* and *non-governmental associations* in the twentieth-first century.

In the contemporary Western world, the cement industry has consolidated into a handful of big companies, and several companies control most of the cement production.[45] In short, the overall industry has been globalised and oligopolised into cross-border multi-facility corporations. This means that many cement plants have been absorbed into large multinational organisations to become local manufacturing divisions that lost their own identities, for example the UK's first cement production plant which started producing Portland cement in 1846 by William Aspin (the son of Leeds bricklayer Joseph Aspin who patented the process of making modern cement in 1824). Eventually this UK plant became part of the French Lafarge cement and construction material group in 2001.[46] It is an obscure industry and there is a dearth of helpful analytical studies that examine a single contemporary industrial cement operation, or that narrate the overall developmental history of the cement industry in any individual country. However, one thing is certain: cement production is a highly political business. For this reason, more often than not, the cement industry of any country is bound up with the governmental politics of the locality. This book sets out to further our understanding by exploring and explaining the history of the Chinese cement industry and shows that it is more than the business history of a bland industry. It is part of a far more complex and significant history of the Chinese state.

The Framework and Structure of This Book

This Introduction begins the process of shifting Chinese Republican history's focus from the traditional perspectives and approaches. The above has given an account of the history of legal or corporate personality itself. The important historical role legal personality played in the eventual modern development of industrial England is thus highlighted. This in turn raises the awareness that both modern governments and companies evolved from incorporated entities (N.B. "incorporation" means conferring an entity, e.g., a company or an organisation, with legal or corporate personality).

This chapter presented the framework and structure of this book and discusses the general relationship between China, cement and corporations. It explains the systemic and structural difficulties facing imperial China since the middle of the nineteenth century, caused by the arrival of corporations from the West. It also points out that larger-than-life historical figures of modern China such as Yuan Shikai, Sun Yat-sen and Chiang

Kai-shek all had major roles and untold stories when viewed from this alternative historical perspective. Rather than telling the history of China from conventional political or social historical angles, this chapter sets out the perspective taken by this book: the centrality of legal or corporate personality in China's historical story, seen from the angle of cement manufacturing corporations, in the making of the modern Chinese state.

This book involves the re-reading of some of the scholarship on early Chinese industrialisation in order to present the new interpretation within a framework that takes account of the effect of corporations in modern Chinese history. The overall argument is presented in three parts. Part One reveals in three chapters how corporate personality was introduced into late imperial China. Chapter 2 sets the scene by examining the strength of the original imperial system before the introduction of the corporations. Chapter 3 looks at the beginnings of a redistribution of central economic power when incorporated companies that could challenge the unincorporated imperial monopolies appeared on Chinese soil. Finally, Chap. 4 explains the relationship between the incorporated Qixin Cement plant and the catalytic role it played in the collapse of the Qing imperial dynasty. Corporations then became part and parcel of the modern Chinese state in post-imperial times.

Part Two (Chaps. 5 and 6) illustrates how the corporation manifested itself as an incorporated government, and Part Three (Chap. 7) illustrates its manifestation as incorporated companies. Chapter 5 details how members of the revolutionary Chinese League (*Tongmenghui*), an organisation that was led by Sun Yat-sen before the 1911 revolution, attempted to monopolise the cement industry, trade and business in the incorporated city of Guangzhou after the fall of the empire, and Chap. 6 shows how they attempted to resurrect state power using this incorporated city within a de facto independent province from 1923 to 1937. Chapter 7 examines historically the existence of two different categories of corporations, viz. private and state, in Republican China and their different inceptions in this period. It then shows how the Nanjing Republican government led by Chiang Kai-shek attempted to limit private corporations in favour of transforming the National Resource Commission into a state ministerial conglomerate that directly owned and ruled over many important emerging state corporations. The final outcome of the civil war between the Nationalists and the Communists is the establishment of the People's Republic of China in 1949, and the work of the National Resource Commission was taken to new heights under communism: the state took over the economy completely. Indeed, by destroying corporations and their distributional consequence of economic power, state power was recentralised and China was thrown back to the 1880s where absolute power in the name of one man, the Emperor, was the norm and where this condition was easily sustainable. This is because there was no legal personality in China; hence, there were no modern corporations.

Notes

1. This follows a structuralist perspective of history; see Stephen Davies, *Empiricism and History*, p. 44.
2. Mary S. J. Gani, *Cement and Concrete*, pp. 2–4.
3. Linda Pomerantz-Zhang, *Wu Tingfang*, pp. 149–50; David Faure, *China and Capitalism,* pp. 62–64.
4. See Colin Arthur Cooke, *Corporation, Trust and Company.*
5. Adolf A. Berle, Jr., *Studies in the Law of Corporation Finance*, pp. 3–8.
6. Adolf A. Berle, Jr., *Studies in the Law of Corporation Finance*, pp. 3–8.
7. Diplomat, Adviser to Presidential Roosevelt and Professor of Corporate Law at Columbia University, 1927–1964.
8. Adolf A. Berle, Jr., *Studies in the Law of Corporation Finance*, pp. 3–8.
9. Colin Arthur Cooke, *Corporation, Trust and Company*, p. 185; Colin Cooke ends his analysis in the Companies Act of 1862 when this important Act of Parliament created the modern English commercial corporation in this manner.
10. L. C. B. Gower et al., *Gower's Principles of Modern Company Law*, p. 97.
11. Albert Venn Dicey, *Introduction to the Study of the Law of the Constitution*, pp. 88–89 and 140; Dicey was Vinerian Professor of English Law at All Soul's College, Oxford, from 1882 to 1909 and taught at the London School of Economics from 1896 to 1899.
12. The Sir Ernst Cassel Professor of Commercial Law at Law Department of the London School of Economics and Political Science and a former solicitor and Visiting Professor to Harvard Law School 1954–1955 and Vice-Chancellor of the University of Southampton, 1971–79.

13. L. C. B. Gower et al., *Gower's Principles of Modern Company Law*, pp. 12–19.
14. L. C. B. Gower, et al., *Gower's Principles of Modern Company Law*, p. 15.
15. David Faure, *China and Capitalism*, pp. 63 and 114; Zhemeisen, "Yingguo gongsi dingli" in Chen Zhongyi, ed. *Huangchao jingshiwen sanbian*, 39/3b-5b, referred to in David Faure, *China and Capitalism*, p. 114.
16. Professor of Jurisprudence, Dean of the Faculty of Law and Vice-Chancellor of the University of Melbourne, 1931–1968.
17. George Whitecross Paton, *A Textbook of Jurisprudence*, p. 349.
18. See William L. Tung, *The Political Institutions of Modern China*, pp. 318–380.
19. David Faure, *China and Capitalism*, p. 51.
20. Modern UK company law does not permit this form of unincorporated share-issuing company; see L. C. B. Gower, et al., *Gower's Principles of Modern Company Law*, p. 297, for an overview of the kinds of company available in the UK and an update in Paul L. Davies, Gower & Davies' *Principles of Modern Company Law*, p. 18.
21. For a discussion of the developed rules for companies and corporations in England and America see L. C. B. Gower, "Some Contrasts between British and American Corporation Law".
22. Zhang Zhongmin, *Jiannan de bianqian*, pp. 131–148.
23. Zhang Houquan, *Zhaoshang Ju Shi*, p. 31.
24. Radhe Shyam Rungta, *The Rise of Business Corporations in India*, p. 274; Zhang Zhongmin, *Jiannan de bianqian*, p. 132.
25. See L. C. B. Gower, et al., *Gower's Principles of Modern Company Law*, p. 297, for an overview of the kinds of company that could be available in the UK and L. C. B. Gower, "Some Contrasts between British and American Corporation Law".
26. David Faure, *China and Capitalism*, p. 48.
27. Xia Dongyuan, *Yangwu yundong shi*, pp. 296–311; Zhang Houquan, *Zhaoshang Ju Shi*, pp. 9–19.
28. On the Self-strengthening Movement's military thinking, see Xia Dongyuan, *Yangwu yundong shi*, pp. 326–338.
29. Zhang Houquan, *Zhaoshang Ju Shi*, pp. 33, 39–40.
30. Zhang Houquan, *Zhaoshang Ju Shi*, p. 41.

31. Zhang Zhongmin, *Jiannan de bianqian: jindai Zhongguo gongsi zhidu yanjiu*, p. 131 n1; Chi-Kong Lai simply took the China Merchants' Company as an outright "corporation" in his dissertation: Chi-Kong Lai, "China's First Modern Corporation and the State: Officials, Merchants, and Resource Allocation in the China Merchants' Steam Navigation Company, 1872–1902".
32. A short but enlightening discussion on the ownership and profits concepts for English joint stock companies can be found in Colin Arthur Cooke, *Corporation, Trust and Company*, p. 172.
33. See the contents page of Albert Feuerwerker, *China's Early Industrialization.*
34. Albert Feuerwerker, *China's Early Industrialization*, pp. 2–5.
35. Zhang Jinfan, *Zhongguo jindai shehui yu fazhi wenming*, pp. 249 and 509.
36. "Zhongxi gongsi yitong shuo" *Shenbao* 25th December, 1887 quoted in Yang Zaijun, *Wan Qing Gongsi yu Gongsi Zhili*, p. 114.
37. Albert Feuerwerker, *China's Early Industrialization*, pp. 1 and 251.
38. Chi-kong Lai, "The Qing State and Merchant Enterprise", p. 142.
39. Chi-kong Lai, "The Qing State and Merchant Enterprise: The China Merchant's Company, 1872–1902", p. 109.
40. Zhang Zhongmin, *Jiannan de bianqian*, p. 136.
41. David Faure, *China and Capitalism*, p. 51.
42. David Faure, *China and Capitalism*, pp. 45–64. Faure believes that the Company Law of 1904 was the last of a long series of events that brought the modern company into existence in China and culminated in the Mackay Treaty of 1902. He believes that the thrust which led to the Company Law came from the barrister Wu Tingfang.
43. Linda Pomerantz-Zhang, *Wu Tingfang*, pp. 149–50.
44. David Faure, *China and Capitalism*, p. 64.
45. The largest companies are: Cemex: http://www.cemex.com, Lafarge: http://www.lafarge.com, Holcim: http://www.holcim.com, and HeidelbergCement: http://www.heidelbergcement.com; last accessed 20 June 2016.
46. A. J. Francis, *The Cement Industry 1796–1914*; "Lafarge Buys Blue Circle to Create World's Largest Cement-Maker" *Financial Express*, 9 January 2001; http://www.globalpolicy.org/socecon/tncs/mergers/010109.htm; last accessed 20 June 2016.

PART 1

Analysing the Challenges to the Ancient Empire

The introduction of the "corporate" or "legal personality" to China in the late Qing and early Republican periods had profound consequences for the course of modern Chinese history, and represents the most important form of institutional organisation in the post-imperial state. This part analyses the resilient nature of the imperial state structure and presents the book's argument that the failure of the imperial empire owes more to internal structural collapse than to external revolutions. After rebellions and reforms had either failed to destroy it or had it rejuvenated, what finally triggered the revolution and demolished the dynastical empire was a decentralisation of industrial power and wealth to corporations. This took place after Western corporations, which became ubiquitous in the Western industrial world, were officially introduced into the body of the ancient Chinese absolutist dynastical order by way of the 1904 imperial reform legislations in the aftermath of the notorious Boxer Uprising.

The Imperial system of government in China was in place for over 2000 years until the Qing dynasty fell in 1911. Why did it fall? Was it simply because there were rebellions? Was it because of domestic court politics? Chapter 2 examines the existential threats to the Chinese imperial ruling system in the nineteenth and early twentieth centuries and surveys the insights of major historians. It then presents the insight that emerged from this work: that despite the decline of imperial rule, this entrenched bureaucratic system, which was inherited from the previous dynasties and backed up by the military system of the Manchu people, was tougher and more regenerative even in decline than has previously been argued. This adaptable imperial system enabled the ruling house to extend its effective governing power for over half a century after their defeat by the British in the Opium War in 1842. Although battered, the imperial structure and the Qing state it supported remained intact and functioning until 1911. What eventually did demolish the empire was a decentralisation of industrial power and wealth when commerical corporations began to form in China.

CHAPTER 2

The Imperial System: Durable and Resilient

The imperial system of government in China was in place for over 2000 years until the Qing dynasty fell in 1911. Despite the decline of imperial rule, this entrenched bureaucratic system, inherited from the previous dynasties backed by the military system of the Manchu people, was tougher and more regenerative even in decline than has previously been argued. This adaptable imperial system enabled the ruling house to extend its effective governing power for over half a century after their defeat by the British in the Opium War in 1842.[1] Although battered, the imperial structure and the Qing state it supported remained intact and functioning. No foreign force showed itself powerful enough to effectively "impact" and wholly destroy this ancient home-grown imperial governing structure.[2] Nor was there any indigenously brewed rebellion that could mount a military challenge large enough to totally overwhelm the sturdy imperial system. All challenges were beaten back by the government in Beijing one way or another.[3] Arguably the empire collapsed structurally. That what eventually did demolish the empire was a decentralisation of industrial power and wealth. This did not happen accidentally but as a result of the considered moves of Yuan Shikai, who craved economic power. In 1904 he helped injected the modern concept of corporate personality into the absolutist imperial order. Such a change poisoned central power and made fragile the imperial ruling structure.[4] This culminated seven years later in the Revolution of 1911 which began as a wrangle over the nationalisation of independently funded and sizable "incorporated" railway

H. Ko, *The Making of the Modern Chinese State*,
DOI 10.1007/978-981-10-2660-7_2

companies in the same year.[5] The historical development of the cement industry illustrates this decentralisation of power which took place behind the scenes. Yuan Shikai can be seen manoeuvring the legislative process as well as being one of the earliest people, if not the earliest person, to incorporate industrial companies for his own benefit. It gives an insight into to how he accumulated his personal wealth which in turn sheds light on his staying power even after being ousted from all offices in 1908 on the death of his patron the Empress Dowager Cixi.[6] In short, the introduction of corporate personality into China created independent power centres. In contrast to the government sustained by tax and other government-imposed income, these corporations were fiefdoms, sustained solely by business income. They have been referred to as "private governments" as opposed to "public" ones in accordance with our usual understanding.[7]

Therefore, creating corporate bodies of any form reduces state power.[8] Once corporate personality was adopted into Chinese law and gradually made available in its commercial format, it absorbed central power and did not facilitate the nationalist cause. After 1904, China only recognised the *commercial form* of corporate or legal personality permitted by the Yuan Shikai-sponsored Company Law.[9] It benefited mostly the imperial officials such as Yuan himself who understood the significance of incorporation and the abstract power of legal personality.[10] Even after the establishment of the Republican state after 1911, a study by William Kirby discovered that the corporate form was unpopular.[11] In another study it was discovered that even after the 1904 imperial Company legislation took effect, the late Qing and early Republican central and local governments continued to establish state industries under the old bureaucratic "government-managed" setup which was created by the Self-Strengthening-movement officials back in the 1870s. Investigating China's early cement industry demonstrates how industrialisation was used by the Manchu imperial dynasty in an attempt to "self-strengthen" its own hold on China and also shows the difference it made to the commercial viability of modern industry. Incorporated companies were used first and foremost by Yuan Shikai in the north. Subsequent developments showed the "deep south" continuing to use the old bureaucratic "government-managed" state format of setting up enterprises. Ironically, however, when Guomindang central planning policies came into being in the mid-1930s, this situation had the advantage that there were few "corporate personalities" to obstruct the recentralisation of power. On the contrary, it actually facilitated nationalism and the development of national industries.[12] However, before a discussion of corporations and its introduction to China can begin, we must look closer at the nature of various challenges that were coming from all sides confronting the imperial state structure in China throughout the nineteenth century.

The Challenge to the Imperial State Structure

The Opium War of 1840–1842's "impact" and effects were confined to the coast and acted as no more than a stimulus or catalyst which provoked challenges from all sides.[13] After this disaster, the first major assault to the imperial system was a wave of peasant rebellions that were always brewing in the far-flung countryside but became open military confrontations after the Opium War. The most serious was the Taiping Rebellion (1851–1864), in which many southern provinces fell under rebel control.[14]

During the Second Opium War (1856–1860), the Emperor Xianfeng fled from Beijing to Chengde when the capital was invaded and the then administrative palace Yuanming Yuan was torched and destroyed.[15] After this further disaster, the empire embarked on the first major phase of imperial reforms by "*yangwu*" reformers under the banner of "Self-Strengthening" (1861–1894). Unfortunately, the Self-Strengthening movement came to an abrupt end when the navy was annihilated by Japan in 1894.[16] After the war, the imperial system faced its second major assault, this time from a totally different class of people: the Emperor himself in collaboration with intellectuals attempted to bring the Empire under a constitutional monarchy. This ended in a *coup d'état* which restored the ex-regent Empress Dowager Cixi as the ultimate power-holder and thus the old imperial structure was maintained. In the aftermath of defeat and with the Self-Strengthening movement in tatters, Cixi authorised military reforms almost immediately with the appointment of Yuan Shikai as the trainer of a "New Army".[17] However, similar to the First Opium War, war, defeat and national humiliation provoked the Boxer Rebellion of 1900. Once again, reforms to the system were embarked upon in its wake. It is in this second major phase of imperial reforms under the policy of *Xinzheng* ("New Policy")[18] that Yuan Shikai shared the responsibility of the reform's implementation with the 64-year-old senior official reformer Zhang Zhidong.[19] Yuan ascended the power structure after the Sino-Japanese War 1894–1895 and became one of the most trusted imperial ministers of Cixi.

The above overview reveals that the imperial system deflected two major assaults to its integrity after the Opium war, one *military* and the other *intellectual*. The Qing Empire and government survived all the foreign encroachments and invasions relatively intact even though humiliating concessions were made. It was never carved up as once anticipated.[20] On balance, the Chinese imperial system under the Manchus remained the only effective ruling system for the entire empire in 1901. Its eventual collapse a decade later in 1911 was caused neither by foreign wars nor by the violent military or intellectual assaults, but rather by the accumulated effect of the two major reform attempts to "strengthen" the imperial system.

More specifically, despite the fact that it took 40 years, the process of industrialisation which began in the 1860s through the Self-Strengthening Movement brought not only modern industries to China, but it also brought the accompanying, although less visible, centrifugal Western legal institution and operational concept of legal personality. The establishment of a completely new Western legal concept provided a state-sanctioned vehicle for local organisation which could be independent of state politics.[21]

The Restored Imperial State Structure

Two important books that discuss the late Qing imperial state structure are Mary C. Wright's *The Last Stand of Chinese Conservatism: The T'ung-Chih Restoration, 1862–1874*[22] and Albert Feuerwerker's *China's Early Industrialization: Sheng Hsuan-huai (1844–1916) and Mandarin Enterprise*.[23] Wright's view is interesting, arguing that the "Restoration" was essentially a conservative movement and its thrust was to revamp and revitalise the old Confucian order. She analysed in detail the efforts of "Restoration" and the restored "Confucian order" during the Tongzhi Emperor's reign. She closely examined the various restoration strategies under the following headings: co-operative policy with the powers, the details of the Confucian restoration, the restoration of civil government, the suppression of the rebellion, the re-establishment of local control, the rehabilitation of the Chinese economy, the Self-Strengthening movement and the modernisation of China's system of foreign relations. She determined that by 1870 much had been achieved in every sector but still "the signs of failure" became apparent soon after.[24] However, as mentioned in the last section, what is plainly missing from such an important analysis is the absence of any detailed consideration of the legal system. For the purposes of her study, it appears to be enough to note that China was run by an imperial system with a weak legal framework with few civil regulations or civil law[25]; commercial entities were without legal status and modern industry was expected to be run from an imperial magistracy (*yamen*).[26]

In a more recent study, Edward Rhoads has shown that not only was there a trend in recentralising authority after 1861, restoring power back to the imperial court, but there was also a parallel trend of "reimperialisation", reinstating power to the Manchu aristocracy. This had often been overlooked by earlier historians. This culminated in the appointment of the "imperial kinsmen's cabinet" in May 1911, five months before the revolution. In his view, even towards the end of the empire, "the Qing court was hardly so impotent as it is usually portrayed".[27] Even though externally weak, its imperial administrative structure was still operational and effective until the end.

Confucian Industrialisation Without Western Civil Law

What Albert Feuerwerker studied was a very important aspect of the imperial structure that was undergoing reform: the Chinese Empire's governmental effort to industrialisation and commercialisation. This is the first major phase of imperial reforms. He studied the China Merchant Shipping Company (CMC), which Li Hongzhang established in 1873. This is the first of a dozen large projects conceived as *guandu shangban* (official supervision-merchant management) enterprises.[28] The general conclusion of Feuerwerker is succinctly summarised by J. A. G. Roberts and represents the established view of historians[29]: The company was intended to compete with British and other foreign shipping which had penetrated China's coastal trade. Furthermore, this could encourage risky investment from Chinese merchants into modern industries. This type of commercial vehicle became the prototype of the *guandu shangban* enterprises. The main features are: (1) Chinese merchants would organise and finance the company; (2) it would be directed by an official manager; and (3) a certain business monopoly would be conferred.

In the case of the CMC, it was a concession for the carriage of tribute rice from the south to Tianjin. This has the effect of officially empowering the company so as to ensure its profitable operation.[30] Furthermore, this form of enterprise combined both traditional/Chinese and modern/Western features[31]: (1) The tribute rice concession derived its origin from the old imperial state monopolies with official backing and bureaucratic management methods, for example, the salt monopoly; and (2) the enterprise was supposed to be ***a joint stock company*** rather than as a partnership or state-owned enterprise. Roberts believes that (1) indicates continuity rather than of change and (2) was a new practice and was brought on by foreign competition.

Feuerwerker regarded the adoption of the ***guandu shangban*** form of organisation as an important reason for the failure of the policy. He suggested that the ***guandu shangban*** enterprises reflected and reinforced the tendency to regionalism. The most marked example of this was Li Hongzhang's creation of a military-industrial empire, based on Shanghai and Tianjin and incorporating his interests in the China Merchants' Steam Navigation Company and the Kaiping coal mines.[32] Feuerwerker regarded Li as more concerned with building up his own power base than being committed to Self-Strengthening in the national interest. He supports his view by referring to the famous controversy which arose in 1888–1889 over a proposal to extend the railway line, which connected the Kaiping mines at Tangshan to Tianjin, to Beijing. The suggested intrusion of a railway into the environs of the capital aroused fierce opposition, which served to mask Li's real objective. He was planning to use the revenue generated by the Beijing extension to continue the railway northwards, thereby bringing Manchuria under his control.[33] Feuerwerker equates ***guandu shangban*** to "bureaucratic management", and the monopolistic privileges were intended to give an advantage against ***foreign competition*** but in practice were used to protect the interests of the shareholders ***against all competition***, no matter whether these are foreign or Chinese. The shipping of tribute rice to Beijing is one example.[34]

Thus, Albert Feuerwerker reached a similar conclusion to Mary Wright by analysing more specifically the CMC and the general industrialisation structure (namely ***guandu shangban*** as an imperial licence to do business) during the Self-Strengthening period.[35] Feuerwerker believes that this failure was due to the anachronistic imperial system of industrialisation based upon Confucian patronage. However, Feuerwerker (and the scholarship influenced by him) did not treat these imperial industrial-commercial enterprises merely as government bureaus emulating a joint stock company. Neither he nor Wright presented any hint of what should have been the fundamental structural requirements for development in a modern state and how China failed to meet them. Instead, in another study of the Qixin Cement Company Limited, Feuerwerker suggested that even with the use of the corporate form after 1904, it was no more than the old patronage system under a different name.[36]

It is contended that the most fundamental requirement of a modern state is to develop modern industries. Yet, in order for modern industry to thrive in the long run, a modern legal system supporting its development must be established. No such analytical focus appeared in *The Last Stand of Chinese Conservatism* because in nineteenth-century China, a "legal system" in the modern Western sense was not part of the imperial structure. China, it can be argued, only had a "justice system".[37] It is further contended that a modern legal system containing the "concept of personality" and corporations is an absolute necessity for any capitalist state (of any religious or cultural bearing). Corporations support the emergence and development of *large* industrial and commercial enterprises and innovative conglomerates. Since the legal system was not particularly emphasised in *The Last Stand of Chinese Conservatism,* the academic debates were locked into the framework defined by that text without in-depth consideration of a legal system or awareness of the consequences of its crudeness.[38]

What this first phase of imperial reforms did achieve, however, was the development of several key industries on Chinese soil and within the entrenched ancient Confucian imperial state system. Despite the substantial economic inefficiencies of the *guandu shangban* mode of operation in the development of industries and commerce, it did nevertheless give China some progress towards modernisation. It also provided an opportunity to train personnel and nurture some technical skills, such as the Fuzhou Arsenal.[39] Furthermore, according to Stephen T. Thomas who gave a positive endorsement to the *guandu shangban* enterprises: By 1895 China had six *guandu shangban* enterprises in core economic sectors, namely China Merchants' Steam Navigation Company (1872), the Kaiping Coal Mines (1877), the Imperial Telegraph Administration (1880), the Imperial Chinese Railway Administration (1886), the Shanghai Cotton Cloth Mill (1887) and the Hanyang Ironworks (1889). There were also 76 modern manufacturing enterprises and 33 coal and metal mines.[40] Hence, it could have formed the foundation of China's eventual industrialisation.

These writers are certainly correct if we take a longer view and a broader perspective. This is because, when the long overdue legal reforms finally arrived with the *Xinzheng* reforms (the second major phase of reforms), many were transformed into large industrial corporate persons or corporations.[41] This silent industrial-commercial revolution and its impact upon politics in imperial and republican China constitute the core of the present discussion.

The Second Major Challenge: Intellectual

The second major challenge to the imperial state structure was an intellectual challenge which gathered momentum after the empire's defeat in the Sino-Japanese War of 1895. For the first time, this gave Chinese intellectuals a chance to give serious consideration to the various problems confronting China. Luke Kwong's revealing work on imperial politics during the "Hundred Days Reform", *A Mosaic of the Hundred Days: Personalities, Politics, and Ideas of 1898*, is the authority on the politics of this challenge to the state and how it utterly failed.[42] Another insightful alternative analysis, however, is offered by Liu Ping of Fudan University.[43]

Liu Ping argues that the "*yangwu*" Confucian intellectuals were marginal characters. This is because they could only rely on commercial and military power to confront the Western intrusions. They were on the margins of a state structure based upon landed lineages, thus indicating that they were critically removed from the structure of state imperial power. Their commercial enterprises and economic activities did not in fact have any actual influence on the centre of state power, nor did they manage to shake the traditional economic structure of China. Without influence, they lacked even the potential to initiate reforms. Moreover, considering their frosty reception of the missionaries and Western culture in general, their struggles and exchange with the West were clearly confined purely to the economic realm.

The defeat by Japan brought humiliation to China and the demotion of Li Hongzhang and it unequivocally declared the intellectual death of the Self-Strengthening movement, spurring on a newer grouping of intellectuals headed by Kang Youwei and Liang Qichao.[44] Meanwhile, Protestant missionaries had also become an increasingly powerful intellectual influence in China. Missionaries such as Timothy Richard and Young John Allen chiefly lived by the pen and their major influence was through publishing.[45] Liu Ping believes that the *weixin* intellectual reformers and the missionaries focused their energies on criticism of the framework of Confucianism, the pillar of Chinese society. Unfortunately, these criticisms only shook the fundamentals of the local gentry's power and their survival but failed to touch the imperial structure. The Emperor *Guangxu* decreed on 23 June 1895 the abolishing of "the eight-legged essays" which destroyed the career paths of traditional scholars. From the start, the *weixin* reform was a movement which had departed from the moral and social order rooted in land and lineages and drifted on the margins of mainstream society. This critical intellectual movement had thus exceeded the sustainability of the imperial state-social structure which naturally caused objections from all sides. Furthermore, the power of the Emperor and his supporters in court was feeble. Thus, whatever the motives behind their call for reforms, they did not have the ability to carry them out.

In the end, from the viewpoint of power and structure, neither the *weixin* intellectual reformers nor the missionaries could enter the structural centre of power. Although they had close contact with the ministers surrounding the Emperor, they either became irrelevant or were scapegoats left on the altar of imperial politics when they bet their lives and future on a powerless Emperor. Indeed, that the *weixin* intellectuals' eventual arrests were followed by summary execution or exile underscores their remoteness from the imperial centre. This also shows their fragility against the backdrop of the colossal state-lineage social structure of the imperial system.[46] The bedrock on which rested the Qing imperial structure was unyielding. Interestingly, not even the Emperor himself could break the structural hold of the system. Therefore, something else was needed to displace this mammoth and ongoing structural concern. This finally came with the legal reforms of 1904: the introduction of corporate or legal personality and the Western corporation.

The Final Challenge: Corporate Personality

The final challenge to the imperial system came in 1904 during the sweeping legal reforms. The first British-trained Chinese barrister Wu Tingfang was appointed to draft a commercial code after the Boxer Rebellion and the signing of the MacKay Treaty of 1902.[47] This was the second phase of major reforms. But why is this apparently innocuous legal matter such a powerful and critical challenge to the imperial structure? In order to answer this question, we must understand the nature of this challenge, and to understand the nature of this challenge, we must first understand the nature of the concept of legal personality and corporations developed in the West through the ages and moreover, no less importantly, how its commercial form became prevalent in the mid-nineteenth century through company legislation.

The Legal Situation in Late Qing China

In the latter half of the nineteenth century, the Empire did not and could not recognise (legally in the system) the existence of any *private corporate entities* that might accumulate and concentrate *economic power*. Neither was there a movement to promote independent industry and commerce, nor was there any active policy to create a generally conducive legal environment for industrialisation. The only real change occurred when the Company Law of 1904 brought in the legal personality concept and injected into the system private and power-sharing corporations in the form of commercial and industrial companies. Despite this development, it was still not an active considered policy of the imperial monarchy. It was an ad hoc measure adopted as a result of the desperate situation after the Boxer Uprising and the signing of the "Boxer Protocol" in which 450 million taels of silver were to be paid to the eight nations involved as indemnity over a course of 39 at 4 % annual interest with the annual payment being equivalent to 20 % of the annual budget.[48]

The present study shows that there was a scramble to introduce a Company Law into imperial China in 1902. This was completed swiftly in 1904 under the auspices of Yuan Shikai and the more senior Qing mandarins Zhang Zhidong and Liu Kunyi.[49] The Company Law was quickly drawn up to become the first piece of modern legislation of the Qing dynastical state even before any hope of the new general legal rules were put in place. These were needed to lay the foundation for modern civil legal relationships. It would take another seven years until September 1911 for a draft Civil Code for China to be completed.[50] Unfortunately, this was just a month before the revolution broke out. An anomaly arose because the imperial state recognised the corporate form of a commercial company but did not have any supporting regulations. These include those dealing with its civil rights and duties; or horizontal inter-corporation civil relationships; or with other legal entities such as a person or government. As a result, the companies incorporated in the late Qing were uncontrollable and wildly independent entities. They were created under the Company Law of 1904 but the complex legal mechanism for regulating the behaviour of companies and corporations that developed over many centuries in the West remained unlegislated and unavailable in China.

A bankruptcy law did follow shortly after the promulgation of the company legislation in 1905 which might have set some limits to the power of these new Chinese corporations.[51] However, unless these companies went bankrupt, there was in practice little restraint against them. In other words, once business firms were formed as incorporated companies they become unassailable and quite independent of the state itself. That is, after acquiring legal personality in accordance with the formalities prescribed in the 1904 imperial Company Law and thus receiving legal recognition by the imperial state as a separate entity: a corporation. This is because the whole system of civil law was non-existent and thus the judicial authority over corporations was ambiguous. The lacuna includes civil litigation procedures on how to bring a corporation to court and subject to its jurisdiction. This was how Yuan Shikai and his economic adviser Zhou Xuexi gained unassailable economic power in a time of legal anarchy. Ironically, the imperial state did not survive the end of empire but imperial corporations did.

State and Corporate Personality

An important study of the relationship between legal or corporate personality and the state was conducted at Oxford in the mid-1920s by Frederick Hallis under the supervision of the Anglo-Russian jurist Sir Paul Vinogradoff.[52] It was published in 1930 as *The Corporate Personality: A Study in Jurisprudence*.[53] Hallis examined the concept of corporate personality and the legal situation in England theoretically and observed that between the state on the one hand and the individual on the other, exist "a great variety of corporations" and that some of these well-organised corporations rival the state in influence on society. He found numerous examples in the nineteenth century of bodies which assumed political responsibilities, such as trade unions, professional associations and large trading corporations. This, he asserted, was the reality in Western society at the time of his writing. Besides, these "new loyalties" have cut across the relation of the individual to the state and have produced demand for a new type of limitation of the state's authority over the interest of society.

Referring to the West, Hallis pronounced that the state had from a certain perspective become a "discredited" institution. There was simply a decentralisation of authority. The law in England had advanced by the 1920s to a point where the state simply had no right of control over the spheres of influence of "modern associations" such as these trade unions and professional associations. These corporate personalities did not become fictitious creations of the state. Furthermore, their powers were neither conceded by nor derived from the state but "inhere in them as living social organisations".[54] Furthermore, there is one concept which is clarified by Hallis that is useful to this historical study of China and concerns the word "person" or "personality". The Latin *persona* from which the English "person" is derived meant originally an actor's mask.

Thus, the Romans in their law used this word to denote the subject of civil rights and duties, meaning that a *persona* can act in the "legal drama". In other words, only a *persona* could be an actor in a play or a party in a legal dispute.[55] And it is this concept of *persona* which we shall see in this story to be so important in the understanding of state power and industrialisation in late imperial and early Republican China. This is because it allowed savvy personalities such as Yuan Shikai to control major industries by concealment and using a proxy, making the concept of *persona* a sword as well as a shield. He could appoint trusted individuals as company officials in the registered corporations during the infancy of commercial development of these industrial companies but hiding their ownership structure behind the veil of corporate personality.

This is a major contrast to the *guanban* (official management) and *guandu shangban* (official supervision-merchant management) enterprises which can always be associated with the patron officials. This structural possibility created by the introduction of corporate personality reduced the danger of provoking an early attack by the state towards the owners. This was the case for Yuan Shikai because his growing political power did indeed pose a potential but serious threat to the interests of other "state actors" such as the Manchu aristocracy which was embedded within the imperial state system apparatus.[56] Therefore, enterprises administered under the auspices of the old *guanban* and *guandu shangban* system constructed the imperial state whilst at the same time, through the corporate personality and corporations, deconstructed the imperial state.

Frederick Hallis, after analysing and comparing many theories of law and state and applying them to the situation of the 1920s, affirms the "reality of corporate persons" that implied a new conception of the state. Undoubtedly this was a result of Britain's industrialisation and transformation towards modernity. He concluded that it is no longer necessary for human associations endowed with corporate personality to require a benevolent concession of the state.[57]

Turning to English corporate law and China, it must be understood that even medieval English law recognises various forms of associations and also recognised the concept of incorporation. At first, incorporation was limited to ecclesiastical and public bodies such as chapter monasteries and boroughs. In the commercial spheres at this time the principal associations were the Guild of Merchants which more closely resembled trade protection associations. Incorporation was not needed to define members' rights and liabilities because each member traded on its own account subject to their obedience to the regulations of the guild. Trading on joint account was carried on through partnerships. The first type of English organisation to use the name "company" was the merchant adventurers trading overseas. The earliest types were the "regulated companies" which were extensions of the guild principle into the foreign sphere. They also retained much of the ceremonial and freemasonry of the domestic guild and each member traded with his own stock and on his own account. While obeying the rules of the company, incorporation was not essential. This is because the trading liability of each member was entirely separated from that of the company and the other members. Later, the partnership principle of trading on joint stock account pervaded the regulated companies. They became joint commercial enterprises instead of trade protection associations. These people started to operate on a joint account and with a joint stock. This was done initially on top of the separate trading by each member with his own stock. Subsequently this was done instead of partnership. The process can be traced in the development of the East India Company which received its first charter in 1600, granting it a monopoly of trade with the Indies which included China.[58]

The East India Company lost its monopoly on trade with the East in 1833. The modern English company legislation which allowed incorporation by simple registration as well as defining a clear distinction between partnership and joint stock companies was introduced between 1844 and 1845. Furthermore, limited liability of incorporated companies was confirmed by the British Parliament ten years later by the Joint Stock Companies Act of 1856.[59] Thus, in the intervening years between the two Opium Wars (1840 and 1860), Britain made great strides in developing a corporate form as a vehicle for commercial exploitation. The effect of this development was brought directly to the Chinese coast by a corresponding 1865 Companies Ordinance of Hong Kong and was resorted to by British firms in the China trade such as HSBC (the Hongkong and Shanghai Banking Corporation), when it was founded. David Faure notes that, throughout the 1890s, elite Hong Kong-Chinese circles felt that there was a need for constitutional and legal reforms. Before Wu Tingfang was appointed to the imperial government, he was in the legal circles in Hong Kong and was a legislator in the colony's Legislative Council. Wu became the vice-president of the newly formed Ministry of Agriculture, Industry and Commerce of the imperial government in April 1903. This was given responsibility for drafting the first Company Law of 1904. It only took Wu nine months from his appointment to the Bureau's presentation of the completed draft bills in January 1904. Faure also believes that an article by George Jamieson, the British Consul in China, on English company law could have served as the model and in this way the Western concept of corporate personality found its way from Europe into China.[60]

The Combined Consequence of the Reforms, 1860–1910

As discussed, the first phase of major reforms involved initial industrialisation based upon the development of *guanban* and then more importantly on the *guandu shangban* forms of enterprise. When the CMC was founded in 1873, the *guandu shangban* arrangement hinged on an "understanding" and that both the government and merchant could "tolerate". Imperial sanction was given in this way and Faure summed up the essence of this imperial outgrowth towards industrialisation and modern commerce from a commerical perspective. He believed that: though the CMC competed with foreign shipping companies, it benefited considreably from being the sole Chinese shipping monopoly granted by the imperial government and under the patronage of Li Hongzhang. This include access to imperial loans, the assured business of tribute rice, faciliated acquisition of valuable wharfing sites and exemption from transit dues for CMC shipped goods.[61]

It is apparent from the present discussion that the *guandu shangban* was a compromise arrangement for the imperial system, a form of *licence* personally overseen by imperial bureaucrats. From an economic perspective, it is ironic that whereas Britain, the first Western country to arrive uninvited in China, extinguished the monopoly of the East India Company in 1833, China adopted just such monopolies 40 years later in 1873. It would be another 31 years before China attempted to adopt a completely new and rudimentary legal system that carried with it a heavily British-influenced company law embedded with corporate personality.

Finally, after Li's fall from central power in 1895 and his subsequent death in 1901, Yuan Shikai gradually took over the "industrial-military complex" of Li Hongzhang and replaced him as Viceroy of Zhili and High Commissioner for Military and Foreign Affairs in North China. Yuan played an instrumental role in initiating the second phase of imperial reforms (*Xinzheng*) by establishing a legal system. In the end, this served more to protect his own interest. Corporate personality and corporations gave him a different *persona* to mask his ambitions. Taking advantage of the patronage such as that conferred upon the CMC and shielding his industrial interest under the legal *persona* of incorporated companies, Yuan was able to establish a mighty powerbase within the imperial state concealed beneath the ruling house. Over time he accumulated enough wealth and strength to withstand banishment to the political wilderness and later returned to the centre to challenge the imperial structure. He was finally powerful enough to mount a personal challenge and helped to bring the Qing Empire to its conclusion in early 1912 while the southern half of the empire was engulfed in revolt. This was sparked not by religious sects or by intellectual uproar but rather by the imperial attempt to nationalise railway corporations.[62]

Notes

1. Mary Clabaugh Wright, *The Last Stand of Chinese Conservatism,* p. ix.
2. For the "impact-response" analytical framework, see Ssu-yu Teng and John K. Fairbank eds., *China's Response to the West.*
3. For the massive but failed mid-nineteenth century Taiping rebellion where much of imperial China's Yangtze River heartland was occupied and costing more than 20 million lives, see Thomas H. Reilly, *The Taiping Heavenly Kingdom*; Frederic Wakeman, Jr., *Strangers at the Gate* gives an account of social unrest and a description of lesser rebellions on the eve of the Taiping Rebellion.
4. Yuan Shikai was in charge of legal reforms and the drafting of the company code which is the commercial form of corporate personality, see Philip C. C. Huang, *Code, Custom, and Legal Practice in China*, p. 34.
5. David Faure, *China and Capitalism*, p. 61.
6. Edward J. M. Rhoads, *Manchus & Han*, p. 171.
7. Arthur S. Miller, *Private Governments and the Constitution.*
8. Frederick Hallis, *Corporate Personality*, p. xiii.
9. David Faure, *China and Capitalism,* p. 64; Zhang Jian incorporated his regional enterprise Dasheng Cotton Mill (Mill No.1) in 1907.
10. The Qing dynasty ex-official, scholar-cum-entrepreneur Zhang Jian registered a cotton mill in 1905 under the new law as an unincorporated company with the Ministry of Commerce and incorpo-

ration in 1907; see Elisabeth Köll, *From Cotton Mill to Business Empire*, p. 124.

11. William C. Kirby, "China Unincorporated: Company Law and Business Enterprise in Twentieth-Century China".
12. Zhao Xingsheng, *Chuantong jingyan yu xiandai lixiang*, pp. 36–40.
13. Mary Clabaugh Wright, *The Last Stand of Chinese Conservatism*, pp. viii–ix; Paul A. Cohen, *Between Tradition and Modernity*, pp. 239–76; Paul A. Cohen, *Discovering History in China*, pp. 9–25.
14. Frederic Wakeman, Jr., *Strangers at the Gate*, pp. 109–149.
15. Wong Young-tsu, *A Paradise Lost*, p. 137.
16. See, S. C. M. Paine, *The Sino-Japanese War of 1894–1895.*
17. Jerome Ch'en, *Yuan Shih-k'ai*, 2nd ed., pp. 30–36.
18. Richard S. Horowitz, "Breaking the Bonds of Precedent: The 1905–6 Government Reform Commission and the Remaking of the Qing Central State".
19. Jerome Ch'en, *Yuan Shih-k'ai*, 2nd ed., pp. 55–76.
20. Victor Purcell, *The Boxer Uprising: A Background Study*, p. 213.
21. A corporation can of course carry on non-commercial businesses but it can be considered to be mainly a commercial and profit-generating enterprise.
22. Mary Clabaugh Wright, *The Last Stand of Chinese Conservatism.*
23. Albert Feuerwerker, *China's Early Industrialization.*
24. Albert Feuerwerker, *China's Early Industrialization*, p. 299.
25. Philip C. C. Huang, "Codified Law and Magisterial Adjudication in the Qing".
26. Albert Feuerwerker, "China's Nineteenth-Century Industrialization: The Case of the Hanyehping Coal and Iron Company, Limited," in *Studies in the Economic History of Late Imperial China*, p. 172; also see Quan Hansheng, *Hanyeping gongsi shilüe.*
27. Edward J. M. Rhoads, *Manchus & Han*, p. 7.
28. Li Hongzhang was the Viceroy of Zhili, fully referred to as "The Governor-General of Zhili and surrounding areas; Supervisor of Military Affairs and Food Production; Manager of Waterways and Director of Civil Affairs".
29. J. A. G. Roberts, *The Complete History of China*, p. 288.
30. Albert Feuerwerker, *China's Early Industrialization*, p. 98.

31. See Chi-kong Lai, "The Qing State and Merchant Enterprise: The China Merchants' Company, 1872–1902".
32. Also see David Faure, *China and Capitalism*, p. 54.
33. Albert Feuerwerker, *China's Early Industrialization*, pp. 13–14.
34. J. A. G. Roberts, *The Complete History of China*, p. 294.
35. Albert Feuerwerker, *China's Early Industrialization.*
36. Albert Feuerwerker, "Industrial Enterprise in Twentieth-Century China: The Chee Hsin Cement Co.".
37. See Philip C. C. Huang, *Civil Justice in China: Representation and Practice in the Qing*, pp. 9–20.
38. Examples of these academic debates include: Jonathan K. Ocko, *Bureaucratic Reform in Provincial China* and John L. Rawlinson, *China's Struggle for Naval Development.*
39. David Pong, *Shen Pao-chen and China's Modernization in the Nineteenth Century.*
40. Stephen C. Thomas, *Foreign Intervention and China's Industrial Development*, pp. 81–108.
41. See Chap. 7. The China Merchants' Steam Navigation Company, however, was incorporated into a large state corporation after Chiang Kai-shek took over power in 1930s; also see Zhongguo di er lishi dang'an guan (The Second Historical Archives of China), *Zhonghua minguo shi dangan ziliao hui bian. di 5 ji, di 2 bian.*
42. Luke S. K. Kwong, *A Mosaic of the Hundred Days.*
43. Liu Ping, "Wu Xu bianfa".
44. See Luke S. K. Kwong, *A Mosaic of the Hundred Days*, pp. 87–90.
45. Timothy Richard (1845–1919) was a Welsh Baptist Missionary Society missionary who went to Shandong province of China in 1870. Young John Allen (1836–1907) was an American Methodist missionary with the American Southern Methodist Episcopal Mission.
46. Luke S. K. Kwong, *A Mosaic of the Hundred Days*, pp. 213–224 and Jerome Ch'en, *Yuan Shih-k'ai*, 2nd ed., pp. 38–43.
47. David Faure, *China and Capitalism*, p. 63.
48. Joseph W. Esherick, *The Origins of the Boxer Uprising*, p. 311.
49. Liu Kunyi and Zhang Zhidong jointly memorialised the throne, Ssu-yu Teng and John K. Fairbank eds., *China's Response to the West*, p. 197; the Bureau of Commerce (*shangbu*) was created in 1903 to oversee its implementation, see Linda Pomerantz-Zhang,

Wu Tingfang, pp. 149–50; David Faure, *China and Capitalism*, pp. 62–64.

50. Zhang Jinfan, *Zhongguo jindai shehui yu fazhi*, p. 509.
51. On some problems of the Bankruptcy Law, see Zhang Jinfan, *Zhongguo jindai shehui yu fazhi wenming*, p. 253.
52. Frederick Hallis, *An Examination of Some Modern Theories of the Relation of Law and State with Special Reference to the Juristic Doctrine of Corporate Personality.*
53. Frederick Hallis, *Corporate Personality.*
54. Frederick Hallis, *Corporate Personality*, pp. xiii–xvi.
55. Frederick Hallis, *Corporate Personality*, p. xx.
56. Edward J. M. Rhoads, *Manchus & Han*, pp. 121–172.
57. Frederick Hallis, *Corporate Personality*, p. 244.
58. L. C. B. Gower, et al., *Gower's Principles of Modern Company Law*, pp. 22–52. Generally, see C. A. Cooke, *Corporation, Trust and Company.*
59. L. C. B. Gower, et al., *Gower's Principles of Modern Company Law*, pp. 22–52.
60. *David Faure, China and Capitalism*, pp. 52, 63 and 114; Zhemeisen, "Yingguo gongsi dingli", referred to in David Faure, *China and Capitalism*, p. 114.
61. David Faure, *China and Capitalism*, p. 50.
62. David Faure, *China and Capitalism*, pp. 47–51; Jerome Ch'en, *Yuan Shikai*, 2nd ed., pp. 90–108.

PART 2

Transplanting the Corporate Idea into Imperial China

Yuan Shikai, his Incorporated Cement Works and other Incorporated Companies, 1890–1912

This part shows that the enterprises founded during the Self-Strengthening Movement in the late nineteenth century may resemble companies at first glance—they issued stocks, for example—but they lacked the legally recognised independent status of a modern corporation with legal personality. As a result, they were subject to political machinations and had no defensive shelter. The Company Law of 1904 changed the situation entirely. Owing to the fact that it was incorporated, the Qixin company controlled by Yuan Shikai was the first major state industry that became independent, and the Qing court lost complete control over an imperial monopoly. This only eroded the imperial government's economic power mildly, but significantly enhanced Yuan's personal financial power. Gaining control of Qixin Cement sustained his influence while out of office and finally enabled him to regain control of the military during the revolution of 1911. Yuan was finally able to press for the child Emperor Puyi's 1912 abdication in Beijing. He took over from the Provisional President Sun Yat-sen and became the first President of the newly established Republic of China.

Chapter 3 opens in 1904, with the arrival of the new imperial Company Law. This allowed Western-type incorporated companies to be formed under China's own laws for the first time in its long history. It then sketches the country's demand for cement, as well as military strongman Yuan Shikai's attempts to find a stable income source to fund his activities and political struggles against his sworn rival Sheng Xuanhuai. Sheng, like him, was a protégé of Viceroy Li Hongzhang, but was for a long time merely managing the imperial monopolies for Li and had no military links. After the death of Li in 1901, however, Sheng Xuanhai gained control of all the big imperial monopolies and consolidated his economic power. Yuan Shikai, however, is shown here to be frantically fighting for a share of the imperial monopolies with only limited success.

This chapter documents the crude beginnings of Chinese cement manufacturing and the uneven path of its initial development. Even though the initiative was state-directed by the empire, early attempts to produce cement were a failure. The difficulty owes much to the lack of understanding of the technology and the product itself (mildly corrosive, bulky, perishable, anhydrous and existing as a hard-to-handle formless powder). The narrative addresses these issues in the 1890s and explains the characteristics of the modern cement industry, and the intricacies of its manufacturing and supply. Furthermore, by telling the story of the fight between Yuan Shikai and Sheng Xuanhuai over the imperial monopolies (railways, telegraphy and merchant shipping) after 1911, this chapter further explains the subtle differences between controlling a big business via an incorporated company and via a company that is not, in particular when the businesses in question were big imperial monopolies.

This chapter also casts light on the many political problems with the imperial monopolies. Many problems of China's early industrialisation before 1904 can be traced back to the absence of incorporation possibilities. This also caused the most important coal industry in Kaiping, in the northern city of Tangshan, to be seized by the British during the Boxer Uprising. This was then incorporated and listed on the London Stock Exchange under English law by the onsite drainage engineer Herbert Hoover. He made a big fortune out of this and became the President of the USA. Finally, this chapter concludes and argues that the problem for China before 1904 was the lack of a Chinese company law that could enable the state to confer legal personality on its own big companies by way of incorporation. Without this, it was impossible to offer Chinese legal protection in the jurisdictional as well as proprietary interests of their businesses.

Chapter 4 opens with a historical observation: Even though Yuan Shikai was ousted from political power in 1909 after the death of Empress Dowager Cixi in 1908, he returned to dismantle the Qing Empire in 1911. How did he sustain his political influence during banishment? This chapter answers the above question by providing a very detailed account of the recovery by Yuan Shikai of the old unincorporated Tangshan Cement Works from the British. This was achieved with the assistance of his right-hand man Zhou Xuexi. This imperial monopoly was taken over by the British during the Boxer Uprising. After repossession of the cement works, they speedily incorporated it to become a Chinese corporation under the Chinese Company Law of 1904. They also renamed it as the Qixin Cement Company Limited. The company was an "immediate success" and made huge profits in a very short time. Significantly, Yuan Shikai finally acquired a privately incorporated monopoly. With this, he found the protected economic engine that would help propel him past all his political opponents. From this time onwards, the cement industry would develop into a major industry in China and play a crucial part in the national modernisation of the new Republic.

In the past, Yuan Shikai was portrayed by historians to have had almighty military power. Many simply believed that he had unconditional and unwavering loyalty of his army subordinates. More elaborate scholarly discussions on the economics of acquisition and maintenance of this power are very rare. No doubt Yuan's military influence is an important explanation, but it was also the economic power created by private corporations that made him powerful. To Yuan Shikai, the Chinese cement industry was an easy takeover target in the early twentieth century. Firstly, it was unincorporated, and hence legally unprotected and could be easily acquired. Secondly, the business was relatively simple and focused: this was a single-product manufacturer. Thirdly, by 1905 he had consolidated his control of the railways, which were crucial for transportation in a bulk industry. Finally, it was an imperial monopoly with only one cement plant in the country and it was inside the province of Zhili that he governed. After 1906, the success of the cement company spurred on the establishment of other large incorporated businesses.

By the time Yuan Shikai was removed from power after the death of Empress Dowager Cixi, Yuan and Zhou Xuexi had already turned the success of the Qixin cement plant into an economic refuge. This refuge was for Yuan's supporters, while Yuan continued to expand into other industries and businesses. The reason why Yuan Shikai was able to make a remarkable comeback was this: by the eve of the 1911 "revolution", he not only possessed an independent, large, incorporated, expanded and very profitable cement company, he also had a whole string of both incorporated and unincorporated private businesses, owned and managed by and in the name of his protégé Zhou Xuexi.

CHAPTER 3

New Corporate Powers: The Accelerator of Imperial Malfunction

Private corporations introduced by the 1904 Company Law contributed to the imperial collapse. A corporate law in the form of the Qing Company Law of 1904 could seriously affect the imperial system. In order to understand this, how the position and status of large industrial and commercial concerns such as the cement plant in question must first be explained. Simply put, there were no *large* and *legally independent* Western-type enterprises in the Qing Empire before 1904. In fact, its mode of financing may have been governmental or private. Despite this, *all* the large industrial and commercial enterprises were *dependencies* operated within the imperial system. There was a single aim: military modernisation to strengthen imperial power.[1] This was the case for Viceroy Li Hongzhang from 1870 to 1896. Under his regime, all enterprises were controlled *within* the imperial *political structure*, thus exposing these enterprises to imperial politics.[2]

This situation was fundamentally altered by the 1904 Company Law. The effects of the law were as follows: commercially, the privilege of monopolistic non-competition was removed from the old industrial and commercial concerns of the Li Hongzhang era dating from the 1860s. This was replaced by a privilege-enforcing competition with other companies. Systemically, this was a granting of legal jurisdiction and an official devolution of political power.[3] This is because corporations, in any format, are analogous in structure and power to modern governments, albeit on a much smaller scale.[4] If one of these corporations expanded to form

H. Ko, *The Making of the Modern Chinese State*,
DOI 10.1007/978-981-10-2660-7_3

a large conglomerate with different enterprises and substantial business income obtained through strategic commercial and industrial businesses, and if it is also controlled by a military grouping sidelined by imperial politics, a volatile situation would develop. This was precisely the case for Yuan Shikai and his cohorts in the last three years of the Qing dynasty from 1909 to 1911.[5] Arguably, their group controlled a large "private government" in the form of an industrial conglomerate. This, unlike Li Hongzhang's enterprises, was independent of the imperial political structure. Yet it was couched within the newly introduced Western-style legal structure of the *Xinzheng* (New Policy) reforms.[6]

Yuan Shikai was the protégé in charge of the military affairs of the powerful Viceroy and Governor-General of Zhili, Li Hongzhang. This was before Li lost this position following the Sino-Japanese War of 1894–5.[7] This war was a disaster which completely annihilated the Chinese Navy that Li Hongzhang had conscientiously built up over the previous 30 years under the banner of the Self-Strengthening Movement.[8] After Li Hongzhang's death in 1901, Yuan Shikai was appointed to this once-powerful position in June 1902. He assumed the same post previously held by Li Hongzhang seven years before.[9] Unfortunately, the position was the same in name only because the "military industrial complex" of Li Hongzhang had been split up long ago into its components after the Sino-Japanese War. It was a three-way split with the military going to Yuan Shikai, the political position of Viceroy of Zhili and High Commissioner for Military and Foreign Affairs in North China to Wang Wenzhao and the economic aspect to Sheng Xuanhuai. They were all protégées of Li Hongzhang.[10]

With the navy destroyed, the major industrial and commercial enterprises which Li Hongzhang had built passed to his other protégé Sheng Xuanhuai. Sheng was previously in charge of commercial affairs in his camp. He had been promoted to "fourth-rank official of the Court of Sacrificial Worship" (*si jing pin tang*) after he had received an imperial audience in October 1896. He gained control of all the big imperial heavy industries. For some years Yuan Shikai had to find ways to politically struggle against an economically entrenched Sheng Xuanhuai. Yuan needed to wrestle economic power from Sheng and his followers and desperately wanted to find alternative income sources to consolidate his position. Finally, Yuan Shikai, through his protégé Zhou Xuexi, discovered a unique old cement plant in 1906 (the first cement plant in China). This was the only heavy imperial industrial monopoly the imperial dynasty had that was *not* in the possession of the imperial government. Hence, it was *not* inside the imperial structure. It had fallen into British control during the Boxer Rebellion but Yuan discovered that the British coal-mining corporation that controlled it did not have any documents to back up their legal possession of the plant.[11] He swiftly seized it and incorporated it under the new Chinese Company Law of 1904 and turned it into an enormously successful *private* monopoly. This was the beginning of the end of the Qing Empire, precipitating too the end of an imperial system which had survived two millennia.

The Cement Industry Begins

Yu Ruiyun, a Xiangshan resident of Guangdong province, made a personal investment of 100,000 taels of silver and built a cement plant along the Wanzai waterway near Macao between 1882 and 1887. This plant was subsequently sold to the British and the production facilities eventually moved to Hong Kong. This became the British-owned Green Island Cement Company on the edge of the Kowloon peninsula.[12] In northern China in 1889, Li Hongzhang authorised the manufacturing of cement next to the Kaiping mines near Tianjin. This plant was mainly intended for military use. It began manufacturing in 1891 but the enterprise failed after one year. It was restarted again after 1901 with limited production when it was taken over by a British company. This company was established by the future American president and mining engineer Herbert Hoover with his employer Charles Moreing. It was registered in London but operated by Major Walter Nathan for this British-registered company in China. Yuan Shikai, who by this time had become a rising military governor and Viceroy of Zhili, was presented by his economic deputy and adviser Zhou Xuexi with a simple retrieval plan, and the plant was confiscated by Yuan Shikai in 1906. It was then incorporated under the Chinese Company Law as Qixin Cement Company Limited.[13]

The difficult operational characteristics of the cement industry are illustrated by this first cement plant of China, in that it failed soon after opening.[14] Yet, after a 15-year break in 1906 it was restarted by Yuan Shikai to become one of the most successful heavy manufacturing industries in China.[15] In the same year, Yuan Shikai's rival and Governor of the southern province of Guangdong, Cen Cunxuan, also established a cement plant in the provincial capital Guangzhou. This venture also failed immediately upon opening in 1909.[16] All three ventures were similar in that they were launched by powerful mandarins of the empire. So what was so special about Yuan Shikai?

In late 1889, Li Hongzhang was notified by Liu, a Daotai of the engineering department of the Lüshun Docks, that the scientist of the Nanjing Arsenal and once consul to the German embassy, Xu Jianyin, had sent a box of soil samples from Wuxi. This was to be tested to see whether it would be fit for cement manufacturing. It was accordingly tested by the Western engineer under the employment of the docks, and Li Hongzhang was sent the test report. Although it was found that the material was not suitable for manufacturing cement, it pointed the way for the Daotai to search for similar raw materials in the north. Liu also heard that a cement factory had been built in Portuguese-controlled Macao. So, in the spring of 1889 he secured two barrels of powder cement from this factory for compressive stress testing (after hydrating the powder and letting it stand to form solid cement blocks). It was found that the quality and strength was as good as British imports. Liu also knew that Li Hongzhang's economic deputy Tang Tingshu's home town, Xiangshan,[17] was next to Macao in Guangdong province. He therefore hoped that Li Hongzhang could ask Tang to enquire about the industrial process, the machineries used, selling price, transportation costs and insurance charges on his next visit home. Furthermore, he suggested that some Macao cement should be brought back to the north for testing in the various official arsenals. Tang believed that it would be more economical and sustainable to buy from Macao rather than import.[18]

Li Hongzhang promptly contacted Tang Tingshu and asked him to do just that: to learn about the Macao operation generally.[19] Tang replied three days later, reporting that he had in fact started to survey the Macao cement factory three years before in the winter of 1886. Furthermore, the proprietor and investor, Yu Ruiyun, was his friend. He detailed the chemical processes and the balanced formula required for the manufacturing of "quality" cement. During those previous three years he had asked the Macao cement plant to make different cement from raw materials imported from different regions. Then, for a couple of years, he conducted numerous detailed stress tests of different concrete blocks made from these different cements using British testing criteria. He also asked the English engineer at the Kaiping Coal Administration, which he was managing at the time, to visit the various "Portland" cement plants in England during a visit home. On his return, Tang discussed with the engineer in detail the conduct and processes of cement manufacturing and testing. In his report to Li Hongzhang, Tang reported that it was exactly two months before in the autumn when he became confident that he had mastered the techniques of production. He had also made feasibility calculations for investing in a cement factory in the north. There were supplies of limestone and an abundance of cheap coal needed for making cement around the Kaiping area in Tangshan. Lastly, he noted that the Macao factory had already failed commercially by this time and there was a takeover bid from Hong Kong.[20]

Five days later on 2 December 1889, Li Hongzhang directed Tang Tingshu to build China's first cement plant, using investment from various military departments. The location was a city north of the treaty port of Tianjin called Tangshan. The main reason given by Li was that there was a military and government need for cement:

> The cement that was made previously using the Tangshan limestone and the beach sand from Xiangshan was tested in Great Britain by reputable technical analysts at the various Portland cement plants. It has been recommended as first class cement because it could withstand 400 pounds of stress. If this is really true, then this cement would be the best in the world. This cement material is a necessity for the construction industry. Therefore, if we can make it ourselves and if it is suitable for our use, the transportation cost would be much lower than buying cement from overseas. Presently it is estimated that the erection of the factory building, purchasing of machinery, hiring of foreign personnel et cetra, would require 50 to 60 thousand taels of silver. It has been said that the landlord of Xiangshan would subscribe to the stock issue. If that accounts for 50 % of the stock subscription, then it would cost no more than 20 to 30 thousand taels. Raising this amount would not be difficult. You, the Daotai, have been negotiating with the landlord, so have you reached an agreement yet? At present, there is a high demand in *official* engineering works for cement. Therefore, every bureau can contribute 10 to 20 thousand taels. The Articles of Association must be promptly drawn up and a date should be determined for the commencement of production to meet the needs. The Macao factory has already shut down and the production passed over to Hong Kong. Unfortunately, the cement produced there is not suitable for use in the north, thus we should slow our purchases from them.[21]

The new cement plant was completed in late 1890.[22] When all the machinery and the foreign consultant arrived, production started in 1891. Unfortunately, Tang died in 1892 and the Kaiping Mines together with the cement plant passed to the control of Zhang Yi who was a close relative of Empress Dowager Cixi.[23] By 1893, the cement plant was shut down by Zhang Yi owing to loses. It failed after only two years of operation.[24] The 100,000 taels of invested capital had been exhausted and it owed the

Kaiping Coal Mines a further 100,000 taels.[25] The *North China Herald* attributed the failure to "graft",[26] but Zhou Xuexi, the future owner who became general manager of the Kaiping Mines in 1900, instead attributed the loss to a bad-quality product.[27] So who had the correct explanation for the failure? The answer is that neither had.

Cement Manufacturing Characteristics

Albert Feuerwerker in his study of this cement plant described cement as no more than an "arid powder".[28] This is accurate and the subject a dry one unless looking at the industrial development of China as a whole. Yet, that is precisely the most interesting aspect of this industry. It is the simplicity of the product, the apparent simplicity of its manufacturing process and the outward simplicity of a predicted general demand that makes this industry extraordinary. Modernising economies would find themselves with a continuous craving for this powder. All modern constructions whether railways, bridges, fortresses, buildings, roads or sewage facilities depend on the availability of cement. Cement is an important element of the modern world and modern city-dwellers are never far away from cement or its building material form: concrete (with aggregates of sand, stones and water).[29] Thus, this industry's attraction as a profitable business investment is substantial, especially when in 1900 there was not a single Chinese production facility.[30] However, this simplicity was deceptive. As mentioned, it would be shown that the secret to a successful cement industry lies not with *internal* management efficiency but in politics *external* to the manufacturing firm because of the characteristics of this industrial product. This is, in fact, a treacherous business despite its innocent façade. At this point a preliminary explanation of the nature of the characteristics of cement is in order.

To begin, the cement industry is a bulk industry with a very heavy industrial product in loose powder form which has to be moved in high volumes. Cement itself thus has no shape and is very heavy and dense. The product has a very limited lifespan in normal atmospheric conditions, the length of which depends on external weather conditions. High humidity will cause it to solidify into pellets initially and any contact with water such as rain drops accelerates this process and renders the cement unusable. Thus, if cement is allowed to be exposed to the open air for even a short period of time, atmospheric water will be drawn in, causing the powder cement to solidify firstly into lumps. Then, if left for too long, the whole consignment will become blocks of rocks moulded in the shape of the container or package. Leakages of the powder, which is common during any transportation, and bad weather will thus cause this very heavy product to be stuck to the ground or whatever that was used to transport it such as a train carriage or a ship. Furthermore, cement is an acidic anhydrite and a mildly corrosive substance that can cause blindness if it enters the eye. Inhalation will damage the lungs.[31] Though not impossible, handling and packaging is nonetheless rather tricky, especially under the pre-modern conditions of Qing dynasty China, when automatic bulk power-handling equipment and specialised transportation had not been invented.

The nature of the cement business is such that those who correctly manage the special logistics and operate in the optimum conditions can expect very high profits in a *continuous* and *simple* operation. If *continuity* can be maintained, this industry can become very profitable in a very short period of time. Getting it wrong would result in extremely expensive *discontinuity* of operation and prohibitively high re-activation costs, as well as endless lengthening of the time to reach quality stability.[32] Such a situation is, therefore, highly likely to cause the speedy collapse of the firm. Thus, the success of the cement industry is predicated upon a continuous, smooth growing supply of this "grey gold" by reliable processes and transportation. Consequently, the industrial business of cement manufacturing is always intricately linked to the local power-holder or the local "baron" (military, bureaucratic, financial, commercial, or robber). This is because, in a backward developing state, it can always be expected that the most powerful local organisation controls this industry because the ability to control the market can help ensure the necessary continuous flow from plant to customers.

So how did Yuan Shikai come to this industry? Why was the cement industry important for a latecomer to the economic realm? Furthermore, how did he and his followers turn cement manufacturing into one of the most profitable industrial companies in the early industrial history of China from 1906? And why did it affect the whole imperial system? In order to answer these questions, we must understand the political battles which Yuan had to fight to consolidate his political power for the "commanding heights" of the nascent Chinese industrial economy in the early 1900s.[33] Paradoxically, he had to seize enterprises which were both *incorporated* and *un*incorporated and his plans were frustrated by the most important coal-mining firm which was *incorporated*. In the end, it was the rediscovery of the Tangshan Cement Works which changed his floundering economic fortunes.

Unincorporated Imperial Monopolies

The large *un*incorporated imperial industrial monopolies were vulnerable to political takeovers. This is clear from the actions taken by Yuan Shikai towards gaining control of them. Yuan Shikai was made Governor of Shandong province in December 1899. On Li Hongzhang's death on 7 November 1901, he was appointed to Li's post of Viceroy of Zhili and High Commissioner for Military and Foreign Affairs in North China.[34] Yuan Shikai gained some political power because he controlled the new military,[35] but economic power resided elsewhere in the control of the imperial industrial monopolies. However, these were not under his control before 1906.

So who were controlling these monopolies, the "commanding heights" of the imperial Chinese economy between 1901 and 1906? A brief summary should help set the scene for discussion: Sheng Xuanhuai, as the Director-General (i.e., the official supervisor for a *guandu shangban* arrangement), controlled the railways (*un*incorporated and within the imperial system), the iron and steel industries (*un*incorporated and within the imperial system), telegraphy (*un*incorporated and within the imperial system) and merchant shipping (*un*incorporated and within the imperial system). The British controlled coal mining (*incorporated* under English law) and cement (*un*incorporated but under the control of the incorporated British coal-mining company).[36] The above shows that, in 1901, just when Yuan Shikai became Viceroy of Zhili, the most important large-scale imperial industrial monopolies were *un*incorporated and held within the imperial system but administered or "supervised" by Sheng Xuanhuai.

In 1901, the Boxer Protocol stipulated that China was banned from purchasing arms for two years. The moratorium was observed by both Yuan Shikai and the Viceroy of Huguang, Zhang Zhidong. Neither of them requested the imperial treasury for arms-purchasing funds during this period, and only local resources were being used to finance the army. Yuan Shikai, however, was desperately looking for alternative finances, not only to pay for his army and to supplement Zhili's provincial revenues but also to consolidate his position within the government and his own influence.[37] In order to consolidate his political power, he turned to the large industries to strengthen his economic power base.[38] Though taking over these were possible, it would take Yuan Shikai a while to clear up Sheng Xuanhuai's influences. This is because Sheng had been in command of these major enterprises since the early days of the Self-Strengthening movement in the 1870s. Sheng Xuanhuai had had nearly three decades to consolidate his hold and to place people loyal to him in these firms. They, together with Sheng, were well dug in as stockholders.[39]

Unincorporated Railways

Yuan Shikai's takeover of an *unincorporated* imperial business proved relatively easy, even with an entrenched Sheng Xuanhuai, but Yuan's control was initially shallow. This is illustrated by the situation of the railways. Upon his appointment to the viceroyalty, Yuan Shikai was also made the commissioner of the nation's railways on 10 January 1902.[40] Originally, authority over the railways rested with Li Hongzhang and Sheng Xuanhuai, with Sheng carrying out the detailed execution work. He was in charge of both building and operating the railway lines. When Li Hongzhang fell from power after the Sino-Japanese War, a deal was struck between Zhang Zhidong and Sheng Xuanhuai. The deal allowed Sheng to continue his work with the railways while also taking on the responsibility of running Zhang Zhidong's seriously loss-making Hanyang Steel Foundry. This "privatisation" received imperial approval in June 1895 and was executed in May 1896.[41] Finally, an *un*incorporated National Railway Company (*Tielu zong gongsi*) was formed and headed by Sheng as Director-General in 1895.[42]

When Yuan Shikai became commissioner of the railways in 1901, Sheng Xuanhuai was ousted. He was sent off to semi-retirement in imperial tradition to mourn his father who died on 24 October 1902 for 27 months until May 1905.[43] Furthermore, according to imperial regulations, he had to relinquish his official posts, which he did without delay. Yet, no one was quite sure whether this applied to a Director-General of an imperial enterprise.[44] It was four years after Yuan became commissioner of the railways in late 1905 that he was ready and determined to force Sheng to resign as Director-General and replace him with Yuan's own protégé, Tang Shaoyi.[45] On 21 October 1905 when the Yellow River railway bridge on the new Beijing-Hankou line was completed, Yuan sent Tang Shaoyi to accompany Sheng Xuanhuai for the final inspection and take possession. Then, a month later, Sheng was accused of mismanaging the Nanjing-Shanghai line and was ousted. Tang was immediately appointed as Director-General on 17 November 1905. After taking full control, the National Railway Company was then simply abolished in 1906![46] It is significant that the *un*incorporated National Railway Company was abolished by Yuan with such effortless ease: an *un*incorporated enterprise, no matter how big, was politically exposed without legal cover. As we shall see later, taking control of the railway was significant because this made controlling of the cement industry meaningful. This is because political power had given Yuan the market for the bulky cement along the railway lines (Fig. 3.1). This stretched from Tangshan to Tianjin and Beijing, and from Beijing all the way across the North China Plain down to the industrial city of Hankou along the Yangtze river.[47]

Unincorporated Telegraphy and Merchant Shipping

The Imperial Telegraphy Administration and the merchant shipping firm CMC were another two important *un*incorporated monopolies which were controlled by Sheng Xuanhuai. There were, however, entirely within the administration of the imperial system.[48] These were eventually taken over by Yuan Shikai and again with relative ease in early 1903. As discussed, the earliest opportunity came during the time when the death of Sheng Xuanhuai's father caused him to temporarily lose his official positions but he managed to cling on to some important commercial appointments. At this juncture, the control of the Imperial Telegraph Administration and the CMC was up for grabs from other officials who wanted to take control as well. Sheng did attempt to defend these enterprises from predators. Firstly, when he heard that Empress Cixi's man Zhang Yi was about to be appointed as Director-General to both firms, he sought help from Zhang Zhidong and Yuan Shikai. Then, subsequently, when Yuan Shikai wanted to take these firms for himself after warding off Zhang Yi, Sheng endeavoured to broker a deal during his meeting with Yuan in Shanghai. He suggested that the Imperial Telegraph Administration should be given to Yuan with Sheng himself retaining the CMC (bureau). He also sought the help of the governor of Shandong province Zhou Fu to act as the mediator. Furthermore, he went to ask Zhang Zhidong for help again. He even asked Grand Councillor Ronglu to stop the Telegraph Administration falling into Yuan's hands by suggesting that it should be administered by the new ministry of commerce. Failing all that, Sheng attempted to make an official buyout more difficult by setting a high value for purchasing the merchant investment and demanding only "cash" for these.[49]

Sheng Xuanhuai's political tactics plainly didn't work. Yuan Shikai never intended to pay. Moreover, there was in fact no reason for him to pay. The CMC was *not* an incorporated firm with corporate personality. It was not even equivalent to a Western *un*incorporated company. It was just

Fig. 3.1 Map showing northern China and the extent of the railways under Yuan Shikai's control in 1906 and hence the size of his inland cement market (Based on Jerome Ch'en, *Yuan Shih-kai, 1859–1916*, p. 8)

a government bureau dressed up as a Western company by taking on some of the outward attributes of Western firms operating in China.[50] Attributes that would have helped Li Hongzhang raise money, such as issuing stocks, were only a clever scheme devised by Li Hongzhang to launch the firm with merchant money. Subsequently, Yuan Shikai secured an edict appointing himself and Zhang Zhidong to oversee the transfer of the Telegraph Administration to official control.[51] Yuan was appointed commissioner in charge of the telegraphs on 15 January 1903 and Sheng was forced to resign as the CMC's Director-General after the lunar New Year in February that year.[52] No cash was paid out to the stockholders as requested by Sheng, but the stockholders (Sheng being the largest) continued to receive the "large dividend to which they had become accustomed".[53] Although Yuan Shikai sent his men, Tang Shaoyi (nephew of Tang Tingshu) and Xu Run (the original general manager of China Merchants before being ousted by Sheng in 1885) to take over the Telegraph and Shipping firms respectively, many of Sheng's people remained firmly fixed in the "companies". It is interesting to note that Sheng Xuanhuai used the word "*gongsi* (company)" to describe these imperial firms but up to this point in time there was no company law in China.[54]

Consequently, even though Yuan Shikai *could* take over these imperial firms easily, because these were *not* separately incorporated and thus *not* protected by clear modern Western-type legislation, he *could not* gain instant absolute control. This is because firms such as the Imperial Telegraph Administration and the CMC had technical operations spanning the length and breadth of the empire. The internal management operations within these firms were large and complicated: the Imperial Telegraphy was at the time an advanced technological company involved in electronic signal transmission and the CMC involved running a complex and expensive logistic operation. These were cross-provincial imperial enterprises with offices and agencies all across the ports of call. Furthermore, in the nepotistic world of the Qing dynasty, many of these were run by stockholders who were friends and relatives loyal to Sheng.[55] For example, Sheng's third brother manages the Imperial Telegraph Administration office in Guangzhou. They needed pacifying with dividends because, in revolt, it might become practically difficult to make these long-distance operations operable.[56]

Therefore, although the *un*incorporated monopolies were easy to capture, in reality, it would take a little time for Yuan to gain complete control. During the three long decades Sheng was Director-General he had made himself the biggest stockholder over the years.[57] Thus, it is not difficult to understand how hollow Yuan's control was immediately upon his swift takeover even when management experts in the respective businesses such as Tang Shaoyi and Xu Run were parachuted in. This is in contrast to the later situation when Yuan managed to take over the old Tangshan Cement Works in 1906. Firstly, cement was almost a new industry because it had failed two years after opening in 1891. So there was no entrenched imperial bureaucrat such as Sheng Xuanhuai in charge. Secondly, the cement industry in general employed fewer people and had comparatively minor operational difficulties internal to the firm.[58] The concern of the small internal management of the Tangshan Cement Works was simply to manufacture a solitary product, cement, and then only one type of it. Yet, the cement industry potentially still had market reach for the whole of China and beyond.[59] In order to appreciate the importance of the infant Chinese cement industry, the situation which had developed at the neighbouring Kaiping coal mines should be understood first.

The Incorporated Coal Mines

The only incorporated enterprise Yuan Shikai had to deal with was in the strategically important coal-mining industry. It is worth scrutinising the coal industry in detail because it is intimately intertwined with the development of the cement industry. Cement manufacturing uses a large amount of coal, and the history of China's cement industry is inseparable from that of coal mining. The Kaiping Coal Administration was established as a "*ju*" (bureau) by Li Hongzhang in 1877. It fell into the hands of the British during the Boxer Uprising and the subsequent events of 1900 and 1901. The British company, the Chinese Engineering and Mining Company Limited, which was formed to take over the Kaiping Mines was incorporated in London by Herbert Hoover and his then principal Charles Moreing.[60] This company was able to operate on Chinese soil by virtue of the extraterritoriality bestowed to its nationals (corporate persons included) by the various "unequal treaties" signed between the two countries since July 1843.[61] All of the other major industries were *un*incorporated in 1901 and, except cement, were held by the Qing government structure, tucked securely *within* the jurisdiction of the imperial system as bureaus and controlled directly by Sheng Xuanhuai. Yuan Shikai was politically powerful and could abolish the *un*incorporated National Railway Company or take over the *un*incorporated China Merchants' Steam Navigation Company and *un*incorporated Imperial Telegraph Administration. However, when he confronted the British-registered Chinese Mining and Engineering Company which controlled the Kaiping Mines and had *full corporate per-*

sonality protection, he was totally frustrated. It was only three years since the singing of the Boxer Protocol and China was in a weak international and military position. Thus, Yuan Shikai made it clear to the British that he had never intended to repudiate the transfer by force but instead opted for peaceful negotiation and litigation.[62]

The Kaiping Coal Administration was also founded by Li Hongzhang in 1877. It was wholly government-operated because the government only needed private capital and not special skills from the private sector to operate a coal mine.[63] The Director-General appointed by the imperial government who was holding office in 1900 during the Boxer Uprising was again Zhang Yi and he was captured by the British during the uprising. After some wrangling, and while under arrest, he transferred all Kaiping's assets to a new London-registered, limited company for "protection".[64] This was without the knowledge of the imperial government and was thus subsequently disputed. Originally, stockholders who lost out in this matter were angry but the anger was contained within the company. When this came to public light in November 1902, Yuan Shikai was alarmed at the loss of China's most "basic" industry under his watch in Zhili.[65] He investigated the situation, speaking to the British Minister to China, Sir Ernest Mason Satow, in early December of 1902 and was shown details of the transfer agreements.[66] A few months later, in March 1903, he debated the issue with the new British general manager T. R. Wynne as well as confirming the authenticity of the legal documents held by the company.[67] Yuan finally memorialised the throne within a few days of 13 March 1903, setting out the whole situation and damning Zhang Yi's incompetence.[68] On the other hand, Zhang Yi had already pre-emptively memorialised to defend himself against criticism in January 1903, two months before Yuan memorialised the throne in March.[69]

Litigation: Fighting the British Corporation

Meanwhile, during his investigation in mid-February 1903, Yuan Shikai contemplated the possibility of legal action against the English company while in conversation with Walter Townley, the British *chargé d'affaires.* The advice from him was that if the English company was legally constituted, which he believed to be so, there was no good legal case for the Chinese government recovering the Kaiping mines.[70] Apparently sensing the gravity of the situation and encouraged by Article 12 of the "Mackay Treaty" signed six months previously,[71] the imperial government appointed Zai Zhen, Yuan Shikai and Wu Tingfang on 22 April 1903, one month after Yuan's detailed memorial to the throne, to draft a Company Law and to "immediately" select the personnel needed to establish a ministry of commerce.[72]

Legislation: Making Chinese Corporations

The Ministry of Commerce was duly established four months later on 9 September 1903.[73] In December 1903, Yuan Shikai informed the British that he had never intended to settle the matter of the coal-mining company by force and simultaneously memorialised the throne again, accusing Zhang Yi of procrastination.[74] A month later, the Company Law was completed and promulgated before the lunar New Year on 21 January 1904.[75] The Company Law was quickly drawn up to become the first piece of modern legislation even before any hope that the new general legal rules laying the foundation for civil relationships were put in place. In fact, Zhang Yi started legal proceedings in London. At the same time, it was decided to urgently draft the new law. On 17 June 1903, two months after the appointment of Zai Zhen, Yuan Shikai and Wu Tingfang, the London solicitors representing Zhang Yi filed a case at the High Court in London.[76] The case was finally heard by the Chancery Division in early 1905 and Zhang Yi won the first case.[77]

The Chinese Company Law was in place by early 1904. Yuan Shikai was thus not impressed by this early 1905 judgement after the promulgation of the new Chinese law. He had already memorialised the throne again in March 1904. Yuan pointed out that according to the memorandum the company was registered in London under English law. That registration, he contended, must be cancelled and that the company must be governed by Chinese law.[78] Of course, nothing happened. Extraterritoriality would certainly not be rescinded by one piece of hastily drafted Qing company legislation. Worse of all, the Court of Appeal in London overturned the lower court judgement in January 1906.[79] Hence, Yuan Shikai's first brush with the power of modern corporate personality was exasperating. The process of untying the legal situation was long, slow, abstract and difficult. Once incorporated (by simple registration in this case), the establishment of corporate personality for a firm offers a shield against external interference.

Unlike *un*incorporated counterparts (such as the National Railway Company, the CMC, or the Imperial Telegraph Administration which were firms operated and held *within* the imperial system and subject to *political* manoeuvres), firms that acquired corporate personality were protected by the modern *legal* institution: civil law enforced by the courts. Whether it was English law that applied through the unequal treaties or an indigenous Chinese law that was applied is not the crucial conceptual or even practical point: the crucial point is whether incorporation had been recognised by the Qing imperial state. English law, and thus the English corporate person, was recognised by the Qing state via the treaties with Great Britain.[80] The concern here is that China was not confronting a modern Western army on its soil but a modern firm, a modern corporation, formed under a modern Western legal system and armed with the shield of corporate personality.

The problem for China before 1904 was the lack of a company law that recognises China's own firms legally with corporate personality protection. The Kaiping fiasco demonstrates how inappropriate the Chinese imperial system had become. It had difficulties in accommodating modern and Western economic institutions that were created by textual foreign law but operating on China's soil. The imperial system was outdated and was in systemic failure. This benefited the legally better-informed Hoover and Moreing. They took advantage and successfully captured a big chunk of China's energy sector. These adventurers benefited immensely from the chronically anachronistic imperial legal system and its very serious legislative stagnancy. In a nutshell, the unchanging but resilient imperial system descended from an ancient agrarian state had clashed with, and lost out to, the modern world that contains new modern corporations. In 1905, it was genuinely "a sticky situation".

Notes

1. Xia Dongyuan, *Yangwu yundong shi*, p. 195.
2. Chi-kong Lai, "The Qing State and Merchant Enterprise: The China Merchants' Company, 1872–1902".
3. C. A. Cooke, *Corporation, Trust and Company*, pp. 15 and 67. What the Company Law of 1904 changed was the granting of "market privilege" to the granting of "jurisdiction" subject to the rules of the Chinese legal system generally. Since China did not have an advanced legal system comparable to what the Western countries had, this created an anomaly whereby companies in the form of corporations became rather independent and lightly regu-

lated by the Ministry of Commerce formed and assigned to control them.

4. Arthur S. Miller, *Private Governments and the Constitution.*
5. See Edward J. M. Rhoads, *Manchus & Han*, p. 178; Stephen R. MacKinnon, *Power and Politics in Late Imperial China*, p. 205; Jerome Ch'en, *Yuan Shih-k'ai*, 2nd ed., pp. 77–89.
6. After the devastation of Beijing and northern China by the occupying foreign armies during the Boxer Uprising of 1901, the Empress Dowager Cixi authorised legal reforms as promoted by a joint memorial by senior officials Liu Kunyi and Zhang Zhidong: The "Joint Proposals of Liu Kuniyi and Zhang Zhidong 1901", see Ssu-yu Teng and John K. Fairbank eds., *China's Response to the West*, p. 197.
7. Jerome Ch'en, *Yuan Shih-k'ai*, 2nd ed., pp. 8 and 18.
8. S. C. M. Paine, *The Sino-Japanese War of 1894–1895*, pp. 197–244.
9. Jerome Ch'en, *Yuan Shih-k'ai*, 2nd ed., pp. 53–76; Stephen R. MacKinnon, *Power and Politics in Late Imperial China,* pp. 23–26 and 53–76.
10. Albert Feuerwerker, *China's Early Industrialization,* p. 66.
11. Xia Dongyuan, *Sheng Xuanhuai Zhuan*, pp. 243–251; Luo Zhaoqian, *Wangqing guandu shangban yanjiu*; Zhou Xuexi, "Qixin gongsi chuangban jingguo" in *QXGS*, p. 27.
12. Green Island Cement Holdings Limited, "Introduction: Compile Profile".
13. Shi Changjun, "Qingzhou, Qixin: shui shi zhongguo shuini gongye de faxiang di?".
14. Yu Lu, "Yu Lu gei Zhou Xuexi de zhawen" in *QXGS*, p. 27.
15. Albert Feuerwerker, "Industrial Enterprise in Twentieth-Century China: The Chee Hsin Cement Co."; Wellington Chan, *Merchants, Mandarins, and Modern Enterprise in Late Ch'ing China*, pp. 114–117; *QXGS*, pp. 153–158.
16. Liu Linrui, "Zou ban Guangdong shimintu chang gongwen shimo jilüe, di er juan", A brief account of the financing arrangement for the establishment of the Guangdong Cement Works by Liu Linrui in *ZJGS3*, p. 325.
17. Present day Zhongshan, Guangdong province, north of Macao.
18. The report from Tang Tingshu to Li Hongzhang in *QXGS*, p. 22.

19. Short order issued by Viceroy Li Hongzhang, High Commissioner for Military and Foreign Affairs in North Chinato Tang Tingshu, *QXGS*, p. 19.
20. The report from Tang Tingshu to Li Hongzhang, *QXGS*, p. 22.
21. The opinion of Li Hongzhang for Tang Tingshu, 1889 in *QXGS*, p. 22.
22. The opinion of Li Hongzhang for Tang Tingshu, 1889 in *QXGS*, p. 25.
23. The Kaiping Mines Administration reporting to Yuan Shikai, Junior Guardian of the Heir Apparent in *QXGS*, p. 50.
24. It will be seen in Chap. 5 that this is normal for a cement plant for those who came in believing that it should be a simple business to operate. "Zhou Xuexi: What happened in the initial founding of the Qixin company?" in *QXGS*, p. 27.
25. See generally Ellsworth C. Carlson, *The Kaiping Mines, 1877–1912.*
26. Ellsworth C. Carlson, *The Kaiping Mines,* p. 51, quoted from the *North China Herald* (18 April 1893), 50:260; (1 September 1893), 51:339–340; (6 July 1894), 53:15.
27. What happened in the initial founding of the Qixin company? by Zhou Xuexi in *QXGS*, p. 26.
28. Albert Feuerwerker, "Industrial Enterprise in Twentieth-Century China: The Chee Hsin Cement Co.".
29. Philip A. Alsop & James W. Post, *Cement Plant Operations Handbook*, p. 77.
30. *QXGS*, p. 19–20.
31. Philip A. Alsop & James W. Post, *Cement Plant Operations Handbook*, pp. 54–67, 80 and 126; David W. A. Sharp, *The Penguin Dictionary of Chemistry.*
32. Philip A. Alsop & James W. Post, *Cement Plant Operations Handbook*, pp. 84–91.
33. "Commanding heights" is a term coined by Lenin and means banking and large-scale industry. See Richard B. Day, "Dialectical Method in the Political Writings of Lenin and Bukharin".
34. Accepted by Yuan in 17th November 1901<TE: Please check.>; Jerome Ch'en, *Yuan Shih-k'ai*, 2nd ed., pp. 62–63.
35. This was achieved by being entrusted to build the modern New Army for the throne after the annihilation of Li Hongzhang's Huai Army and his navy; Jerome Ch'en, *Yuan Shih-k'ai*, 2nd ed., pp. 29–43.

36. This was caused by the unpaid debt from the 1890s owed to the mines; therefore it was occupied together with the coal mining company. Xia Dongyuan, *Sheng Xuanhuai Zhuan*, pp. 247–256; Ellsworth C. Carlson, *The Kaiping Mines,* pp. 57–83; Luo Zhaoqian, *Wangqing guandu shangban yanjiu*, pp. 57–83; *QXGS*, pp. 26–27.
37. Jerome Ch'en, *Yuan Shih-k'ai*, 2nd ed., pp. 62–63. Jerome Ch'en believed that Yuan Shikai needed money for his military but the sums involved were too big for Yuan Shikai to finance himself. Other materials show clearly that the state paid for his regiments and that the state remained in control of who headed the various armies: see Stephen MacKinnon's calculations in Stephen R. MacKinnon, *Power and Politics in Late Imperial China,* pp. 103–116. Yuan remained a servant to the imperial dynasty and at its mercy and direction: Edward J. M. Rhoads, *Manchus & Han*, p. 7. However, amassing income in industrial production would boost his *economic* position and hence his *political* position in court, as well as providing security for his supporters.
38. Jerome Ch'en, *Yuan Shih-k'ai*, 2nd ed., p. 64.
39. Albert Feuerwerker, *China's Early Industrialization*, p. 85.
40. See *WQJB*; Jerome Ch'en, *Yuan Shih-k'ai*, 2nd ed., p. 66.
41. Jerome Ch'en, *Yuan Shih-k'ai*, 2nd ed., p. 68; *WQJB*, pp. 656 and 679; Xia Dongyuan, *Sheng Xuanhuai Zhuan*, p. 128.
42. Xia Dongyuan, *Sheng Xuanhuai Zhuan*, p. 146.
43. Jerome Ch'en, *Yuan Shih-k'ai*, 2nd ed., p. 69; Xia Dongyuan, *Sheng Xuanhuai*, p. 248; Albert Feuerwerker, *China's Early Industrialization*, p. 73.
44. Luo Zhaoqian, *Wangqing guandu shangban yanjiu*, p. 122.
45. *WQJB*, pp. 953–954.
46. Albert Feuerwerker, *China's Early Industrialization*, p. 77; Jerome Ch'en, *Yuan Shih-k'ai*, 2nd ed., p. 84.
47. Jerome Ch'en, *Yuan Shih-k'ai*, pp. 67–69.
48. For general discussions, see Albert Feuerwerker, *China's Early Industrialization*, p. 190; Luo Zhaoqian, *Wangqing guandu shangban yanjiu*, pp. 121–133; Xia Dongyuan, *Sheng Xuanhuai Zhuan*, pp. 50–64 and 68–89; Zhang Houquan, *Zhaoshang Ju Shi: Jindai Bufen*, pp. 39–54, 141–147.
49. Luo Zhaoqian, *Wangqing guandu shangban yanjiu*, pp. 122–124 and Xia Dongyuan, *Sheng Xuanhuai Zhuan*, pp. 249–252.
50. See Chap. 4.

51. Albert Feuerwerker, *China's Early Industrialization*, p. 198.
52. Luo Zhaoqian, *Wangqing guandu shangban yanjiu*, p. 126.
53. Albert Feuerwerker, *China's Early Industrialization*, p. 199.
54. Xia Dongyuan, *Sheng Xuanhuai Zhuan*, p. 249.
55. Albert Feuerwerker, *China's Early Industrialization*, p. 85.
56. The China Merchants' Steam Navigation Company was operated from Shanghai by Sheng Xuanhuai since 1873. It was documented in Zhang Houquan, *Zhaoshang Ju Shi* that the Hankou office depended on Sheng's relatives to operate.
57. Albert Feuerwerker, *China's Early Industrialization*, pp. 84, 130–131.
58. Philip A. Alsop & James W. Post, *Cement Plant Operations Handbook*, pp. 54, 82–88, 92–94 and 145–148.
59. Qixin was the only cement manufacturing facility in China until September 1920 when Liu Hongsheng formed his Shanghai Cement Works, Limited in Shanghai; "The development of the Shanghai Cement Works, Limited" in *LHS*, pp. 76–77.
60. Ellsworth C. Carlson, *The Kaiping Mines*, p. 61; The Memorandum and Articles of Association of the Chinese Engineering and Mining Company Limited dated 20 December 1900 in *KMS*, pp. 140–144.
61. Article II Treaty of Nanking, 1842; Li Yumin, *Zhongguo Fei Yue Shi*, pp. 84–106.
62. Ellsworth C. Carlson, *The Kaiping Mines*, pp. 84–106; Letter from the Under-Secretary of Foreign Affairs F. A. Campbell to the Chinese Engineering and Mining Company Limited 18 January 1904 in *KMS*, p. 254.
63. The report from Tang Tingshu to Li Hongzhang in *QXGS*, p. 22.
64. Letter from Gustav Detring to Charles Moreing, 14 August 1898 in *KMS*, pp. 54–55.
65. For further information on the Dragon flag incident, see Ellsworth C. Carlson, *The Kaiping Mines*, pp. 86–87.
66. Letter from Yuan Shikai to the General Manager of the Chinese Engineering and Mining Company Limited in China T. R. Wynne, 13 March 1903 in *KMS*, p. 235.
67. Ellsworth C. Carlson, *The Kaiping Mines*, pp. 97 and 99.
68. Yuan Shikai's first memorial to the throne 13 March 1903 in *KMS*, pp. 235–237; *WQJB*, p. 874.
69. Ellsworth C. Carlson, *The Kaiping Mines*, p. 99.

70. Ellsworth C. Carlson, *The Kaiping Mines*, p. 97.
71. Signed September 1902. This updated the treaty of 1858 regulating the commercial relationship between Britain with China. Subsequent treaties signed with the USA in August 1903 and treaties with Portugal, Germany and Italy contained a similar provision. p. 1; David Faure, *China and Capitalism*, p. 63; Li Yongsheng *Qing Mo Zhong Wai Xiuding Shangyue Jiaoshe Yanjiu.*
72. *WQJB*, p. 878; Negotiations with the other Western powers based upon the MacKay treaty also began in June 1903, two months after the imperial appointments; see Zhongguo jindai jingji shi ziliao congkan bianji weiyuanhui, *Xinchou heyue dingli yihou di shangyue tanpan.*
73. *WQJB*, p. 888.
74. Yuan Shikai's second memorial to the throne in November 1903 in *KMS*, pp. 248–250.
75. *WQJB*, p. 901.
76. Statement of Claim filed at the High Court of Justice, Chancery Division, "His Excellency Chang Yen-mao and the Chinese Engineering and Mining Company of Tientsin (plaintiffs) and Chales Algernon Moreing, Bewick Moreing & Company, and the Chinese Engineering and Mining Company, Limited (defendants)" in *KMS*, pp. 239–246.
77. Ellsworth C. Carlson, *The Kaiping Mines*, p. 105.
78. Ellsworth C. Carlson, *The Kaiping Mines*, p. 106; Judgement of the Chancery Division, High Court of Justice delivered on 1 March 1905 in *KMS*, pp. 275–284.
79. Yuan Shikai's third memorial to the throne 31 March 1904 in *KMS*, pp. 261–262; Ellsworth C. Carlson, *The Kaiping Mines*, p. 106.
80. Li Yumin, *Zhongguo Fei Yue Shi*, pp. 2–13.

CHAPTER 4

Yuan Shikai and His Cement Corporation: The Flight of State Power

Yuan Shikai was ousted in 1909 from political power, but he returned to dismantle the Qing Empire in 1911. How did he sustain his political influence during banishment? Traditionally, the military power view is the perspective offered by historians. Yuan Shikai was portrayed to have had almighty military power through the loyalty of his army subordinates but more elaborate discussions on the economics of acquiring and maintaining this power is rare. No doubt Yuan's military influence is an important explanation but it was also through the economic power created by private corporations that made him powerful. The Chinese cement industry offered many advantages to Yuan Shikai in the early twentieth century. Firstly, it was unincorporated. Secondly, the business was relatively simple and focused because it was a single-product manufacturer. Thirdly, by 1905 he had consolidated his control of the railways which were crucial to any bulk industry. Finally, it was an imperial monopoly with only one cement plant in the country and it was inside the province of Zhili that he governed. However, initially, Yuan did not know that it was unincorporated under British law and thus it was unprotected by treaty and extraterritoriality, meaning it could be easily captured by him. This fact was only pointed out to him by Zhou Xuexi in 1906.[1]

H. Ko, *The Making of the Modern Chinese State*,
DOI 10.1007/978-981-10-2660-7_4

The British Connection

In early 1905, Yuan Shikai was an economically frustrated man. Yuan's economic base remained confined to the relatively impoverished province of Shandong and the strategic province of Zhili. He tried but was unable to unseat the British from the vital Kaiping Mines in Zhili. In contrast, his rival Sheng Xuanhuai was still, at this moment, heading the National Railway Company. He was also in full control of the large and important Hanyang Steel Foundry in Wuhan, which Yuan had "officially" taken over from Zhang Zhidong.[2] Furthermore, Sheng had been Li Hongzhang's deputy for 30 years and naturally inherited Li Hongzhang's power base in Shanghai and all the enterprises originating in Li's Self-Strengthening movement.[3] Thus far, Yuan could not stop the large dividends that were still being distributed to the stockholders of the Imperial Telegraph Administration and the CMC.[4] The largest stockholder of these monopolies was Sheng Xuanhuai. In other words, the "commanding heights" of China's economy still rested with Sheng Xuanhuai and Major Walter Nathan, manager of the British coal company. Yuan Shikai was frustrated and was fully aware of this because he told his economic deputy Zhou Xuexi.[5]

Zhou was sent by Yuan to Japan in 1903 to study Japanese industrialisation and the country's currency system. On Zhou's return, Yuan established a mint and adopted many of the Japanese practices in the province of Zhili which was under Yuan's administration.[6] In 1904, Yuan and Zhou established many small industrial firms in Zhili and made apparent attempts to industrialise the province that would strengthen Yuan's political position.[7] Yuan also relied partly on him to deal with the British in the London court case to retrieve the Kaiping mines.[8] By early 1906 there was apparently no hope of retrieving the Kaiping Mines because all options had been exhausted. The incorporated British company had a total monopoly on coal in northern China. Yuan Shikai's economic fortunes seemed rather dim because he had absolutely no control over the price of coal used by his armies, railways, shipping company or so many other industries. In reports from Zhou Xuexi to Yuan Shikai, Zhou pointed out that "the price of Kaiping coal had gone up while the quality had gone down, a situation which had brought great hardship to the Chinese navy, the government arsenals and units, industries and the people".[9] In the strategic energy sector, Yuan was totally at the mercy of the British company. Sheng Xuanhuai, on the other hand, had by this time new coal mines in the south along the Yangtze River, being therefore well equipped to supply the Hanyang steel works which Yuan had no power over.[10] It was at this point that Zhou Xuexi presented a simple plan to Yuan and in a few short months the British lost the cement plant to Yuan Shikai on 3 October 1906.[11] Both the Kaiping Mines and the Tangshan Cement Works were controlled by the British, but without incorporation, the cement works were as vulnerable to Yuan Shikai's power as Shen Xuanhuai's *un*incorporated imperial monopolies.

Back in the chaotic days of 1901, Herbert Hoover and Charles Moreing not only took advantage of the situation to occupy and take over the *un*incorporated Kaiping Coal Mines, they even sold all assets to the newly incorporated English company.[12] At the same time, they also occupied the *un*incorporated Tangshan Cement Works. The pair incorporated the Kaiping Mines in London but strangely did not do this for the Tangshan Cement Works.[13] This was the only imperial monopoly that was neither in the imperial structure nor successfully captured by the British (i.e., by incorporating it as a British company under English law). Why had they been so careless? In fact, they were not careless. They could not have incorporated it even if they had wanted to. In order to understand this, we have to understand how Qing commercial firms were conceptually and practically constructed in an environment without civil law.

A careful look at Kaiping would reveal that the only reason why the Qing government-owned Kaiping Coal-Mining Administration was being taken over without public notice was because it was an *un*incorporated bureau in business. There was no civil law concept in Chinese law and thus no corporate-personality concept. The imperial government did not regulate commercial activities by any general civil law because the Great Qing Code was essentially a penal code, for which it follows that it was not possible to have a public register of commercial firms.[14] The lack of a company law did not seem serious to the imperial government at the time. Besides, the use of the vague *guandu shangban* practice suited the imperial structure's centralisation of authority so that there was no dissemination of economic power. No one had yet appealed for the legislating of a modern company law before the 1900 Boxer Uprising and the Kaiping problem.[15] In the monopolies such as the original Tangshan Cement Works established in 1889, the rights, duties, power and benefits of the various "organs" such as those between the stockholders and the directors, or their interrelationship were merely regulated by a private contract. More precisely these were private constitutions with contractual effects for internal regulations. These private constitutions were the "Articles of

Association" (*gongsi zhangcheng*) of each individual firm. They were legal because the imperial state *did* recognise contractual agreements. In other words, the Chinese state, under its own established laws, recognised contractual associations but conferred no such thing as a separate legal personality to commercial firms before the Company Law of 1904.

In 1901, the British did not incorporate the Tangshan Cement Works because they did not have the Articles of Association and other company documents of this firm.[16] Although they still took it and fired it up for production just the same, without possessing the official Articles of Association they didn't even know what was written on it. All the British management knew was the stockholding distribution as recorded in the accounting books. They had no proprietary rights and were mere occupiers analogous to squatters on land without title deeds. The Articles of Association and other important documents were in fact removed from the offices of the cement works and were hidden away by the plant chemist, the German engineer Hans Günther.[17]

Günther was an engineer introduced to Zhou by Detring while he was still general manager of the original Kaiping Coal-Mining Administration. Zhou employed Günther before the Boxer Uprising and he stayed on in his job after the takeover by the British.[18] Although the British did make great efforts to obtain the documents, they failed. Therefore, without these important title documents they could not claim "good title" or ownership. Accordingly, they were unable to transfer company ownership or the assets to any newly incorporated English company as they had done for the neighbouring coal mines. This is because it was necessary for them to comply with the strict requirements of English law's legal formalities. In the end, it was impossible to incorporate the Tangshan Cement Works into any new English company following the Kaiping Coal-Mining Administration precedent. All along, Günther held out and refused to hand the documents over to the British. In the end, he presented these to a very grateful Zhou Xuexi instead.[19] With the documents in his possession, Zhou was able to inform Yuan Shikai that the day of the recovery, or more precisely, Yuan Shikai's own possession, of the cement works was in sight.[20]

Repossessing the Cement Plant

There was a depressing mood surrounding the attempted recovery of the Kaiping Coal Mines by Zhang Yi's London litigation: Moreing and the British company appealed to a higher court. The Court of Appeal ruled that under English law the memorandum of February 1901 could not give Zhang greater authority than that which could be exercised by a general manager who was concurrently a director. Therefore, there was no way he could have regained absolute authority. By the beginning of 1906, the Kaiping problem was at a standstill. It stood at the same point as three years earlier when Yuan sent in his first memorial. After this judgement, the British were even more firmly entrenched.[21]

Unlike the Kaiping Mines, however, the Tangshan Cement Works was unincorporated. It did not have the protection of a separate legal personality and thus had no access to the British court system. In mid-1906, about three months after the English Court of Appeal judgement of 25 January 1906, Yuan Shikai was informed by Zhou Xuexi of this happy fact and they almost immediately declared ownership. They seized management control of the cement works in just 22 days and took physical possession in exactly three months.[22] It was Yuan's good fortune that Zhou had in his possession the Articles of Association. Also in the bundle of documents given by Günther to Zhou was an agreement that licensed the cement works to Detring personally for "safekeeping" during the Boxer Uprising. It specifically stated that all that was required for repossession by the original proprietor was "three month's notice".[23] The situation at this time was summarised succinctly by Zhou Xuexi:

> When I became the general manager of the Kaiping mines [in 1900], I asked Detring of the custom service whether our country could manufacture cement and he recommended a German named Günther to me. Günther examined the limestone during his survey of the Tangshan region and reported that the material is suitable for the manufacturing of cement. At the time I was promoted to General Manager of the Kaiping Coal-Mining Administration. Hence this fact was reported to the Minister of Beiyang to raise capital for restarting the cement works. As a result, Mr. Li Ximing was appointed to manage this business and Günther was appointed as the plant chemist. Then, during the Boxer disturbance, it was occupied by the British together with the Kaiping Administration. Although Günther and Li remained in employment, the operation was funded by Kaiping which led to the loss of control of the cement works to the foreigners. I was away in Shandong for three years and when I returned [in 1903] Shikai had become the Minister of Beiyang. By then, he had been negotiating with the British on the return of the cement plant but could not reach any settlement. Shikai deeply lamented the difficulty of retrieving the Kaiping Coal Mining Administration and the Tangshan Cement Works. Then I told him

> that the cement works is *not* the same as Kaiping because Mr. Li Ximing made an agreement which stated that it could be retrieved by simply giving two month's notice.[24] Furthermore, it was I who originally [in 1900] reported to the then Minister of Beiyang and applied for official permission from the [then] Minister of Beiyang [Yu Lu] to restart cement production.[25] Therefore, there was official record of this and I suggested to him a possible scheme that should be viable in retrieving the cement works. I proposed to Shikai that he should give me a top down order to retrieve this plant; he agreed that we should order Günther not to obey orders from [British] Kaiping and I will *assume official responsibility* to bear all expenses of the cement works.[26]

Once Yuan Shikai and Zhou Xuexi decided that they were going to take over this *un*incorporated cement works, the whole series of events took place at lightning speed. Zhou did an estimate of the cost and potential business profits which he sent to Yuan on 3 May 1906.[27] The agreement "pawning" the Tangshan Cement Works to Kaiping had a break clause of three months' notice and Detring was the one who signed the original. He was supposed to but failed to ask permission from the then Minister of Beiyang.[28] So the next day on 4 May, Zhou wrote to Detring for assistance to issue a termination notice to the British company and to notify Nathan that Zhou Xuexi himself had been appointed to "assume official responsibility" of the cement plant by the authority of the new Minister of Beiyang (i.e., Yuan Shikai). This was duly carried out by Detring (who agreed to send the termination notice only upon a commission of 20 thousand taels!) and he confirmed the issuance of the notice to Nathan on 23 May 1906.[29] Two days later, on 25 May, Zhou met Li Ximing and Günther who were still working for the company and a "command order" was issued to them "by hand" to notify them that Zhou himself was taking over from that particular day onwards, thus securing management defection within two weeks.[30] Following the terms of the contractual agreement Detring signed in 1901, the physical repossession would take place three months from that date on 26 August 1906.[31]

Nathan had no intention of giving up the cement plant. However, he was apparently caught by surprise. The company was *un*incorporated and he did not have any documents to prove that their company had proper title to the cement works. Yet without the knowledge that Zhou Xuexi was given the company documents by Günther, he wrote on 12 June 1906 to Yuan Shikai, claiming ownership. He could, however, only give a vague description how the Kaiping Mines were related to the Tangshan Cement Works. He claimed many things including that: "it was a conscientious effort to plan and build the plant" and that it was "beneficial to the railway constructions and provided employment to workers". There were also fixed selling contracts which must be honoured with agents et cetera. Furthermore, he claimed that the selling of cement relied on the coal-selling agents of Kaiping at major commercial centres. The success of the British company's cement business was only achievable because the cement was sold side by side with coal. Therefore, he argued that repossession by Zhou Xuexi would not only create a problem in finding working capital for normal daily operations but would also make the loan from the British coal company payable immediately. Nathan warned that the income from the cement plant wouldn't even cover the loan interest and that other shareholders' rights should be considered as well. He remarked that:

> It must be noted also that this cement works was formed by issuing shares: 20 thousand taels were official investment; our company 20 thousand taels; other shareholders 60 thousand taels; and altogether 100 thousand taels. From the perspective of shareholding, both the official shares percentage and our own percentage are smaller than the wider shareholders' percentage. Do you think it is reasonable for Daotai Zhou simply to repossess without taking into account the interest of the other shareholders? Therefore, I would suggest that before Daotai Zhou makes any further moves, we should call a general shareholders meeting to discuss the matter and I ask that Daotai Zhou to attend.[32]

This was followed by a letter on 23 August 1906 from the British mining company, which had acquired ownership of Kaiping under English law. They refused to accept the power of the Minister of Beiyang, denying that he could have jurisdiction over the cement works.[33] They, however, gave no legal grounds. Physical possession was entered into on the 26 August 1906.[34] The British minister in China did attempt to intervene, but without any corporate protection this came to nothing.[35] Finally, Yuan Shikai declared complete victory by giving Zhou Xuexi official permission to operate as General Manager on 3 October 1906.[36]

A preliminary conclusion can be drawn by this time in 1906, as Yuan and Zhou now had over three years of litigation experience behind them. After repossession of the cement works, they speedily incorporated it to become a corporation legally under the Chinese Company Law of 1904 and renamed it the Qixin Cement Company Limited.[37] Yuan Shikai finally had a private incorporated monopoly and with this he found the protected economic engine that would help propel him past all his political opponents. The company made big profits in a very short time.[38] When Yuan was removed from power after the death of Empress Cixi, Zhou Xuexi and Yuan Shikai had already turned the success of this cement plant into an economic refuge for his camp while continuing to expand into other industries.[39] By June 1908, Yuan and Zhou had already successfully established and incorporated a rival Luanzhou Coal Mining Company Limited adjacent to the old Kaiping Mines.[40] This was made possible because Yuan and Zhou had found a way to openly challenge the British without diplomatic consequences, employing the modern corporate form and limiting the negotiations as far as possible to a corporation-to-corporation level. When Yuan fell from power in January 1909, the Luanzhou company was already up and running and together these enterprises were fast multiplying into a large conglomerate outwardly under Zhou and with Yuan staying behind the scenes.[41] This partly helped Yuan and his people to withstand later imperial court battles and retribution from Sheng Xuanhuai. More importantly, Yuan Shikai's eldest son, Yuan Keding, remained as a high official in the Ministry of Agriculture, Industry and Commerce. This ministry had power to authorise and reject commercial incorporation in China. The ministry was headed by Yuan Shikai's protégé Tang Shiyi as Minister and Yuan Keding as Secretary. Yuan also maintained daily contact with his son by courier and thus Yuan Shikai could still control who could incorporate in China and thus protect his commercial interest and cement monopoly even after his ousting in 1908.[42]

Cement and Yuan Shikai

As can be seen, the cement industry in China began its life in one of the most complex periods in Chinese history. Cement, though "an arid powder", was an industrial tool introduced from the West. From the time following Yuan Shikai and Zhou Xuexi's recovery of the Tangshan Cement Works, the cement industry would develop into a major industry and play a crucial part in the national modernisation of China. Its profitability and the success of Yuan's economic front man Zhou Xuexi was amazing. It was an immediate success. The company fully subscribed in less than six months. Zhou's friends were very ready to accede to his request for an initial capital of 1,000,000 taels. By September 1907, the company repaid in full both the principal and interest of the 400,000 taels government loan. In 1907, the first year the company paid out dividends, they amounted to 18 %. Furthermore, the annual dividend between 1908 and 1911, including the 8 % guaranteed dividend or *guan-li*, was a "fantastic" 16 % return. The company report for 1910 was self-congratulatory of the business success and confident of its performance in the future. In other words, Qixin was overflowing with cash very quickly after re-establishment.[43]

Qixin became China's largest cement company with output and sales growing steadily from 1906 to 1907 until the mid-1930s. The company's plant and equipment were constantly improved and modernised, and historians considered it to be the best in the industry. The management team was capable and stable, and company profits were large and steady, hence providing lucrative dividends for those who invested in the company. In the history of this firm, it never depended on foreign loans for operating funds or capital equipment. This simply was most unusual for an early Chinese industrial enterprise which mostly ran into severe operating difficulties. Yet, previous historians such as Albert Feuerwerker who studied Qixin merely attributed its success to passive political "patronage" and objective economic reasons,[44] while Wellington Chan noted Qixin's success but did not seek to explain the reasons behind the company's success. The true reason, however, lies more in the partnership of Yuan Shikai and Zhou Xuexi.[45]

Overview of an Industrial Business

So why was Yuan Shikai so successful in this industry when Li Hongzhang failed? The explanation lies in the special nature of this industry constrained by the unpleasantness of the product. The primary reason for the growth of the cement industry was that, once the production process itself had been solved (e.g., by the acquisition of automatic Western equipment), the industry became a monopolistic creature which fell in line with the *modus operandi* of warlords, bandits and revolutionaries, that is, local or geographical control. Local heavy industry, local raw materials (coal and limestone) and local markets suited the characteristics of a perishable, bulky, low-value (in relation to weight) and high-volume business that was not susceptible to foreign or inter-provincial competition in line with G. William Skinner's analysis of China from a macro-regional angle.[46] The difficulty the management faced was not the production process but the control of the logistics of raw material and fuel supply as well as the logistics in supplying the customers.[47] What Feuerwerker did not identify in his analysis was the fundamental reason for the growth of this industry in late Qing and in the Republican periods. It was not down to "first mover advantage" or government "patronage", which Feuerwerker placed as the prime or primary explanations. Neither was it completely Adam Smith's "invisible hand" of the market, nor was it the "visible hand" of Alfred Chandler's "management revolution". Rather it was the power to control and influence the market which was the deciding factor.[48]

In late Qing dynasty and Republican China, it could be expected that demand was, on the one hand, spurred by population growth and urbanisation and it was the natural market demand of cement which led to huge profits for importers. On the other hand, it was the management of the logistics of the market and not the production (which in any case had been fully automated since the turn of the century) that a local administration or a local military strongman such as Yuan Shikai could perform well. Yuan could muster enough protection as well as threats because he controlled the local armies, administration and, most importantly, the railways. For example, Yuan would go on to control the mining of raw materials (in 1907 he built up a new Luanzhou coal mine).[49] He could offer protection to facilitate the transportation of raw materials from mines to factory and then from factory to markets by the railways he controlled and he obtained tax exemptions from the throne.[50] In sum, he could brutally protect the industry and hence the revenue for himself, for his military and for the local administration, which in turn consolidated their rule and enhanced their power projection capabilities across other provinces.

Analysed from this market perspective, it is fairly easy to see that generally during the late Qing or Republican periods, a local power would almost certainly rely on their advantageous position to swiftly take control of the local cement industry if they were able to and protect this potentially very lucrative industrial business.[51] This would be the same whether it be a foreign "imperialist", a local military power (Yuan Shikai) or a militarised national political party (Nationalist or Communist) or central government. They would then subsequently attempt to use the large profits generated by this industry to finance their armies or build up other more sophisticated heavy industries with stable demands such as that of coal mining, nitrate fertilizers and sulphuric acid.[52] Feuerwerker overlooked this point in his analysis of the Qixin Cement Company in the Republican period. In his articles he listed the members on the Board of

Directors of Qixin and several were also top managers at the major local railways. He saw these directors as representing the railways as customers and interpreted this as further indication of official patronage for Qixin's cement sales.[53] However, these railway representative directors were there, arguably, not only as customers but also as a part of the market control apparatus of a cement plant which served the landlocked markets in and around the North China Plain.

In his analysis of this first fully operational cement works in China, Feuerwerker correctly pointed out that cement is a "highly standardised product for which the required raw material is widespread and the manufacturing technology relatively simple and generally accessible" and that "even the relatively inexperienced management characteristics of an early stage of industrialisation is capable of producing at a profit cement generally free of major technical defects". Furthermore, "the technology employed, in the form of plans and machinery, was almost entirely imported". Additionally, "the supply and quality of its raw materials were not dependent upon agricultural output".[54] These points confirm the point that the importance lies not in the techniques and management of production but in the *control of the market.* This *modus operandi* is the same despite physical, geographical and environmental variations across continental-size China. This is shown by the subsequent development of the cement industry in different parts of China.

Firstly, as pointed out above, in northern China where bulky products could only travel by rail, the presence of railway executives from several important railways on Qixin's Board of Directors implies that the railways were another means to control the cement market conditions. This contrasts with the situation of the Guangdong Cement Works (the second operational cement works in China) located in Guangzhou city. This is in a delta region with myriads of waterways where traffic was difficult to patrol let alone control. Therefore, any attempt to control the cement market there could only rely on the control of the wholesalers. In the dry north where inland transportation for bulky materials was limited to the reaches of the railways, controlling the railways equated to effective control of the market. Thus, the sudden rise of production in 1906 coincided with the opening of the Beijing-Hankou Railway line and Yuan's capturing of the cement works and the railways. This is because Yuan could extend Qixin's market all the way down to Hankou across the North China Plain from its base at Tangshan.[55] In short, by simply enjoying a transportation monopoly, Qixin controlled the distribution network and thus the whole market to the exclusion of all other manufacturers in its sphere of influence. Guangdong's waterways and the natural difficulties in controlling transportation on them did not allow the same reliance on single points of control for physical logistics of cement imports and its end products. The control of the market had to be through other means, that is, by targeting the wholesalers.[56]

Then, looking further into the 1920s, the Shanghai Portland Cement Works Company Limited (the third operational cement works built in China), located in Shanghai at the southern end of the North China Plain, was established in Shanghai in 1920 and faced the same industrial logistics but in yet another form. Under the shelter of a corporation, the Shanghai businessman Liu Hongsheng, who built this manufacturing facility, was able to transform himself from a mere selling agent of coal into one of the richest and most influential industrialists in China.[57] Knowing that a steady supply of coal was crucially needed as fuel for his cement company as well as to maintain his coal-selling agency, he made use of the corporate veil, hiding behind the registered corporate *persona* while he expanded his business from behind the scenes but continuing to be personally employed as a coal-selling agent for the Kailuan Mines (also see Chap. 7). His associate Chen Baoqi testified to this:

> The East China Coal Mining Company, Limited was formed by Liu Hongsheng investing and taking over the Jiawang Coal Mining Company. At that time Liu used Huigong Capital Syndicate as the front and organised a new capital investment group that invested 800,000 yuan. Owing to the fact that Liu was at that time the manager of the Kailuan Sales Office, he avoided an overt conflict of interests by staying *behind the scenes*. He put up the money and employed his close associates, Li Bake, Cao Yutang, Hua Runquan, Xie Peide, Xu Jinggan, Jiang Shanshou, Cheng Weidu as Promoters of the company. He also appointed Hua Runquan, Lu Yinfu and Wang Jianxun as Directors.[58]

Quietly at first, he succeeded in creating one of the biggest corporate conglomerates in Shanghai with interlocking companies and even incorporated a subsidiary bank to finance his own business.[59] He did not control any railways, but the cement produced by his incorporated Shanghai Portland Cement Works Company Limited could be shipped in bulk up the Yangzi River which was navigable up to the city of Hankou. Hankou was a major market on the northern banks of the Yangtze River for Qixin's cement that could be delivered directly by rail from 1906 onwards. However, cement from the Qixin plant could not reach Shanghai directly because no railway crossed the Yangtze until after the People's Republic was established in 1949. This strategic strength allowed Shanghai Portland Cement to threaten Qixin and forced it to negotiate a corporation-to-corporation market control cartel.[60]

Any cement that reached Shanghai in the Republican Period had to be "double-handled". Qixin was an inland cement plant and not situated at a seaside or riverside location. This illustrates that any cement produced must be first loaded on to trains for the initial leg of the journey, then loaded onto ships or barges and then unloaded from these when they arrived at their destination ports. It did not matter where the cement was to be loaded onto ships; it could be a river port at a point where the southbound railway met the Yangzi River or at a northern port such as Tianjin. The crucial point is that the cement would be double-handled or even triple-handled for Shanghai-bound deliveries, adding considerable cost to its transportation. In the bulk business, this seriously weakened the competitiveness of the northern cement producer. As a consequence, cement produced locally in Shanghai was competitive and in this way forced Qixin into the cartel arrangement, thus creating an oligopoly. The two corporations divided the market into the north and south with Shanghai Portland relinquishing the Hankou market and Qixin ignoring the Shanghai market. Both of them played to their own strengths and protected their home (or base) market.[61] They succeeded in keeping profits high instead of letting market forces reign.[62] Once again, the dominant producers, collaborating on transportation and hence supply, successfully controlled the market within their spheres of influence. Put succinctly, the legal development in the north from the 1900s to the 1930s devolved state power to corporations such as the Qixin Cement Company Limited and Shanghai Portland Cement Works Company Limited which they used to forward their corporate self-interest and power independent of state intervention. The only difference between them is that Qixin was a company that was devolved top-down from the imperial government into the ownership by individuals and Shanghai Portland was a firm built bottom-up by an entrepreneur.

Lastly, in Guangdong, a cement plant was built by the Qing Government in its final years. This cement plant, the Guangdong Cement Works (and its successor the Xicun Cement Works), remained government-owned from Imperial through to Republican times, unlike its northern and eastern brethrens (see Chap. 5). Guangdong's waterways facilitated commerce but this province lacks the natural barriers to market entry for non-local cement. It experienced many difficulties and successive local governments wrestled with the market through trial and error. This continued until the "Central Government" left Guangdong with the Nationalist Northern Expedition of 1926–7. Once the post-1925 Guangdong provincial government and the local warlord managed to consolidate its hold on political power, the cement industry became a provincial market-control success and the engine of rapid provincial industrialisation.[63] Therefore, we can see that, although the geography and circumstances may be different, the fundamentals of this industry are always the same and great success in the south owed not to the successful management of the production process but once more to the control and manipulation of the market.

End of Empire

The year 1906 was a crucial year in the political career of Yuan Shikai. This is when Yuan recovered the old *un*incorporated old Tangshan Cement Works with the assistance of Zhou Xuexi and re-establishing it as the *incorporated* Qixin Cement Company Limited. This has been overlooked in past scholarship. Jerome Ch'en's examination of Yuan Shikai in 1961 painted him as the central character in the "factional quarrels" and "personal relationships" of the time. His narrative portrayed the general circumstances that were surrounding the rise of this dominant official.[64] In his 1980 study, Stephen R. MacKinnon developed further Jerome Ch'en's historical understanding, going deeper into Yuan Shikai's political positions as Governor-General of Zhili province and Beijing official from 1901 to 1908. He focused on his achievements as reformer in Zhili and the power and conflicts within the imperial court until Yuan was ousted in January 1909.[65] Furthermore, Edward Rhoads set out Yuan's dismissal within an ethnic Manchu-Han power struggle. Here an economic view is offered.

It has seldom been noted but back in 1902 Yuan Shikai was not the only favourite of the Empress Dowager Cixi. In late 1902 she allegedly said the disastrous events of the 1900 Boxer Uprising gave her an opportunity to find two junior but loyal officials: one was Cen Chunxuan and the other was Yuan Shikai. She described them as brave, courageous and young. Whereas Cen pacified the disturbances in Guangdong and Guangxi in the south, Yuan dealt with the foreigners in the north and recovered Beijng and Tianjin. The Empress was assured that these two able officials would be able to accomplish things and should put her heart at ease for the coming 20 years.[66]

Cen Cunxuan was Governor-General of Sichuan province (1902–1903, 1907–1908), Liangguang (1903–1906) and Yungui (1906–1907).[67] While he was the Governor-General of Guangdong and Guangxi provinces and stationed in the rich trading port and provincial capital Guangzhou, Cen was urged to organise a new military force: the Guangdong New Army, just like that which Yuan Shikai had assembled in the north.[68] He was just as "energetic and reform-minded" as Yuan Shikai.[69] Like Yuan Shikai, he was also very active in economic development while as Governor-General in the various provinces where he was stationed.[70] Simply put, Cen rivalled Yuan for the Empress Dowager's attention and favour.[71]

Before further discussing the political struggle between Cen Chunxuan and Yuan Shikai, it is necessary to point out that during the course of the imperial dynasty, many officials were ousted and such officials seldom had a second chance to return to imperial office. Cen Chunxuan belonged to this category. The only two late Qing officials that were able to return after ousting were Sheng Xuanhuai and Yuan Shikai. Not only did they return but they returned with a vengeance and caused havoc for the imperial dynasty. The reason why these two Qing officials could come back was because of their sustained influence in the imperial court maintained by their individual economic power. The more entrenched and senior was Sheng Xuanhuai, whose economic power and influence were overt, namely his wealth through his investments and continuing control of some of the *un*incorporated imperial industrial monopolies. By 1907, while out of political power, Sheng too began to shield his interests with legal or corporate personality by incorporating the industries that he had managed to retain control of, such as the creation under the 1904 Company Law of a multi-business corporation, the Hanyeping Coal and Iron Company, Limited.[72] But what about the relatively lightweight and less entrenched Yuan Shikai who didn't seem to have any apparent personal interests in the enterprises? The list of Qixin directors in the early period includes no member of Yuan's immediate family; historical research led to the belief that the family had some stocks. Furthermore, from the late 1920s onwards, one of Yuan's sons emerged onto the board of directors.[73]

Thus, in contrast to Sheng Xuanhuai, it was not at all hard for Yuan Shikai to conceal his economic power behind the mask of the corporate persona of a private company. This was apparently an attempt to avoid takeover attacks by presenting incorporated companies as purely economic concerns. Of course, this commercial subtlety, commonly employed by the modern business community to avoid government monitoring, is precisely one of the characteristic advantages of corporate forms of organisation. However, even so, once Yuan gained complete control of the Tangshan Cement Works in the autumn of 1906, where he was poised to gain a very large recurrent income from this monopoly, everybody felt threatened.[74] This is because he already controlled the strategic railways in 1905 and was now moving swiftly to establish a new coal mine right next to Kaiping.[75] Moreover, he also had six divisions of the Beiyang New Army under his command.[76]

There were two separate and independent attacks on Yuan at the same time; one from the Manchu faction led by the military man Tieliang and the other from Cen Chunxuan's faction. There was no conflict between Yuan and the imperial government over the control of the Beiyang Army until 1906. Rather suddenly during the winter of 1906, a struggle for control developed which highlighted Yuan's and the Beiyang Army's dependence upon Beijing for administrative and financial support. At the imperial court, Grand Councillor Qu Hongji made attacks on both Yuan and his ally Prince Qing. At the same time, there were simultaneous heated debates at court about governmental reorganisation, increased centralisation and introduction of a constitutional government. Yuan had always been a supporter and beneficiary of centralisation policies previously and was allied to Tielang. By November 1906, however, Tielang changed to support a Manchu faction which wanted to place control over Han Chinese officials such as Yuan, and the two men fell out openly. Meanwhile, all this was canvassed under the name of centralisation.[77]

The immediate effect of this struggle was that Yuan Shikai lost four of the six divisions of the army which he was administering to Tieliang. More interestingly, Tieliang ordered that the Second and the Fourth divisions (the two divisions that remained under Yuan in Zhili) be *solely supported financially by Yuan's Zhili administration* and not by the imperial government.[78] This was obviously designed to strip Yuan of his military might but to leave him two divisions to wear down his financial resources in his provincial stronghold of Zhili. However, these struggles ended with Yuan's victory half a year later: By August 1907, Tieliang was removed as Grand Councillor and was in due course isolated by Yuan and Prince Qing. Yuan managed to surround Tieliang with his men even within the Ministry of War where Tielang was head, severing his direct authority over the troops. The whole struggle between the Grand Councillors (Qu Hongji vs. Prince Qing) and the Governors-Generals (Cen Chunxuan vs.

Yuan Shikai) turned in favour of Prince Qing and Yuan quite suddenly in late May 1907.[79]

The attacks ended as suddenly as they started. More importantly to our discussion is that it is clear that Cen Chunxuan was indeed threatened by Yuan Shikai's profitable cement works in Tangshan and thus clearly disturbed by his economic power. This is because he also suddenly wanted a cement plant for Guangdong and he memorialised the throne in 1906 and obtained imperial approval to construct a cement plant in the provincial capital Guangzhou.[80] During the struggle, initially Cen and Qu had the upper hand. Cen was granted an audience with the Empress Dowager on 1 March 1907. Two days later he was appointed by the Empress as the president of the Ministry of Posts and Communications on 3 March 1907. There he removed Yuan Shikai's men from the ministry as he began to take control of this imperial economic administrative organ. However, his and Qu's fortunes changed for the worse when the Empress Dowager moved against Cen and Qu. Apparently, she was acting on Prince Qing's trumped-up charges of collusion with the exiled 1898 radical intellectual *Weixin* reformers Kang Youwei and Liang Qichao.[81] Cen left Beijing to return to Guangzhou in June 1907 but was summarily dismissed as the Governor of Guangdong and Guangxi on 12 August.[82] The construction of China's second cement works in Guangzhou (*un*incorporated) was not completed until late in 1909, long after Cen was ousted from power in 1907. Yuan Shikai suffered the same fate as him in January 1909 after the death of the Empress, but unlike Cen, he was able to make a comeback in 1911.

The reason Yuan Shikai was able to make this remarkable comeback was this: by the eve of the 1911 "revolution", he not only possessed an independent, large, incorporated, expanded and very profitable cement company, he also had a whole string of businesses both incorporated and *un*incorporated, owned and managed by and in the name of his protégé Zhou Xuexi.[83] After 1906, the success of the cement company spurred on the establishment of large incorporated businesses. It made selling of shares to raise capital in subsequent entrepreneurial ventures easier because investors were more forthcoming.[84] In the years between 1906 and 1911 Qixin supported Zhou's further expansion into other industries. This created a modern incorporated conglomerate of the most profitable industries which was loyal to Yuan Shikai and mainly in the province of Zhili. For example, after successfully incorporating the Tangshan Cement Works into the Qixin Cement Company Limited in 1906, Zhou and Yuan went on to establish other incorporated enterprises such as the aforementioned Luanzhou Official Mining Company Limited (1907), the Luanzhou Mining Land Company Limited (1908) and the Tianjin Soap Manufacturing Joint Stock Company Limited (1908). In 1907 they also established the Beijing Water Works Joint Stock Company Limited after Yuan was summoned to Beijing to become a Grand Councillor. This was a move intended to curb his political power by moving him "upstairs".[85]

By 1907 in the province of Zhili, Yuan Shikai and Zhou Xuexi had established 85 sub-provincial Boards of Industry, bureaus and factories and actively promoted economic development within the 142 prefectures (*fu*), sub-prefectures (*ting*), departments (*zhou*) and districts (*xian*). The total investment reached 425,200 taels of silver. Up to 1911, there were 134 factories in Tianjin and the total capital invested was 13 million yuan.[86] The province of Zhili became a model of the New Policies (*Xinzheng*) as promoted by Yuan Shikai in court and every province sent study and investigative groups. It became a province where "the new political power would rise" and Yuan Shikai praised Zhou Xuexi as "diligent, farsighted, successful and was able to capture the applause of the media". This was dubbed the New Policy of Zhili province (*Zhili xinzheng*). It greatly enhanced Yuan's political reputation as well as jealousy and fear of him among his enemies.[87] Throughout the remaining years of the Qing dynasty, however, Qixin remained independent under incorporation and the most profitable. In other words, Qixin provided, in the first instance, actual, immediate and direct income from 1906 onwards and, secondly, a successful business reputation for raising further capital. This directly helped boost the industrialisation of Tianjin and the province of Zhili.[88]

The industries established through the Boards of Industries from 1903 were many *un*incorporated companies and after 1905 incorporated industries, but they were generally small and politically insignificant. The provincial Bureau of Industry established many light industries such as: the Quanye Iron Factory, the Quanye Industrial Exhibition Bureau, the Government Paper Mill, the Education Product Manufacturing Bureau, the Tianjin Dyeing and Weaving Company, the Tooth Powder Company, the Tianjin Glass Company, the Xingye Printing Company, the Tianjin Soap Company, the Wanyi Company for the manufacturing of blankets, the Beiyang Tobacco Company, as well as eight weaving factories across the province of Zhili and two wood-processing workshops.[89] It was, however, the large incorporated concerns in which he was involved, and particularly the extremely profitable ex-imperial monopoly, the Qixin Cement Company Limited, that was most significant politically. This provincial industrialisation fortified Yuan Shikai's "private" economic power which was independent of the state but tucked within his industrialising "home" province of Zhili. When, in 1909, he was removed completely from political, military and "public" economic power, he was still able to carry his supporters and allies in private corporate industries, thus ensuring their survival and maintaining his influence. It was very difficult for other imperial politicians to seize this conglomerate of incorporated companies. This was the Noah's Ark for Yuan's collaborators and supporters, captained not by Noah but by Zhou Xuexi while Yuan took a back seat. Company records showing the background of those in control of Qixin Cement Company Limited revealed the political connections.

The biographical data of 29 out of the 39 principal officers and members of Qixin Cement's Board of Directors between of 1907 and 1948 shows that there were: firstly, four sons of Yuan Shikai. At least one son was a director of Qixin Cement from 1927 to 1948. Secondly, 12 of the 29 were minor officials in the Qing dynasty (of these, five or more worked directly under Yuan). Thirdly, eight were in high office of the Republican Beijing government when Yuan Shikai was president from 1912 to 1916 (these include three ministers of finance, a minister of war, two vice-ministers, a minister of agriculture and commerce, a governor of the Bank of China, a provincial governor, and the director of several major government railroads). Fourthly, five of the twenty-nine were high government officers between 1917 and 1927 (all counted in the previous eight: among these were two acting prime ministers, a minister of war, a minister of interior, a minister of foreign affairs, a minister of agriculture and commerce, a vice-minister and an important railroad official). Fifthly, one of the 29 was active in both the 1912–16 and 1917–27 periods and he continued serving as minister to Washington, delegate to the League of Nations and ambassador to the Soviet Union. Lastly, these 29 had interests in at least 25 other industrial, commercial or banking firms, primarily in north China.[90]

It must, however, be stressed that these people were only the "management" of this incorporated firm. The identities of the shareholders are difficult to ascertain because in an undeveloped legal system using a rudimentary share registration system, company shares could amount to no more than "bearer shares", that is, the ownership in reality belongs to the bearer or any actual holder of the share certificate like cash where the real owner's identity appears nowhere registered. This is another facet of the corporate persona in practice. It is clear that Yuan Shikai could continue to maintain his influence because he had "private" economic power in his hands. He could do so even without any formal official position or rank in government and controlling no state industry like Sheng Xuanhuai.[91] In late Qing China, power, as Hallis predicted, had been distributed to corporations which were situated between the state and the individual.[92] The imperial Chinese state by the necessity to legislate for a company law which carried with it recognition of corporate personality. This had inadvertently protected Yuan Shikai's economic power, even after he fell from political power. Whereas those without economic support, such as Cen Chunxuan, would fade away into the political background and then pass into historical obscurity, Yuan Shikai not only survived, he also returned to the centre of political power to dismantle the Qing Empire.

Yuan was recalled to put down the rebellion in the city of Wuhan (consisting of the triple cities of Hankou, Wuchang and Hanyang) in October 1911, but initially he refused to follow the order. Yuan was then offered the Premiership of the Cabinet before he would agree to return. His army arrived in Hankou by train in late October 1911 and crushed the armed mutiny on the north side to the Yangtze River. Yuan, however, did not pursue and claimed that the troops were exhausted and needed resting. Thus, he did not cross the Yangtze and the Han Rivers to take over the parallel cities of Wuchang and Hanyang on the other two shores. This was his decision even though he had better armed and trained troops that far outnumbered the revolutionaries which were already in disarray and on the defensive. The naval commander Sa Zhenbing whose ship sailed up the Yangtze as part of Yuan's task force believed that the battle for Wuhan could have been victorious for the empire. For Yuan Shikai, however, an incomplete victory strengthened his hand in his ongoing negotiations with the Qing court. Thus, General Feng Guzhang was reined: He was ordered to stop the chase.[93]

At this point Yuan Shikai negotiated with both the Qing court and the revolutionaries. The final outcome of these negotiations was that the infant Emperor Puyi abdicated and Yuan Shikai became the President of the new Republic of China.[94] It can be seen that the arrival of private incorporation enabled Yuan Shikai to capitalise an economic power base and to become an effective and highly successful powerbroker. Hence, to state it succinctly, the once absolute imperial central power had taken flight, indirectly brought about by the introduction into China of Western-type corporations equipped with legal personality (Fig. 4.1).

Fig. 4.1 President Yuan Shikai of the Republic of China—Coin minted in the ninth year of the Republic (1920)

Notes

1. What happened in the initial founding of the Qixin Company? in *QXGS*, p. 27.
2. Sheng was still controlling the Hanyang steel company. Although it was still operating at a loss, Sheng began mortgaging the company's assets bit by bit to borrow huge sums from Japan. Albert Feuerwerker, "China's Nineteenth-Century Industrialization: The Case of Hanyehping Coal and Iron Company, Limited" in *Studies in the Economic History of Late Imperial China*, p. 165; Jerome Ch'en, *Yuan Shih-k'ai*, 2nd ed., p. 68.
3. Albert Feuerwerker, *China's Early Industrialization*, p. 75.
4. Albert Feuerwerker, *China's Early Industrialization*, p. 199.

5. What happened in the initial founding of the Qixin company? in *QXGS*, p. 26.
6. *ZXJ*, pp. 25–49. Stephen R. MacKinnon, *Power and Politics in Late Imperial China*, pp. 163–179.
7. See generally Tianjin shi dang'an guan, *Yuan Shikai Tianjin dang'an shiliao xuan bian*.
8. Stephen R. MacKinnon, *Power and Politics in Late Imperial China*, pp. 163–164.
9. Moreover, "immediately after China had recovered the Qixin cement plant from the foreigners, Nathan, the General Manager of the British company, had twice raised the price of coal, making it difficult for the Chinese cement company to operate profitably", see Ellsworth C. Carlson, *The Kaiping Mines*, p. 108.
10. Albert Feuerwerker, "China's Nineteenth-Century Industrialization: The Case of Hanyehping Coal and Iron Company, Limited," in *Studies in the Economic History of Late Imperial China*, p. 174.
11. The Opinion Given by Yuan Shikai to Zhou Xuexi dated 3 October 1906 in *QXGS*, p. 35.
12. Ellsworth C. Carlson, *The Kaiping Mines*, pp. 67–68.
13. The Reply from Zhou Xuexi to the Kaiping Coal Mining Company Limited dated 15 September 1906 in *QXGS*, p. 34.
14. Registration of firms in England serves two purposes: firstly, it confers corporate personality to commercial firms, with or without share issuance, and secondly, it keeps a public record of the share ownership.
15. Li Kunyi and Zhang Zhidong jointly memorialised the throne; Ssu-yu Teng and John K. Fairbank eds., *China's Response to the West*, p. 197.
16. Zhou Xuexi, *Zhou Zhi'an Xiansheng Zixu Nianpu*, p. 38.
17. Report submitted to Yuan Skikai, Junior Guardian of the Heir Apparent, by the Chinese Engineering and Mining Company, Limited dated 12 June 1906 in *QXGS*, p. 29.
18. Zhou Xuexi was the Zongban (General Manager) of the cement plant at that time before the trouble started; What happened in the initial founding of the Qixin company? in *QXGS*, p. 26.
19. Zhou Xuexi, *Zhou Zhi'an Xiansheng Zixu Nianpu*, p. 38.
20. What happened in the initial founding of the Qixin company? in *QXGS*, p. 26.

21. Ellsworth C. Carlson, *The Kaiping Mines*, p. 106.
22. Report to Yuan Shikai dated 24 May 1906 in *ZXJ*, p. 219.
23. Order by hand to Li Ximing and Kunde dated 25 May 1906 in *ZXJ*, p. 217.
24. This is apparently a typing mistake because it was three months' notice instead of two.
25. A brief order to Zhou Xuexi from Yu Lu in *QXGS*, p. 27.
26. What happened in the initial founding of the Qixin company? in *QXGS*, p. 26.
27. Submission to Yuan Shikai concerning matters for the expansion of the cement company, dated 3 May 1906 in *ZXJ*, p. 215.
28. This situation is not dissimilar to the disputed Kaiping Administration's transfer; the second letter from Zhou Xuexi to Detring, dated 15 May 1906 in *ZXJ*, p. 217.
29. Zhou agreed to pay Detring on 28 May 1906; the second letter from Zhou Xuexi to Detring, dated 15 May 1906.
30. Order by hand to Li Ximing and Kunde, dated 25 May 1906 in *ZXJ*, p. 217.
31. The second letter from Zhou Xuexi to Detring, dated 15 May 1906 in *ZXJ*, p. 217; the third letter from Zhou Xuexi to Detring, dated 28 May 1906 in *ZXJ*, p. 218; Report to Yuan Shikai, dated 24 May 1906 in *ZXJ*, p. 219.
32. Report submitted to Yuan Skikai, Junior Guardian of the Heir Apparent, by the Chinese Engineering and Mining Company, Limited, dated 12 June 1906 in *QXGS*, pp. 29–30, p. 30.
33. Letter from the Assistant general manager of the China Mining and Engineering Company, dated 23 August 1906 in QXGS, p. 32; letter from Kaiping's lawyers Meng Shen and Dr. Gan, dated 3 September 1906 in *QXGS*, p. 33.
34. Letter from Zhou Xuexi to Detring attached to the reply, dated 26 September 1906 in *ZXJ*, p. 224.
35. Letter from Detring to Zhou Xuexi, dated 24 September 1906 in *QXGS*, p. 35.
36. Yuan Shikai's dismissal of the matter in Yuan's order to Zhou Xuexi in *QXGS*, p. 35.
37. Submission to the Viceroy of Zhili concerning opening a case file concerning the drafting of the Articles of Association of the Tangshan Cement Joint Stock Company upon full subscription of issue shares, dated 26 August 1907 in *ZXJ*, pp. 228–236.

38. Albert Feuerwerker, "Industrial Enterprise in Twentieth-Century China", pp. 273–308; Wellington Chan, *Merchants, Mandarins, and Modern Enterprise in Late Ch'ing China*, pp. 114–117; QXGS, pp. 153–158.
39. Albert Feuerwerker, "Industrial Enterprise in Twentieth-Century China", p. 296.
40. Ellsworth C. Carlson, *The Kaiping Mines*, p. 109; the dispatch from the Governor-General of Zhili Yan Shixiang to the Luanzhou company, dated 8 May 1908 in *KMS*, pp. 323–326.
41. Wellington Chan believes that Yuan Shikai benefited by using his family as shareholders; see Wellington Chan, *Merchants, Mandarins, and Modern Enterprise in Late Ch'ing China*, p. 116.
42. Stephen R. MacKinnon, *Power and Politics in Late Imperial China*, pp. 196–208.
43. Wellington Chan, *Merchants, Mandarins, and Modern Enterprise in Late Ch'ing China*, p. 115.
44. Albert Feuerwerker, "Industrial Enterprise in Twentieth-Century China" in *Studies in the Economic History of Late Imperial China*, p. 273.
45. Wellington Chan, *Merchants, Mandarins, and Modern Enterprise in Late Ch'ing China*, p. 115.
46. G. William Skinner, "Presidential Address: The Structure of Chinese History". Skinner correlated long-term regional cycles of growth and decline to macro-regions and his approach is generally acceptable here in this study.
47. In Guangdong, it was discovered that the market was not free but was controlled and manipulated by a revolutionary government corroborated by a local warlord. See Chaps. 5 and 6.
48. Since the 1980s American understanding of business history has been dominated by the ideas of Alfred Chandler Jr. and centred upon the permanence, power and continued growth of managerial hierarchy in a business organisation thesis: the "visible hand" of management was responsible for industrial growth and not the "invisible hand" of Adam Smith's free market. For China, however, the debate focused upon the role of the Chinese government. See Alfred D. Chandler, *Strategy and Structure: Chapters in the History of the Industrial Enterprise*; Alfred D. Chandler, Jr., *The Visible Hand*; Alfred D. Chandler, Jr., with the assistance of Takashi Hikino, *Scale and Scope*, and Thomas K. McCraw ed., *The Essential Alfred Chandler*.

49. Ellsworth C. Carlson, *The Kaiping Mines*, p. 107; the dispatch from the Governor-General of Zhili Yan Shixiang to the Luanzhou company, dated 8 May 1908 in *KMS*, pp. 323–326.
50. *QXGS*, pp. 93–94.
51. *RCC4*, pp. 1509–1511.
52. Xie Yingming, "Shengying gongye gaikuang ji yishu", pp. 219–240.
53. Albert Feuerwerker, "Industrial Enterprise in Twentieth-Century China", p. 293.
54. Albert Feuerwerker, "Industrial Enterprise in Twentieth-Century China", pp. 273–281.
55. Hao Qingyuan, *Zhou Xuexi Zhuan*, p. 122; Albert Feuerwerker, "Industrial Enterprise in Twentieth-Century China", p. 275.
56. See Chap. 5.
57. See Chap. 7.
58. Oral account of Chen Baoqi, dated April 1962 in *LHS* v. 1, p. 258.
59. LHS v. 1, pp. 281–297.
60. LHS v. 1, p. 187.
61. LHS v. 1, p. 194.
62. LHS v. 1, p. 199.
63. See Chap. 5.
64. See Jerome Ch'en, *Yuan Shih-k'ai*, 2nd ed.
65. Stephen R. MacKinnon, *Power and Politics in Late Imperial China.*
66. Stephen R. MacKinnon, *Power and Politics in Late Imperial China*, p. 44.
67. He Ping and Li Ludian, *CCWJ*, p. 523.
68. He raised a small army but was forced to disband due to lack of funds and poor quality; Stephen R. MacKinnon, *Power and Politics in Late Imperial China*, p. 109; Edward J. M. Rhoads, *China's Republican Revolution*, pp. 77–79.
69. Stephen R. MacKinnon, *Power and Politics in Late Imperial China*, p. 35.
70. *The Late Qing Economic Chronicle* records many entries of Cen Chunxuan's various economic activities.
71. Stephen R. MacKinnon, *Power and Politics in Late Imperial China*, p. 83.
72. See Albert Feuerwerker, "China's Nineteenth-Century Industrialization" in *Studies in the Economic History of Late Imperial China*, p. 175.

73. Wellington Chan, *Merchants, Mandarins, and Modern Enterprise in Late Ch'ing China*, p. 116.
74. Note that Yuan Shikai had already established control over the railways in 1905; *WQJB*, pp. 953–954.
75. Ellsworth C. Carlson, *The Kaiping Mines*, p. 107; Yan Shixiang, "1908 nian 5 yue 8 ri Zhili Zhongdu Yang Shixiang zha Luanzhou gongsi wen" in *KMS*, pp. 323–326.
76. Jerome Ch'en, *Yuan Shih-k'ai*, 2nd ed., p. 63.
77. Stephen R. MacKinnon, *Power and Politics in Late Imperial China*, p. 114.
78. Stephen R. MacKinnon, *Power and Politics in Late Imperial China*, p. 114.
79. Stephen R. MacKinnon, *Power and Politics in Late Imperial China*, pp. 86–87.
80. The office of economic affairs of Guangdong province, "Construction in Guangdong in the last 5 years", in *ZJGS3*, pp. 325–6; A brief description of memorials to the imperial court for the establishing of the Guangdong Cement Works in *ZJGS3*, pp. 332–333.
81. *Stephen R. MacKinnon, Power and Politics in Late Imperial China*, pp. 84–87.
82. See Chap. 5.
83. See generally *ZXJ*; *Tianjin dang'an wang*, http://www.tjdag.gov.cn; last accessed 21 March 2012.
84. *QXGS*, p. 26.
85. Wellington Chan, *Merchants, Mandarins, and Modern Enterprise in Late Ch'ing China*, p. 117.
86. Zhang Xueji, *Yuan Shikai Mufu*.
87. Tianjin shi dang'an guan, *Yuan Shikai Tianjin dang'an shiliao xuan bian*.
88. Wellington Chan, *Merchants, Mandarins, and Modern Enterprise in Late Ch'ing China*, p. 117.
89. See generally *ZXJ* and *Tianjin dang'an wang*, http://www.tjdag.gov.cn; last accessed 21 March 2010.
90. Albert Feuerwerker, "Industrial Enterprise in Twentieth-Century China", p. 296.

91. Sheng Xuanhuai continued to head the Hanyang Steel Foundry even after being ousted by Yuan Shikai from the other imperial monopolies and eventually incorporated it in 1908 after he returned to power on the death of Empress Dowager Cixi and the removal of Yuan Shikai from the political scene.
92. Frederick Hallis, *Corporate Personality*.
93. Edward J. M. Rhoads, *Manchus & Han*, p. 178.
94. Tang Degang, *Yuan Shi Dang Guo*.

PART 3

The Making of a Modern Incorporated Government

Sun Yat-sen, his Unincorporated Cement Works and the Incorporated City of Guangzhou, 1912–1937

Fifteen years after giving up the Presidency of the Republic in 1917, Sun Yat-sen, the father of modern China, arrived in the capital city of his home province Guangzhou to start another revolt. He located his headquarters in the city's cement works, which was a relic of the Qing imperial industrialisation programme and the only industrial enterprise in the city of Guangzhou. This part shows that Sun Yat-sen and his party did not embrace incorporated industrial companies in the late 1920s and early 1930s. Instead of allowing private corporations to develop freely, the city acted as a corporation and developed industries aggressively. Market success and consolidation of economic power reversed the post-imperial trend. Yet, this could only be achieved by the complete government takeover of the market by force, starting with cement and then eventually for all products. Without creating or employing modern corporations, an entire command economy in Guangdong province of Republican China was instigated by Sun Yat-sen. It was built from one single cement plant that was Sun's revolutionary headquarters and which was situated in a newly recognised as legally corporate Guangzhou city. Sun Yat-sen lived above the shop but never embraced private enterprises or capitalism.

Chapter 5 examines this chaotic period when Sun Yat-sen went to base himself in Guangzhou three times (July 1917, November 1920 and March 1923). He lacked military power and was on the brink of bankruptcy. There, he endeavoured to raise an army for a military expedition to unify China. Fortunately, when Sun was out in the political wilderness, there was a legal change in China: Cities were declared to be legal persons (or corporate persons) by the policy of the Municipal Autonomy System (*shi zizhi zhi*) promulgated by Republic of China President Xu Shichang in July 1921. This means that foreign banks could legally lend to any newly incorporated self-governing city. While Sun Yat-sen was in residence in Guangzhou during his second return to the city in 1921, he took advantage of this new Municipal Autonomy System to establish the Guangzhou City Council, which subsequently became the government. Suddenly, he had a corporation with legal personality under his control. He allowed it to be headed by his son Sun Ke. By October 1921, this gave him, through his son, an economic lever to real power. Sun was then able to bypass the local warlord Chen Jiongming's monopoly of all political and military positions and his opposition to the northern expedition idea.

The creation of the Guangzhou City Council in 1921 gave Sun Yat-sen borrowing powers for the military in the name of city development. He died in 1925 but he laid the foundation for state power reconsolidation: he created a city corporate for regaining political power and he took over the cement works for recapturing economic power. After his death, these legacies were both in the hands of his former secretary Lin Yungai. Lin dutifully pressed on with the unfinished quest and put into practice the idealism that Sun had set out.

This chapter shows that, unfortunately, using the city as the corporate vehicle to manage a cement business is problematic. Attempts to control the market through legislation were also fraught with complex unforeseen difficulties. In the end, the industrial optimism of Sun Yat-sen, as executed by the stoic effort of Lin Yungai after Sun's death, only had limited success. Despite this, the province staggered onwards without using private incorporated companies for developing major industries. The province, however, subsumed economic development under one incorporated city.

Chapter 6 shifts the focus to the recovering of state power. In stark contrast to Qixin Cement Company in the north, the Guangdong Cement Works in the south was an abject failure between 1909 and 1932. So, how did cement suddenly become an enormously profitable business in Guangdong from 1932 onwards? The answer lies with the foreign investment hype following the construction of the symbolic Pearl River Bridge by officials who were former revolutionaries inside an incorporated city government. This is arguably an icon of modernity for Guangzhou, comparable to the Eiffel Tower for Paris or the Golden Gate Bridge for San

Francisco. The influx of investment propelled the economy forward and empowered the Guangzhou City Government. Hence, the contextual economic circumstance is the cause of business success. Even without any marketing effort, the cement will sell under overheating economic conditions. The former revolutionaries of Sun Yat-sen's defunct organisation in Guangdong province, the Chinese League (Tongmenghui), were led by Sun's former assistant and secretary Lin Yungai after Sun's death in 1925. Lin stumbled upon this model of development that attracted huge investments directly from the overseas Chinese. Investing in many other industries, they relentlessly used the incorporated city to recover state power lost after the imperial collapse.

The story then turns to explaining how the former members of Sun Yat-sen's Chinese League in collaboration with the "warlord" Chen Jitang used the Guangzhou City Government within the province as the corporate vehicle to re-establish central state power. In the process, hearts and minds were discovered to unite not under Sun Yat-sen's nationalist ideals but by the sight of the technologically advanced electric-driven double lever bascule Pearl River Bridge that can automatically open up to let ships through. This is a potent symbol of Chinese modernity in the 1930s built by the city, which is a genuine modern corporate institution. Unfortunately, all this modernisation was destroyed by war when the Japanese invaded in 1938. This ended Sun Yat-sen and his followers' revolutionary legacy in the city of Guangzhou. After the war, Chiang Kai-shek's Nanjing Government took over control and Guangzhou lost its independence forever.

CHAPTER 5

Sun Yat-sen and His Unincorporated Cement Works: Revolutionaries in Business

This part explores the history of "bureaucratic capitalism" in Republican China when company law was not used (i.e., no private corporations). This took place in Guangdong province before and after revolutionary leader Sun Yat-sen's death in 1925. Instead, a municipal corporation was used as the vehicle. After the 1911 "revolution", the Guangdong Cement Works (the second operational cement plant in China) was captured and used by Sun Yat-sen to enter into commercial activities to generate revenue. His revolutionary followers continued to use the Guangdong Cement Works in the same way after his death. The city government was at the centre of these activities and no commercial incorporated private industrial companies were employed. In other words, this is an early Republican example of the modern "state-ownership" of enterprises.

The city was declared to be a *legal person* (or a *corporate person*) by the policy of the Municipal Autonomy System (*Shi zizhi zhi*) promulgated by Republic of China President Xu Shichang in July 1921. This declared a city to be legally denoted as such until the Municipal Organisation Law (*Shi zizhi fa*) of 1930.[1] What is most important is the fact that Sun Yat-sen wasted no time and established an autonomous city council within three months under his southern breakaway government. Effectively, he established a city government in the capital city of his home province Guangzhou. This move directly reversed his and his followers' fortunes and made the Northern Expedition led eventually by Chiang Kai-shek possible.

As will be seen in this chapter, incorporating a city (or municipal) government carries with it financial benefits. Here, the city government was

H. Ko, *The Making of the Modern Chinese State*,
DOI 10.1007/978-981-10-2660-7_5

used as the corporate vehicle to own and manage the cement business. Subsequent expansion into other industrial businesses followed the same pattern. In other words, an corporated public government was employed as the commercial vehicle. This differs greatly from private corporations in that the city possesses governmental power that includes legislative and police powers. In Guangdong, this power could be exercised or abused to sell goods and make money. After Sun's death, his followers in the city government attempted to force cement sales up by issuing restrictive legislation against competitors in the marketplace. This was market control but it did not go as planned and only succeeded in starting a commercial war with the local cement merchants. The city government was competing with the merchants for profits and it encountered serious difficulties in this capacity. These government officials were diehard revolutionary ex-members of the Chinese League (*Tongmenghui*) that was set up by Sun Yat-sen to overthrow the Qing Empire and they were surprised, bewildered and confused by the intense commercial confrontation that broke out with the merchants.[2]

The Birth of the Guangdong Cement Works

In China, between 1882 and 1887, a Xiangshan resident Yu Ruiyun made a personal investment of 100,000 taels of silver and built a cement plant along the Wanzai waterway near Macao. This plant was subsequently sold to the British and the production facilities eventually moved to Hong Kong. It became the British-owned- and Hong Kong-incorporated Green Island Cement Company on the edge of the Kowloon peninsula.[3] In northern China in 1889, Li Hongzhang established the Tangshan Cement Works for use in the construction of the mines. Tangshan began manufacturing in 1892 and by 1906 it had purchased two horizontal rotary kilns from equipment manufacturer F. L. Smidth of Denmark that supported continuous production, boosting output of cement to 40,000 barrels. As shown in Chaps. 3 and 4, this plant subsequently became the Qixin Cement Company Limited.[4] The Guangdong Cement Works was built in Guangzhou between 1906 and 1909. It was established by imperial edict and wholly imperial facility operated by the Guangdong provincial government.[5] This plant did not install advanced horizontal rotary kiln available at that time but bought a technically backward manual batch-processing German technology with vertical kilns. This design was purchased because of inexperience of the officials in charge of construction and its backwardness was only discovered after the plant was built.[6] The Guangdong Cement Works was a genuine disaster and made no profit in operation during its functional lifetime. So how did this fully government owned cement manufacturing plant change the meaning of industrialisation in China? How did cement manufacturing in Guangzhou city overcome extreme difficulties to become enormously successful? The answer lies in war and politics.

The Government-Owned Guangdong Cement Works

This is the facility that Yuan Shikai's rival Cen Chunxuan wanted. The cement plant in Guangzhou (or Canton), southern China, was officially authorised to be established on 29 April 1906. This is also the same month that Yuan Shikai is taking over the old Tangshan Cement Works from the British. The Governor of Guangdong Province, Cen Chunxuan, arrested an officer of the Guangdong Customs Office, Zhou Dongsheng. Zhou was accused of, among other corrupt activities, the illegal quarrying of limestones in Feishuyan situated in the county of Huaxian to the north of Guangzhou. The limestones were delivered to the British-controlled Green Island Cement Company in Hong Kong for the manufacturing of cement. This was obviously a lucrative business opportunity because the cement manufactured in Hong Kong had been selling very profitably in Guangdong as well as in other parts of China. Thus, further quarrying was immediately prohibited and Cen memorialised the court, seeking permission to buy machinery and to establish this cement plant on the land confiscated from Zhou Dongsheng. It was officially stated that the profit earned from this plant could be used for the funding of education in Guangdong province. The plant took four years to construct and the governorship passed to Zhou Fu and then to Zhang Renjun during this time.[7]

The difficulty in constructing the plant was felt from the start. A cement plant has to be built in ways that will accommodate the nature of the cement industry's logistics. For a river port such as Guangzhou, it had to be built alongside the waterways for ease of transportation of the bulky raw materials and the bulky manufactured end products. Thus, it was decided in July 1906 that an area in Caofangwei along the river shores opposite Guangzhou be chosen as the cement work's location. The requisitioning of this land took almost two years. Cai Shoukang who was entrusted with the task of selecting the land intended to pay 70 taels for the 100 *mu* inland paddies and 100 taels for the 140 *mu* marine paddies in the land requisition. Yet some owners led by Li Desan refused to sell.

It was only after Zhang Renjun, the then governor, agreed to allow an increase in compensation to 80 taels and 120 taels for the land and beach paddies respectively that the matter was resolved in 1908. The site was on the sandy beaches along the waterfront of the Pearl River. Therefore, these had to be filled with extra sand and gravel to level the foundation. It was up to nine-feet high and a lot of gravel was used to complete the foundation. Furthermore, the office buildings and the workshop where the heavy machinery was to be built required digging to 16–30 feet underground. Lastly, to create a firm foundation wooden piles mixed with concrete were driven into the ground.[8]

The construction of the plant soon ran into financial difficulties. The initial lump sum for construction, which was diverted by Cen from the Guangdong-Guangxi Salt Administration, Reconstruction Bureau, Guangdong Customs and the salt *likin*, amounted to 1.2 million taels. By the spring of 1908, during the construction period, continuous short-term borrowings of one to two years from merchants and various government branches were necessary to continue the construction work. Eventually, it was only with the personal support of the governor Zhang Renjun that construction was made possible.[9] Worse, the machines bought from the German equipment manufacturer Krupp via their agents in China were discovered to be obsolete. Krupp sold an obsolete 25-year-old English manual batch-processing cement-manufacturing design to Guangzhou which employed eight vertical kilns. This was reported to the provincial government by Liu Ruilin. Liu was the Shanxi Assistant Daotai who was sent to oversee the plant in 1909 after he had toured the Green Island Cement plant in Hong Kong and Macao, and the Qixin Cement plant in the north.[10] While a permanent German engineer had to be employed at high cost in the Guangzhou plant to *manually* supervise the production process, all the other plants bought new fuel-efficient and fully automatic rotary kiln processes from the Danish firm F. L. Smidth.[11]

Furthermore, to add salt to an already bad wound, the Guangzhou process could only produce 30–50 barrels per day, a fraction of its stated capacity of 500 barrels per day in the purchasing contract.[12] After production began on 15 May 1909, a dispute broke out between the management and the German engineer that the Krupp selling agent recommended. Liu Ruilin condemned the engineer as incompetent and by November of that year he claimed to have mastered to some extent the production techniques and was overseeing the manufacturing process himself. The plant under his watch was working at 60 % capacity, producing 300 barrels of cement each day. The engineer, however, claimed that the quality of cement produced was low.[13] Liu was able to make detailed observation during his visits to the other cement plants. Certainly, he did make simple but reasonable calculations relating to the production cost and so adjusted the pricing structure of the Guangzhou cement after analysing in detail the competitive strengths and weaknesses and cost structures of home and foreign cement.[14] By 1912, the then manager Xia added four fans to the kilns to increase efficiency and the yield increased to 400 barrels per day, thus enabling the plant to reach financial breakeven point.[15]

The cement industry in Guangdong followed neither the *guandu shangban* (official supervision-merchant management) format of the Tangshan monopoly, nor was it incorporated under the Company Law of 1904. Instead the Guangdong Cement Works was originally established by the Qing government to be a *guanban* (government-managed or official-management) enterprise and no stocks or shares were issued. In the Republican period, this Qing dynasty built enterprise continued initially as *guanban* and was *never incorporated*, but it went through periods of *zhaoshang chengban* (invitation to merchant-management) and *guandu shangban* (official supervision-merchant management) formats of management. This plant remained *guanban* until 1919 and then shangban (merchant-managed or merchant-management) from 1920 to 1927. It became *guandu shangban* in 1928 (see Table 4.1). The revolutionary Guangzhou government eventually adopted a form of what can be called neo-*guanban* (neo-official management). This is a model substantively adapted from a comparative study of the government-run enterprise systems of American and European cities. This neo-*guanban* format was implemented extensively and had short-term successes in Guangdong in the 1930s.

It must be carefully noted, however, that this *guandu shangban* format in the late 1920s bears little resemblance to the format of the Qing Dynasty *guandu shangban* format of the same name. The Republican *guandu shangban* format for the Guangdong Cement Works was no more than a leasing arrangement with a provincial government-appointed supervisor stationed at the company. Unlike the *guandu shangban* of the CMC in the Qing Dynasty, no shares were ever issued. The cement works was *on loan* to the merchants so that the government would have a share in the profit if it so arose. In the *zhaoshang chengban* (invitation to merchant-management) format, the government basically leased the plant and equipment out to the merchants for a fixed monthly rent but with an official overseeing the firm. Therefore, it can be thought of as neo-*guandu shangban*.

Table 4.1 The demise and resurrection of the unincorporated Guangdong Cement Works

Year	*Management type*		*Status*
1904	*guanban*	Official	Established
1909–1912	*guanban*	Official	Production starts 1st management team under Liu Ruilin (*Lost money and left*)
1913	–	–	No production
1914	*guanban*	Official	2nd management team (*Lost money and left*)
1915	*guanban*	Official	3rd management team (*Lost money and left*)
1917	*guanban*	Official	Sun Yat-sen's takeover of office block and 1st management team under Liu Ruilin returns but resigned soon after (*Lost money and left*)
1918	*guanban*	Official	4th management team (*Lost money and left*)
1919	*guanban*	Official	5th management team (*Lost money and left*)
1921	*zhaoshang chengban*	Merchant	Leased to the Huiqun Company (*Lost money and left*)
1923	*zhaoshang chengban*	Merchant	Leased to a merchant named Tang (*Lost money and left*)
1924	*zhaoshang chengban*	Merchant	Leased to a merchant Zhang Zhuyin (*Lost money and left*)
1924–1927	–	–	No production
1928	neo-*guandu shangban*	Official supervision – merchant management	Cement works on loan to merchants but with an official stationed in the firm. Cement Works now under Construction Dept. (*Lost money*)
1931–1932	neo-*guanban*	Official	Merged with new Xicun Cement Works, achieved phenomenal success that paved the way for Guangdong going fully into industrialisation (*Became a highly profitable business*)

In 1912, the plant only made a little profit and by 1914 it was under new management, and then another new management team again in 1915 but still without success. By 1917, Liu Ruilin was back and he fired the German engineer to save money but the provincial Governor Zhu Qinglan mortgaged the whole plant to the Bank of Taiwan on Shamian Island for 3 million yuan, which led to Liu resigning in protest. In 1917, 1918 and 1919, three different managements took over but the government-managed *guanban* plant continued to suffer losses. It was under merchant-management (*shangban*) from 1921 and it was initially leased to the Huiqun Company for 350,000 yuan per annum but lost 400,000 yuan in the first ten months. In 1923, a merchant name Tang tried his hand but he too failed. In 1924, yet another merchant Zhang Zhuyin lost 70,000 yuan as a contractor of this business. There was a stoppage of three years until 1927 when another Zhengxing Company lost 90,000 yuan in a few short months of operation. In 1928, the plant was transferred to the Construction Department and subsequently changed to a *guandu shangban* enterprise and operated by the Puyi Company with both the provincial government and company investing. The cement works again ended up losing the investment and eventually reverted back as a *guanban* enterprise in October 1931 after a ten-year round trip.[16]

At a glance it may seem odd that so many different companies took over the plant year after year but all lost tremendous amounts of money. Yet the cement works never failed to find new contractors under the initial *shangban* (merchant-management) arrangement except for the three years from 1924 to 1927. So why did the business lose money in both *guanban* and *shangban*? Why were there willing *shangban* investors all the time? And finally why and how did this *guandu shangban* enterprise become *guanban* again and why is it eventually super successful under this model of operation? To understand the development of the cement industry in Guangdong and to understand this business, we must look to the broader *political context* (this chapter) and the *general economic circumstances* (next chapter) beyond the spotlight on the management aspect of this manufacturing industry, as well as scrutinising the nature and logistics of cement marketing. A good starting point is Sun Yat-sen's takeover of this Qing dynasty cement works in 1917.

Sun Yat-sen's Takeover

Sun Yat-sen became Provisional President of the newly created Republic of China on 1 January 1912. However, soon afterwards he had to surrender his post to Yuan Shikai. Yuan's subsequent death in June 1916, after a botched attempt to make himself the emperor in the same year, together with another attempt by Zhang Xun to restore the Qing Dynasty Emperor Puyi to the throne in July 1917, plunged the new Republic into "warlord" rivalries.

During this chaotic period Sun Yat-sen went to Guangzhou in his home province three times (July 1917, November 1920 and March 1923). He lacked military power and was on the brink of bankruptcy. There, he endeavoured to raise an army for a northern expedition to unify China. On the first occasion, he was ousted by Cen Chuxuan and Cen's Guangxi province clique. These people were running the affairs of Guangdong after the empire fell. Soon, Sun returned with the "warlord" Chen Jiongming and Chen's military in November 1920. He declared himself the legitimate President of the Republic of China and brought a section of the legislature with him, only to be driven out again by Chen's *coup d'état* in 1922. However, Sun returned again in 1923, driving Chen Jiongming out of Guangzhou with his new allies, the Yunnan "warlord" armies. On the first and third occasions (1917 and 1923), he decided to headquarter and reside in the elegantly designed office block of the then idle and *un*incorporated Guangzhou Cement Works. This was situated on the opposite shores of the Pearl River and he "borrowed" this facility.[17] Sun declared very clearly that he was "temporarily borrowing two office blocks" and that "this will not disrupt the normal business operation of the cement factory and that this should continue as usual."[18]

The Creation of the Guangzhou City Council 1921: Legal Personality Arrives

While Sun Yat-sen was in residence in Guangzhou during his second return to the city in 1921, he took advantage of the new Municipal Autonomy System (*Shi zizhi zhi*) idea promulgated in July 1921 to establish the Guangzhou City Council. Suddenly, he has a corporation with legal personality under his control. He allowed it to be headed by his son Sun Ke. This is perhaps the most crucial turning point in the revolutionary history of the Republic of China that has been overlooked by previous historical research. It is certainly difficult to appreciate this without an understanding of corporations. This certainly is a crucial moment in the pre-communist history of Guangdong Province, though this was not obvious in 1921. It seems that it was Sun Yat-sen's absolute powerlessness that forced him to make this creative move to establish a city council for Guangzhou. This was achieved in October 1921. It gave him, through his son, a short-term lever to actual power, bypassing Chen Jiongming's monopoly of all political and military positions.

Subsequent events would show that it had two major effects. Firstly, Sun Yat-sen gave his son Sun Ke and other members of the Chinese League, which had no military arm, a foothold in government with legal personality to continue their cause well into the mid-1930s. Secondly, by introducing genuine urban renewal and development, he inadvertently created a higher local demand for building materials including cement. Urban renewal projects could also be alternatively used as an excuse and smokescreen for large-scale corporate borrowing to fund Sun's military aims. Furthermore, by choosing his headquarters in a cement plant from 1917, Sun Yat-sen became obsessed with this industry. His industrialism was clearly espoused when he declared that China should build an infinite number of cement plants along the banks of the Yangtze River in his 1920 writing, "The International Development of China".[19] More importantly to the Guangdong cement industry, this section of his work was translated into Chinese for publication by Sun's secretary, Chinese League member and future Mayor and Provincial Governor, Lin Yungai. This part will show that it was Lin who tried to use the special characteristics of the cement business to propel Guangzhou and thus the wider province to rapid industrialisation.

In late November 1920 after Chen Jiongming drove the Guangxi clique out of Guangzhou, Sun Yat-sen returned to Guangzhou for the second time. Here he re-established the Guangzhou Military Government to counter the government in Beijing. In April 1921 he was elected President of this new "national" government by the remnants of the 1912 National Assembly. Unfortunately, his legitimacy was in serious doubt and his government received no recognition from any foreign states. The "warlord" Chen Jiongming who helped reinstate Sun Yat-sen, however, was concurrently Army Commander, Interior Minister, Commander-in-Chief of the Guangdong Military Forces and the Governor of Guangdong Province. As such, real power was not in Sun's hands but firmly in the hands of Chen.[20]

Despite this, Sun Yat-sen established a city council for Guangzhou in Nandi on 15 February 1921. His son Sun Ke was installed as the first Mayor, and together with the Guangzhou City Council,[21] the Guangzhou Public Works Bureau was created under it. This was headed by Sun Ke's hometown classmate who attended the University of Illinois, Cheng Tiangu. Both were Chinese League members.[22] Soon city planning began in earnest but without funding. On the surface, it all seemed to fit in very well but Sun Yat-sen at this juncture was in reality little concerned with urban renewal. With Chen Jiongming controlling everything, the newly created city institution gave him the cover to legally borrow money from foreign governments and banks in the name of the Guangzhou City

Council to fund his other activities. This city via its Public Works Bureau was a perfectly legitimate legal entity in the eyes of institutional lenders.

On 15 June 1922, a day before Chen Jiongming's *coup*, Cheng Tiangu was urgently summoned by Sun Yat-sen to the presidential palace around 6 pm by a telephone call:

> When I arrived, there was a secret meeting of the military leaders and I had to wait until 8 pm before the Premier emerged from the meeting to see me.[23] He promptly pulled out a "Sino-Japanese Loan Agreement" from the document bag he was carrying and said to me, "The situation is urgent, the wording is long and tedious, it is really not necessary for you to read it in full, sign it immediately, so that I can draw money straight away to tackle the present circumstances." I said, "But what kind of agreement is this? How is the money to be drawn? Could you briefly explain to me please? I am at your service no matter what happens." Then the Premier said, "This is a Five million yuan local loan for the city development and the setting up of the Yongjiang hydroelectricity plant, that's all." Then I said, "Isn't that within the jurisdiction of the provincial government and not my responsibility?" The Premier answered, "No, this is actually requested by the Japanese, *they are giving credit to the city authority* and its public works department, so after you have signed, it will be passed to Sun Ke for signing." And then he solemnly continued, "Tiangu, let me tell you truthfully, this is actually for the purchase of military equipment to deal with the present grave political situation, so don't be suspicious." I was delighted that the Premier was so candid with me and I signed at once without further ado.[24]

The next day the alliance between Chen Jiongming and Sun Yat-sen completely broke down when Chen Jiongming staged a rebellion to topple Sun Yat-sen and ransacked the Presidential Palace. Sun Yat-sen fled to Shanghai and Sun Ke and Cheng Tiangu fled to Hong Kong. However, by January 1923 the situation was reversed and Chen Jiongming was relentlessly pursued by all the other military forces supporting Sun Yat-sen. This included "warlord" armies from Yunnan, Guangxi and Guangdong provinces. Under such circumstances, Chen retreated east from Guangzhou to the strategic city of Huizhou on the banks of the East River. The "warlord" armies from the three provinces entered Guangzhou on the morning of 16 January. The "warlord" Shen Hongying entered first and took the strategic highlands of the city. The Yunnan and Guangxi armies took over all the governmental departments and agencies that generated income. This was the situation when Sun Yat-sen returned to Guangzhou after Chen Jiongming's *coup* was over.[25]

Chen Jiongming's eventual eviction from Guangdong brought Sun Yat-sen back to Guangzhou in March 1923 but the Presidential Palace located at the foot of the scenic hill Guanyinshan was torched during the 1922 *coup*. Therefore, once again Sun returned to the Guangdong Cement Works and used it as his revolutionary base. In this old headquarters, he re-established a military government there as he had done in 1917.[26] On that previous occasion, Sun declared that he only required the office buildings of the Guangdong Cement Works for his headquarters. This time, however, he was desperate to take actual control of this cement works and its income. Unfortunately for him, even though his headquarters were in the factory office blocks, he was powerless to assume control of the business. The Yunnan army faction that had become the squatter landlord of this facility was unwilling to surrender it to Sun Yat-sen.[27] At this time, Sun Yat-sen desperately needed funding. This was because all of Guangzhou's income-producing government departments and agencies had been captured by the different "warlord" armies. These forces had expelled Chen Jiongming from the city and they were simply not turning over revenue to Sun's government.[28] Soon after the founding of the Whampoa Military Academy in May 1924 and the arrival of the Soviet adviser Mikhail Borodin in June, however, the Yunnan faction volunteered to return the ownership of the plant to Sun Yat-sen's "Central Government" on 1 July 1924.

In a letter to Sun Yat-sen surrendering the cement works to his government, the Yunnan army commander Fan Shisheng described it as "the most successful enterprise of all the official enterprises of Guangdong Province"[29] and explained that they were stationed there "in order to protect it from illegitimate occupation by friendly military armies and from damage by undisciplined forces". The Yunnan army's excuse for continually occupying the cement works was that they needed the income to "buy meals" and to pay compensation to the families of those Yunnan soldiers killed in the recent battles within Guangdong. Thus they decided to "contract the cement works out to private companies and rely on this to provide sustenance".[30]

Sun Yat-sen annotated this letter with the words:

> The Finance Committee is requested to send officers to take delivery of the transfer, and to deliberate on the appropriate detailed measures. Previously, the cement works in Hong Kong expressed a willingness to buy our limestone in its entirety and double our profits as compared to our own manu-

> facturing. We could request Chen Youren to negotiate with the Hong Kong cement works again.[31] If the Hong Kong cement works still has the intention to *purchase all our limestone*, we will shut down this plant and build another one along the North River; otherwise alternative measures should be considered. In addition, we must reply to praise Fan. Signed Sun Yat-sen.[32]

The letter is interesting because it shows the perception of the cement works and a glimpse of the general situation at the time. It also exposes the impotence of Sun's dealings with the "guest" armies, the general financial predicament of his government and how he finally took complete control of the Guangdong Cement Works in 1924. It also importantly reveals that, upon receiving the above letter from Fan Shisheng, Sun instantly requested the Finance Committee of the Military Government to dispatch officers to take delivery of the cement works to the Central Government. In a meeting duly convened on 4 July 1924, the Committee resolved that the Ministry of Finance would appoint the Finance Department, which was headed by Lin Yungai, to take delivery of the plant.[33] Sun Yat-sen finally took control of this cement plant completely a few months before he left the city in late 1924 for negotiation with the northern "warlords" in Beijing.[34] However, he was never to return to his government inside the Guangdong Cement Works because he died from terminal cancer while in Beijing on 12 March 1925.

The Guangdong Cement Industry Before Sun Yat-sen's Death

In 1921, the cement plant became what the City Council dubbed a "merchant-management" (*shangban*) operation, beginning from Chen Jiongming's reign to the Yunnan force's occupation of Guangzhou. However, throughout this period the merchant contractors were all reported to have lost large sums of money. How could this be so? The letter from Fan Shisheng to Sun Yat-sen indicated that the cement works could go into normal operations. Furthermore, from the point of view of market demand, there was a continuing market for this modern building material in the early 1920s. The reasons for the loss of investment and to the previous question of why there was no shortage of contracting merchants may now be explained.

The answer lies with the very nature of this industry during the 1920s and its relation with the market. When Sun Yat-sen arrived in 1917 there was no production. Stoppages were frequent and this was because during the early *guanban* period the plant managers were basically struggling to master the technology and the yield was low. Spare and replacement parts were a major problem. These had to be imported from Hong Kong because there was no local supporting metal works industry. Worse, they had to be paid for in foreign exchange, either in Hong Kong dollars, sterling or German Mark.[35] It is not difficult to understand why merchants were willing to invest as contractors during the *shangban* policy period after Chen Jiongming took over Guangzhou. Examining the computation of Liu Ruilin illustrates the attraction. He calculated that the cost of core raw materials for the Guangzhou plant was much lower than for the Green Island Cement plants in Hong Kong and Macao, up to 36 % lower for limestone due to proximity and 68 % lower for the additive "mud". The source of limestone was stable, estimated to last at least 200 years, and Guangzhou had sole use since its confiscation.[36] This lucrative proposal was very alluring to merchant investors.

According to these figures, it should not have been difficult to make large profits but they simply did not materialise. The reason was that merchants who were only specialised in trading activities, however complicated, were involved in nothing more than the buying and selling of goods. Unfortunately for them, the cement business turned out to be far more complex than simple trading. It also had concealed hazards and traps for the unwary newcomer. It had already evolved into a capital-intensive modern manufacturing industry at that time. The old manual technology of the Guangdong Cement Works required high capital input. Cement manufacturing is also a high-volume business which means that a large circulating or working capital is always required. Worse, it is a bulk industry with a manufactured product which had a very short lifespan (owing to inherent chemical characteristics and worsened by the simple packaging techniques of the 1920s) and came in a very difficult-to-handle powder form. This means that transportation, handling and storage logistics were the main hidden costs behind the rosy profitable picture. The product could not be stored for lengthy periods or in humid weather (such as that in sub-tropical Guangdong) and there would have been limited storage facilities on the plant site. This is because the cooling processes would have taken up most of the silo space. It follows that once cooled, the cement must be packed and sold quickly or perhaps somehow "taken away" to make space for the next batch of production. It is essential in this industry to maintain a continuous flow of product out of the plant to allow for the inflow of pre-ordered and continuous shipments of bulky raw materials such as coal and limestone.[37]

Neither did their calculations show the huge cost of disposal incurred when sub-standard, low-quality cement was produced (it did not matter whether the cement produced was sellable or not; it still cost money to transport it either to the customer or to the dump), nor could it possibly show how the pressure to remove the manufactured product out of the plant before the "expiry date". Typically, this would have led to the cement work selling on credit and ultimately failing to receive payment in full or at all. If the wholesaler fails to sell it on, even returning slow stock after several months of non-payment would not have been useful owing to the product's short lifespan. These unforeseen logistic problems and difficulties were concealed traps laid for the merchants whose backgrounds were in trade and who were therefore unaware of the technicalities and requirements of this heavy industrial enterprise. They were simply lured into the merchant-management (*shangban*) system by the calculations and seeing the business through their own eyes as traders.[38] It is clear from Fan Shisheng's letter that the Yunnan forces were acting only as *owner* of the plant, receiving short-term stable periodic rent without regard to its long-term commercial success and bearing none of the risk mentioned above.[39] To them, the Guangdong Cement Works was "the most successful enterprise of all the official enterprise of Guangdong" because it was the merchant *investors* who lost out in this merchant-management arrangement.[40] This model was clearly not suitable for long-term industrial development during this period of history.

The cement business in 1920s Guangdong was then a treacherous business. There were hazards everywhere for the unwary newcomer. In order to understand how this industry functioned, the classic traps must be scrutinised. Interestingly the annotated remarks of Sun Yat-sen on the letter from Fan Shisheng demonstrate one classic trap for an industrial novice such as Sun Yat-sen. The suggestion by one cement manufacturer to another nearby manufacturer, who shares the same local market, to completely buy out their raw materials, that is, the limestone, was the cheapest way to neutralise the competition. This was an attempt to eliminate the competition from Guangdong Cement Works and shut it down completely and to prevent the development of the whole web of logistics and business networks required for the successful operation in this industry. A second slightly more expensive method would have been to buy all the clinker, the semi-manufactured ungrounded cement, so that the competition could not develop a wholesale or retail network which may grow into threatening competition. The third and even more expensive method to neutralise competition would have been to buy out all the cement produced by the Guangdong Cement Works so that it could not develop a brand of its own and so that no wholesalers or middlemen could obtain the cement and develop their own brand. If all the above failed, the fourth method would have been to negotiate a cartel in order to divide up the market and to maintain an oligopoly.[41] If even this last effort proved futile, there would be a price war and it would have been likely that the cement would have had to be sold at below cost in order to keep the plant running above the threshold volume of production. For example, a price war and then a cartel were the situation and solution of the cement industry in northern China as will be discussed in the case between Qixin Cement and Shanghai Portland Cement during this same period in the 1920s.[42]

After Sun Yat-sen's Death

In the few years that Sun Yat-sen was in this cement works, he plotted and laid the groundwork for the eventual northern expedition of 1925. This was eventually led by his protégé Chiang Kai-shek. Furthermore, Sun Yat-sen's ultimate control of the cement production in 1924 also paved the way for the rapid industrialisation of the province and this was led by some of his most loyal revolutionary followers in the Chinese League (*Tongmenghui*) after his death in February 1925.

After Sun Yat-sen's death, the members of the Guangzhou Military Government were then divided into two newly created governments, as well as joining the existing provincial government which was reorganised in 1925. These were the national Nationalist Government headed by Wang Jingwei, the Guangdong Provincial Government headed by Xu Chongzhi and the Guangzhou City Government headed by the ex-minister of foreign affairs of the Central Military Government and the son of the Qing Minister and British-trained barrister Wu Tingfang, Wu Chaoshu.[43] While his followers in Guangzhou prepared for the Northern Expedition, this cement business, now in the hands of the civil government, unfortunately could not contribute any income because it was shut down following the loss incurred by its operator Zhang Zhuyin. He had lost 70,000 yuan of his investment in 1924.[44] The government was at a loss in dealing with this industrial business and a long period of trial and error ensued and continued into the early 1930s.

When Sun Yat-sen returned to Guangzhou back in 1923 after the "warlord" Chen Jiongming was driven out, he began to consolidate his power. This was after his collaboration with the Soviet Union began and he finally took control of the Guangdong Cement Works in 1924. Sun Yat-sen promptly allocated it to the Provincial Government but the government could do nothing to breathe life into this commercial enterprise. It was the City Government which attempted to control the market for cement. This was executed through the 1928 city government which was controlled by the surviving members of the Chinese League who were dedicated followers of Sun Yat-sen. In the 1920s, the Guangdong Cement Works was the only major government-owned manufacturing industry in Guangdong. However, the market for its products was in the hands of the cement-import merchants because they controlled the distribution market. Thus, it is not difficult to understand the viewpoint of a local government faced with a financial crisis and desperate to instigate industrialisation. The merchants appeared to be wicked and were definitely the obstacles and it naturally followed that they must be tamed. So, what methods were employed to control them? Additionally, is controlling the market of an industrial product the magical formula for general industrialisation? The history, structure and methods of control will be expanded in the remaining pages of this chapter.

Government in Business I: Market Control

Up to this point, the market was operating under a classic absolute *laissez-faire* environment. China at the time in 1925 had no national industrial product standards and was still in its infancy *vis-à-vis* the development of law.[45] Many commercial legal concepts of modern society simply had not arrived in China. There was no building law and mercantile practices operated under the ancient principle of "let the buyer beware" (*caveat emptor*). On another level, the new Guangzhou City Government adopted a cabinet committee system. The Mayor's office was now legally named the Chairman of the City Government and his cabinet was the Executive Committee. The Chairman of Guangzhou City, Wu Chaoshu, following in his father's footsteps, was also a Barrister-at-law who had qualified in England.[46] Immediately upon taking office at the new Guangzhou City Government, Wu used legislation to control commercial activities. He passed into law the *Guangzhou City Regulations for the Banning of*

Cement Sales.[47] This sought to regulate the totally unchecked market of this important and increasingly popular modern building material.

Regulations for the Banning of Cement Sales 1925: Here Comes the Law

This piece of legislation was an early attempt to regulate this wayward free market. There were only nine articles and the provisions were modest. The regulations achieved limited success but this formed the basis and legal foundation for the eventual manipulation of the entire provincial market in later years. The *Regulations* required that firstly, all the cement sold in Guangzhou City of whatever brand name must obtain the consent of the Guangzhou Public Works Bureau. This is evidenced by the issuance of a certificate after passing the relevant tests at the Bureau.[48] Secondly, that all brands of cement must be sold as it was originally packed and no mixing of different brands or types of cement should be allowed. This was an attempt to stop low-quality cement from being mixed into good-quality cement or such worthless impurities such as sand being added into the bagged or barrelled cement.[49] Thirdly, no packaging, be it barrels or bags, should be opened to extract cement, and overweight bags or barrels were no excuse.[50] Fourthly, it was also required that once hydrated lumps appeared in the cement, it should not be sold and that these should not be "hammered back into powder" and resold.[51] Fifthly, all cement sellers were required to register with the Bureau and obtain a licence free of charge to sell cement.[52] Lastly, there was a maximum fine of up to a thousand yuan and a permanent ban in selling cement for those who failed to comply.[53]

In 1925, cement was generally used in the construction of buildings, roads and sewers. There were reported cases that houses and warehouses were collapsing during construction and new pillars buckling under the weight of constructing the next floor. On investigation by the Public Works Bureau, it was discovered that the main cause was the low quality of cement used and it was common for the cement seller to add sand, mud and other cheap impurities into the product. It was also common for the powdered cement to hydrate and solidify into small stones in humid weather or when exposed to rain and mist. The hydrated cement lost its cementing power, but merchant sellers could employ workers to hammer these lumps back into powder and re-bag them as good cement.

The Public Works Bureau carried out raids on cement sellers and found that almost all sellers were involved in such unethical practices. A number of raids on warehouses exposed many kinds of malpractices. In one raid, girls hammering the solidified cements were caught red-handed, and re-bagged cement was found sitting on weighing balances. In another, the accounts confiscated showed the volume of cement sold by the merchant far exceeded the volume he had originally bought. One merchant hid the accounts in his Shamian Island (foreign concession) office outside of the Public Works Bureau's jurisdiction with another being visible under a foliage of scribble in an attempt to conceal the fraud. Some were found to be selling a certain brand of cement but had never imported or purchased any of this particular brand; they were faking high-quality cement with a low-quality one. Arrests were made of eight larger merchants but Wu Chaoshu lamented that there were hundreds of cement sellers in the city and what the government could do was limited.[54]

The regulations were made as a result of *bona fide* concerns that modern housing constructions in the unregulated environment of Guangzhou were threatening the life and property of its citizens. However, these merchants reported the matter to the Control Yuan a few months later, accusing the Public Works Bureau of acting inappropriately and beyond its powers. The merchants of Guangzhou in 1925 were not an easy community of people to deal with. This was the same community which Sun Yat-sen had to put down by military force only two years before and was to rise again in 1926.[55]

The Guangzhou City Government of 1928: Lin Yungai Taking Charge

The creation in 1925 of the Guangzhou City Government from its predecessor, the Guangzhou City Council, was decisive in the development of the cement industry and the subsequent provincial industrialisation process. There are several reasons for this. Firstly, China was at war and before 1928 the successive provincial authorities during this period paid little attention to local economic development. Their leaderships were dominated by ambitious military and political leaders aspiring to the top echelons of political power. Many were only using Guangzhou as a springboard for their various political or military careers. The city authority, however, was more stable, paid serious attention to urban redevelopment and ushered in an era of large-scale public works. Secondly, the upgrading of this city council to a city government conferred on it more power to issue local laws and regulations.[56] This allowed it to promote its interests with minimal direct interference from higher tiers of government or military leaders. Finally, perhaps out of political coincidence, it quietly became the stronghold of the remaining Guangdong Chinese League members and gave them the institutional leverage to stay in power and perhaps to pursue the economic ideals of Sun Yat-sen, at least initially, in their home province of Guangdong.

The Guangzhou City Council was fought over by the two factions of Guangdong Chinese League members, those belonging to the "elders' faction" led by Hu Hanmin and those belonging to the "princeling" faction led by Sun Ke. The jostle was sometimes fierce: for example, Lin Yungai representing the elders, was made Mayor on 8 February in 1923 but was ousted by Sun Ke, who was determined to resume office as Mayor when he returned from Hong Kong after Chen Jiongming was driven out of Guangzhou following the *coup*. He took office and doubled up as the director of the Public Works Bureau because Cheng Tiangu refused to return to the directorship. Cheng Tiangu was avoiding taking sides in the wrangle and went away instead to assist in the founding of the National Guangdong University where he became Dean of the law faculty. He would subsequently return to take the helm at the bureau eight years later in 1931, becoming Mayor at the same time.[57]

The two factions alternately held the Mayor's office.[58] Sun Ke, after he occupied this office for the third time, however, had to resign in early 1927. This was when he had to leave with the Central Government to Wuhan as the Minister of Transport. It was only after Sun Ke's departure that Lin Yungai took control of the city administration, barring a brief disruption in November 1927 when a leftward-leaning Guangxi clique took power over the Provincial and City governments.[59] Lin had consolidated his position by January 1928 when he was confirmed as the Mayor of Guangzhou for the third time and headed both the Provincial Government's Finance and Civil Affairs departments. Once in power, Lin made full use of the City Government's legislative and administrative resources to transform the now-deserted cement plant into the driving force behind provincial industrialisation.

The Powerful Supplementary Procedures of 1928: Lin Yungai Squeezing

Lin Yungai led the Guangzhou City Government for the third time from 7 January 1928. After Sun's death, the financial troubles of the government did not die with him. The Central Government had now left Guangdong for Wuhan and then Nanjing and were there squeezing the city of Shanghai together with other places for financial resources in support of the Central Government as well as to the completion of the Northern Expedition.[60] Finances in Guangdong remained tight and Lin was entrusted with the task of finding the money as financial chief. His appointment to the Finance Department had put him in control of the Guangdong Cement Works and the appointment to become the Mayor of the Guangzhou City Government gave him control over the Public Works Bureau.[61] This was a unique combination of two civil offices and created formidable power and facilitated his push for industrial development.

Lin Yungai's government was in just one industry: cement. It was estimated that the cement market in the whole of Guangdong Province was around 3000 barrels per day but the maximum daily production of the Guangdong Cement Works was only 400 barrels.[62] Worse, since its completion in 1909, the cement works had been hit by successive failures (see Table 4.1). None of the operators was successful, seldom did this factory work at full capacity and stoppages were common. In 1928, Lin Yungai had unmistakably declared that it was his government's intention to keep the government cement plant in business. This is because it was the "only" state enterprise of Guangdong province. Furthermore, this factory had "historical value" and could be used to steer government policies in its dealings with the free market. Unfortunately, this factory was out of business for a long time when he took office and Lin Yungai identified the flood of imported cement as the root cause of its woes.[63]

Lin Yungai acted swiftly after he came into office. Within the first month he began to draft a supplement to the 1925 regulations promulgated by Wu Chaoshu to give his government greater legal power. It was acknowledged by the Public Works Bureau that the promulgation of the 1925 regulations had generally been ignored by the merchants and traders. Lin tabled a draft *Supplementary Procedures to Regulations for the Banning of Cement Sales*, in the form of an opinion from the Director of Public Works Peng Hui, at the Executive Committee of the Guangzhou City Government on 16 February. The important sections are listed here[64]:

Section 1

The Public Works Bureau ("this Bureau") hereby determines that the *Licence required for selling cement shall be renewed annually* within the month of January of each year, or shall be renewed when there is a change of manager of the business. The Licence shall be returned for cancellation on cessation of business. There shall be a renewal printing fee of five yuan.

Section 2

The representative General Manager of cement companies and owners of retail shop businesses *shall declare to this Bureau the location of the shop, the location of its warehouses and the storage location of the cement stock at the issuance of the renewed Licence.* Officers shall be dispatched for inspection at anytime as this Bureau thinks fit.

Section 4

Upon receiving the said tender information this Bureau may dispatch Bureau officers in conjunction with the General Manager of that particular brand of cement for inspection at the construction site. *Police officers shall be requested to arrest the building contractor according to law upon any discovery of unlawful activities.* The arrestee shall be allowed bail upon surety by a licensed shop business.

Section 6

Any delivery of cement consignment must be reported to this Bureau within 24 hours of such entering a warehouse. This Bureau shall dispatch officers to the shop within 24 hours of receiving such reports. The shop shall make arrangements for the officer to extract samples at the warehouse for testing at this Bureau. The sample shall not exceed 5 pounds.

Section 9

Any breach of the Regulations for the Banning of Cement Sales and this Supplementary Procedure shall be *fined* a minimum of 50 Yuan and a maximum of 500 Yuan for the first offending act; and shall be fined a minimum of 500 Yuan and a maximum of 1000 Yuan and a *prohibition* to carry on business for six months for any second offending act; and shall be fined 1000 Yuan and a *permanent prohibition* to carry on business for any third offending act.

These supplementary procedures were duly passed by the Executive Committee immediate upon introduction to the meeting and forwarded on to the City Legislative Committee. They were also duly passed on 2 March 1928 by the Legislative Committee and came into effect on 13 March. The Public Security Bureau and the Public Works Bureau were specifically ordered to carry out the new requirements stipulated in the 1925 *Regulations* and the *Supplementary Procedures* stated above. With these orders the Mayor Lin Yungai declared war on the market.

Initial Reactions to the Supplementary Procedures[65]*: Lin Yungai Unmoved*

The Public Works Bureau took action without further delay and immediately issued notice of the latest legal amendments and that the Bureau would enforce the registration without hesitation. Since it was already mid-March and the stipulated renewal period for the new rules was in January, he promptly gave the merchants, traders and shop proprietors until the end of March to complete the compulsory renewal. If they failed to comply, the fine imposed by section 9 of the *Supplementary Procedures* would be levied on the offender.

The cement merchants and traders were understandably up in arms. Through their trade association the Cement Merchants Trade Association (*Yanghuihang tongye lianjutang*) pleaded with the City Government. In their opinion, the new rules were so restrictive that it would "suffocate" their businesses. They also doubted whether there was a need for such draconian regulations or whether there was such a proliferation of malpractices among the traders as implied by the *Supplementary Procedures.* They were hoping that the government would first withdraw the *Supplementary Procedures* and that the Public Works Bureau would review each clause in consultation with them before promulgation. The Trade Association could just about tolerate four sections of the new *Procedures* (sections 3, 5, 7 and 8) but found sections 1, 2, 4, 6 and 9 stated above totally unacceptable. Thus, they were requesting the complete deletion of these five sections. The merchants also believed that these sections were open to distorted interpretation and/or outright misinterpretation. Therefore, they detailed their worries on each section and appended them to their pleading for the Mayor's perusal.

Lin Yungai was unmoved and instructed the Public Works Bureau to draft and send a detailed explanation of each section in reply to the Cement Merchant Trade Association's demands. Neither was he moved by the formal criticism from the Public Security Bureau. Since the *Supplementary Procedures* now obliged the cooperation of the police force, the Public Security Bureau objected to it on grounds that on the one hand, it was the job of the Public Works Bureau to ensure cement or other building material quality and thus fell outside their law enforcement responsibility. On the other hand, those responsibilities on the criminal breach of law such as fraudulent acts of counterfeiting goods fell squarely into the criminal jurisdiction of the police.

The Public Security Bureau argued articulately that the police force and the police magistracy were the law enforcement agencies of the City

Government and would be the more appropriate branches of government to handle the arrest, custody and judicial hearings of those offenders. Furthermore, their agencies had all the specialised facilities such as custody cells, court rooms and legal personnel as well as experience in dealing with the multitude of cases arising from the various Bureaus of the city government. Put simply, the Public Security Bureau was unhappy as to why the Public Works Bureau was given criminal law enforcement powers and why the police should be responsible for building material quality. They objected to the *Supplementary Procedures* on the basis that they were causing confusion regarding the individual authority and powers of each government department.

The Public Security Bureau's complaints were sound and reasonable. There were no legitimate reasons for the Public Works Bureau to be given wide law enforcement powers but for the fact that it had become the institution used by Lin Yungai to carry out his work, that is, to control the cement market by heavily regulating the cement merchants' activities. Lin Yungai urged the two Bureaus to come to a workable settlement but did not give way to the merchants. In the end, sections 3 and 4 were removed as a compromise but this, in reality, did not have any effect to his plans.[66] The Public Works Bureau always had a special position within the City Government and the survival of which, as well as its effectiveness as an administration, was reflected chiefly by the effectiveness of this Bureau since the establishment of the city government.

Assaults on the Merchants in 1928 and 1929: Lin Yungai's Wrath

In analysing the cement industry of Guangdong and its expansion from 1928, it could be seen that it does not concern good business management or marketing. The officially operated *guanban* cement firm's management was chaotic. Its expansion or success fell squarely on an industrial administrative structure that would effectively enable a civil government (dominated by revolutionaries and collaborating with a local "warlord") to participate in industrial production and commercial business acting in the manner of a corporate person. At the Dasheng Cotton Mill in Nantong, Elisabeth Köll found a retreating central state that offered local industrialists the opportunity to be involved in both business and politics.[67] In Guangdong, however, owing to the particular political context, it was exactly the opposite. The state was far from retreating but was in fact fast advancing towards industries. On the one hand, like Dasheng in Nantong, the cement works in Guangdong were a local enterprise of Guangzhou. On the other hand, it was not local industrialisation by a family firm which maintained old practices and personal control. Instead, local industrialisation instigated by Sun Yat-sen's revolutionary followers did their utmost to revolutionise the provincial system under nationalism. At times, their desperation reached the point of being unrealistic and totalitarian. For example, they even tried to ban rumours using City Government directives.[68] In the words of Lin Yungai as Mayor of the City Government in 1928:

> The Guangdong Cement Works is the only national enterprise in our Guangdong province. It is not only our guide and teacher of the market, it also of historical significance. Previously, owing to various reasons, it has laid idle for many years with no production. This allowed imported cement to dominate the market in our cities. The size of this loophole is increasing daily and is distressing to those people who are conscious of the situation. Since there is an urgent need to maintain *national* industrial enterprises, it is now ordered that the Enterprise Department (*shiye ting*) and the City Council (*shizheng ting*) forcefully *ban rumours* that would damage our *national* product. This would help to maintain this government enterprise….Apart from carrying out this order, it must be announced to the citizens to let them know that the cement works is one of our *national* enterprises. Therefore, as the citizens of our *nation*, it is of utmost importance that they must not create rumours to deliberately sabotage and obstruct the sales promotion of our *national* product.[69]

Lin Yungai may or may not have understood the problems but his understanding of cement production technicalities or industrial management was not decisive. Simply put, he already had his mind completely set on forcing the market to accept the local output. He showed absolutely no concern about the quality of the manufactured product. In April 1928, armed with the new *Supplementary Regulations* of March 1928, Lin began his ferocious charge towards the cement merchants in the market. The offensive began on 18 May 1928 after the publication of the report by the Director of Public Works, Peng Hui: *The Public Works Bureau Cement Strain Test Report.* However, this was no simple strain test report at all but a declaration of the new duties of the Bureau. He noted that cement was an important material required in the building industry and that his bureau was in charge of public works and had administrative duties over all construction works including the duty to prohibit construction. It follows that in order to facilitate the convenient use of cement, the Bureau had to "test fully and ban strictly". All cement in the market was to be tested in turn and the results announced on a chart. The Bureau would set the minimum standard of stress-strain pressure that each was required to meet and demanded that those that could not meet the minimum standard be used only for plastering walls. It suggested that:

> Before purchasing cement it is best to consult the annexed list and choose wisely for safety reasons; nevertheless, the most important selection criteria must be to choose national products (*guohuo*) so that our right to profits remains within our country.[70]

Cement as an industrial product, it seems, did not benefit much from the rise in nationalism and the consumer enthusiasm for the "buy Chinese" sentiments. Yet, the City Government in its quest to control the cement market employed this "national product" concept just the same. It is also arguable whether the cement made from the Guangdong Cement Works and it successor the Guangdong Xicun Cement Works could be said to be "national product". This is because the products are made by foreign imported machines. The former employs German equipment from Krupp and the latter a Danish turnkey system from F. L. Smidth.[71]

These tests were in fact fakes and Peng Hui was so bold to make clear that thenceforth the Public Works Bureau would be performing tests on cement to help purchasers to choose "safe" as well as "national" products. That is, eliminating non "national" products. The report also declared that the French "Dragon" brand cement failed three consecutive tests at the Public Works Bureau. Hence, on 23 May 1928 it was banned from the market for one year and all shops were given 30 days to sell their remaining stock. Three weeks later in on 1 June 1928 the Bureau took action to enforce the ban and seized a ship which belonged to the Dongan Shipping Company while it was unloading its shipment of Dragon brand cement. The shipment was seized because it was not declared to the Public Works Bureau as required by the *Supplementary Procedures*. It was discovered that deliveries were made to several retail shops both in Guangzhou and the surrounding counties outside the provincial capital. The shops in Guangzhou were found to be in breach of the new laws and were fined from 20 to 100 yuan accordingly on 9 June.[72]

The provoked merchants, however, refused to be subjugated and their wholesaler's association pleaded to the City Government on 19 June to have the order annulled.[73] Not only did the merchants plead in person at the city government, but their association also requested help from the French Consul in person who demanded that the consignment be retested in public in the presence of a French chemist.[74] The French Consul then pressurised the Provincial Government to allow such a request. In August 1929, the City Government abolished the committee system and Lin Yungai as Mayor of the city "temporarily" lifted the ban on Dragon brand cement and ordered the Public Works Bureau to carry out this order on 30 August.[75] This was reported to the Provincial Government in October 1929.[76] The French followed up to force the City Government to follow testing procedures as directed by them.[77] This, however, was turned down bluntly by Lin Yungai as "too complicated".[78] It may appear that Lin Yungai had become lenient or that he had lost the battle with the merchants but in fact he had merely changed his tactics.

On 17 August 1929, the Public Works Bureau caught another company, the Dalonghao Company, selling counterfeit cement.[79] They were supposed to have *mixed* poor-quality cement with good cement which was explicitly banned by both the 1925 *Regulations* and its *Supplementary Procedures.* This approach had the advantage that it did not question the quality of the manufactured products. The conflict between the City Government and the merchants escalated to the point where angry merchants refusing to pay fines were arrested and imprisoned.[80] This tactic was continuously employed for 12 months until August 1930 when Cheng Tiangu was officially appointed as the Director of the Public Works Bureau and the City Construction Committee Chairman.[81] He ordered two independent tests of the Guangdong Cement Works' Lion & Globe brand but the cement passed neither of these tests.[82] Lin Yungai was enraged and he openly lambasted Cheng in an official mayoral order criticising him for helping "enemy imports", stating that he should not have taken independent samples from retail outlets. He should have obtained samples directly from the cement works instead. This, Lin claimed, was because there could be a possibility that shops were selling remixed "counterfeits".[83] However, sometime later the poor quality of the Lion & Globe brand from the *guandu shangban* Guangdong Cement Works was explained. It was eventually found to be mixing and adding foreign cement into its own products. That is, it was selling foreign cement in Lion & Globe packaging.[84]

It is ironic that Lin Yungai's dry nationalism and his relentless effort to fight the wholesale merchants in support the local cement works amounted to little. By protecting the market and granting a monopoly to a single enterprise, he was only unconsciously assisting the merchants who had control of the cement works to perform cement trading under the disguise of industrial manufacturing. Hence, directly defeating his own revolutionary endeavour to support "Guangdong's only national industry" and pursue the hope of industrialisation.[85] It had become clear that his single-minded attempt to control the wholesalers in support of the Guangdong Cement Works would not in itself create the necessary momentum for Guangzhou to leap into industrialisation. The solution to industrialisation was located not merely in *market control* but also in *market expansion*. That is the reason why Lin Yungai's persistence and perseverance did appear to pay off in the end when he unwittingly stumbled upon the doorway to industrialisation. This is all because he appointed Cheng Tiangu to head the Public Works Bureau and Cheng instigated development in Guangzhou using his own clever ways.[86]

Government in Business II: Selling Cement

It is a rule in the cement industry that once production started, it is not impossible to manage production or pricing of the product. This is despite the difficulties, animosity and complications during the construction and manufacturing process. The real difficulties always lie in actually marketing and selling the cement. So how did a government sell a major industrial product in the 1920s and 1930s? Is an incorporate government suited to this?

The Prospect of **Guandu Shangban**

As seen earlier, under *shangban* (merchant-management) operations, the merchant contractors had no hope of making a profit. Then, what about under *guandu shangban* (official supervision-merchant management)? When the last *shangban* merchant contractor, Zhenxing Company, finally failed in the middle of 1927,[87] the responsibility for the Guangdong Cement Works was then transferred to the Provincial Construction Department. This was newly headed by the Chinese League daredevil pilot of the 1911 revolution Ma Chaojun.[88] Ma arrived in Guangdong in February 1928 and assumed the helm of the Construction Department in June.[89] This was immediately upon the appointment of Lin Yungai (he too was a participant in the 1911 revolution and Chinese League member) as the Mayor of the Guangzhou City Government in January 1928.

With Ma and Lin acting in tandem they immediately set out an agenda to revamp the cement industry of the province. While Lin set off to use the City Government's power to tame the cement market by legislating tough regulations as well as tightening enforcement,[90] Ma laid out a detailed plan and took actions to build a new automated cement plant. By this he hoped to solve all the previous pollution problems and make cement manufacturing in Guangdong as efficient and smooth as that of automatic Qixin Cement.[91]

In the interim, before the new cement plant could be built, the old Guangdong Cement Works was changed to *guandu shangban*. A merchant Puyi Company was allowed to operate the plant by an investment of 150,000 yuan for a contracted period of three years. The Provincial Government appointed an officer Huang Chengyu as the factory manager. According to the contract there would be equal profit-sharing between the Provincial Government and the merchant investor and production began in January 1929.[92] Soon afterwards, in mid-1929, Ma Chaojun left Guangdong for other duties and the Commissioner of the Construction Department role passed to Deng Yanhua, who was an army commander.[93] Deng displayed no appetite for quickly building the new cement plant. Although contracts for the purchase of equipment had been signed, loan agreements had been negotiated and the plant site decided by Ma before he transferred office, Deng sat on the project to build a new plant and did nothing until he was pushed a year later by higher authority in 1930.[94] Thus, it is apparent from the actions of Deng that not everybody in the provincial administration shared Lin and Ma's sense of the urgency of industrialisation. In particular, this was the case after the departure of Ma.

From early 1928, Lin Yungai and Ma Chaojun attempted to push for industrialisation. By late 1929, however, Lin had to invite back to Guangzhou the ex-Director of Public Works and Chinese League member Cheng Tiangu to deal with the stagnating situation. It was fortunate for Lin because Cheng had recently resigned as head of the China Custom Duties in Beijing.[95] Cheng was made the Acting Director of Public Works when he arrived in Guangzhou and then officially the Director in June 1930. He was also appointed as the Chairman of the newly established Guangzhou City Construction Commission at the same time.[96] The Commission at once summoned the Secretary of the Construction Department, Deng Yanhua, before it on 4 June 1930 to give reasons for the lack of progress in the construction of the new cement plant. He gave a less than satisfactory verbal answer and claimed that the project was too big and that those civil engineering firms who had tendered for the project were either inexperienced or had no working capital.[97] Nonetheless, the construction process of the new plant resumed after the hearing in July 1930.[98]

In mid-1929, the City Government was instigating the increasingly effective legal controls on the cement merchants. They used the *Supplementary Procedures* to help their local cement manufacturer. This was while Cheng Tiangu was reinitiating his massive urban modernisation program which had stalled in early 1923.[99] By mid-1930, Cheng's return and the resumption of his extensive road-building programme in Guangzhou caused an upsurge in the local economy. The factory manager of the old cement plant Huang Chengyu and the military commander Deng Yuanhua were determined to tap into this lucrative market for cement. Huang petitioned the Guangdong Provincial Government with the help of Deng.

In August 1930, Deng, acting as the Government Supervisor of this *guandu shangban* industrial enterprise, submitted a petition to the provincial government. This was redirected from Huang, written in the capacity of the cement works' Government Supervisor and titled: "Please Order the General Use of Lion & Globe Brand Cement". This was a request asking the Provincial Government to *order* the use of their Lion & Globe brand of cement in all road-building works in the drive to renew the city. They obtained an order directed to the Guangzhou City Government to demand the Public Works Bureau purchase cement solely from the *guandu shangban* Guangdong Cement Works. They calculated that, in the road-building plan which began in May 1929, over a million yuan had already been spent by the City Government. Furthermore, there was a specific term in the road-building contracts stating that the Lion & Globe brand belonging to the *guandu shangban* Guangzhou Cement Works must be used in such works. However, up to that point no contractor had been willing to purchase any Guangdong "national" cement, even when it was clearly stated in the contract. There were inquiries but no contractor bought any cement![100]

The Provincial Government was "utterly bewildered" and simply could not understand why such a "superior quality" government supervised production had no market.[101] This was so even after many official orders and appeals from the government. Furthermore, the Provincial Government simply could not understand why "the yearly Guangdong imported cement market of 700,000 barrels (2000 per day) could not accommodate the 182,500 barrels per year (500 barrels per day) production from the *guandu shangban* Guangdong Cement Works". Neither were the initial retail sales nor the subsequent wholesale sales meeting the provincial government's expectation. The government simply could not understand why the cement works was not operating at full capacity.

Thus, Huang Chengyu pleaded to the Provincial Government that they should invoke Article 8 of the Memorandum of Association of the *guandu shangban* arrangement for the Guangdong Cement Works which stated that all government agencies *must* purchase cement for construction works from this cement works. He hoped that the Provincial Government would "formally order" the Public Works Bureau in Guangzhou and all its subsidiaries in provincial towns and counties to purchase their Lion & Globe brand cement. Furthermore, the failure of these local government departments to comply must be punished by the Provincial Governments. He even blamed the failure on the Public Works Bureau for failing to issue rules enforcing the interests of the "national product". Additionally, Huang wanted to compel all branches of the provincial local government that contracted out public works to report to the Provincial Construction Department, that is, Deng Yanhua's Department. He wanted them to report the amount of cement required upon the signing of the contracts. This information would then pass to the cement works. Subsequently, when the contractors went to purchase cement the Department would then issue a receipt. On completion of the construction work, the receipt would have to be presented to the final inspection officer. Failure to do so, Huang wished, would lead to a denial of the final inspection of the relevant construction work and thus, no payment for the work done from the government could be received.[102]

The suggestions may be naïve commercially, but it can be seen that Huang Chengyu was serious from his close collaboration with Deng Yanhua. It was *not* in Deng's interest to build a *new* cement-manufacturing facility quickly because he was working closely with the appointed supervisor of the *old* cement works. Much of the difficulties at the cement works could be attributed to conflict of interests arising from this unsophisticated or even primitive *guandu shangban* arrangement. There were few checks or balances on the powers of the supervisor or the provincial minister. In a booming market driven by government investments, such as that in 1929, all that *guandu* (official supervision) did was to tempt the merchant to do the minimal but to use government influence to find a market for its production. Merchants, with their voracious appetite for profits, would calculate how they could do the minimum but reap the maximum return. Hence, if petitioning the government led to an easy market for their goods and maximum their returns, then that would become their course of action. In *guandu shangban* of the 1920s, the government official should be supervising the manufacturing enterprise but where were the tools of commercial supervision such as auditors? What were the definitions of the supervisor's duties? What were the parameters of the supervision such as employment law and contracts? There seems to be none.

A Wasted Effort?

National politics caused a change in the provincial government. On 28 February 1931, Chiang Kai-shek placed the Cantonese Guomindang elder Hu Hanmin under house arrest. This caused an immediate crisis in the party and Central Government. Two months later on 28 April 1931, the Guangdong Governor, also an old Chinese League comrade and military commander, Chen Mingshu sneaked out of the Province to Hong Kong. This is because he was suspected to be a supporter of Chiang Kai-shek.[103] The governorship was taken over by Lin Yungai and the military by Chen Jitang. Deng Yanhua also left office and the Tsinghua University and US-educated Hu Jixian was appointed by Lin Yungai as the new chief of the Construction Department.

The new administration sent personnel to the cement works and made a thorough assessment of the situation. It was reported that there were serious discrepancies in the company accounts and the books did not balance. Interest payments were wrongly booked; commissions were paid on purchases of raw materials but were not entered into the books; circulating capital was used for maintenance of machinery explicitly in breach of the government contract; no new machinery was added as had been agreed with the government; the raw materials purchased were unreasonably expensive which raised the cost and reduced the profits. During the two-and-a-half years of *guandu shangban* (from January 1929 to August 1931) the plant had been shut for 350 odd days for "maintenance of the kilns". However, 6400 tons of coal had been bought which far exceeded what the plant was supposed to use. Hu Jixian in his report to the Provincial Government predicted that the fictitious wages paid were incalculable because he presumed that these must have been enormously exaggerated to reduce the 50 % profit entitlement of the government.[104] The merchant contractor pleaded to the government to allow it to continue operations but the City Construction Committee chaired by Cheng Tiangu resolved that the contract must be rescinded.[105]

So what happened? A report by the Construction Department of 1930 *Five Years of Guangdong Construction & Development* gave the following account of the Guangdong Cement Works:

> From [1928], that cement factory was administered by the Construction Department. Under Director Ma Chaojun...With the support of the provincial executive committee, he changed the administration of it to *guandu shangban* to enable the plant to compete more profitably. It was invested in by the Puyi Company, adding smokeless motors and fans thus pushing the production to *above* 500 barrels per day.[106]

However, the maximum capacity of this cement works was investigated by Ma Chaojun himself in 1928 and was determined by him to be 400 barrels per day.[107] In order for this cement works to produce any cement at all under this *guandu shangban* arrangement there was only one way and Lin knew:

> The Puyi Company could not produce enough cement and they constantly added in foreign imports.[108]

Lin Yungai knew all along what was happening at the Guangdong Cement Works. It was such an open secret that when Huang Chengyu petitioned the provincial government to force the Public Works Bureau to adopt the Lion & Globe brand as the official cement, Director Cheng Tiangu ignored the order. He deliberately tested the Lion & Globe brand twice independently at the Public Works Bureau and found that the cement failed the quality test twice.[109] The Guangdong Cement Works suffered from quality problems because of the backward, manual, batch-processing, vertical kiln system of cement production. This means that it was possible to produce cement but almost impossible to produce *quality* cement. In the end, selling the Lion & Globe brand cement was all about politics and market control, forcing the entire market into buying the lower-quality product.

Uncontrollable Merchants

If we look at it from another angle, we may understand what actually happened. Merchants trade and they treated the industrial business in a mercantilist way. They were not revolutionaries seeking to industrialise the nation but were there to make money. The merchant in this *guandu shangban* case invested a large sum of money and his aim was no doubt to recuperate in the shortest possible time and then make some profit after recuperating the invested sum. Given the set-up, if he could generate a profit by speculating in coal, he would definitely have speculated in coal; if buying clinker from Hong Kong was cheaper than producing it in Guangzhou, he would definitely have bought clinker then ground it at the plant; if it turned out that trading the cement was far more profitable than making the cement at home, he definitely would have traded. Nevertheless, he still would have done all the above using the Lion & Globe brand because this brand was the only brand protected by government in Lin's market-controlling mechanism.[110]

Furthermore, if they could find a way to siphon off profits and not pay the government such as distributing profits every month to all employees; they would have done just that. The monthly division of profits among employees, the bloated purchasing prices and salaries all demonstrate the failure of the *guandu shangban*.[111] It could be said that this failure owed much to the lack of government rules for supervision. However, the root of the problem must be the very difference in *expectation* between government officials, such as Lin Yungai, who had a long-term revolutionary cause, and the trading merchant contractors, who would have aimed for short-term profits. Regardless, *guandu shangban* was definitely hopeless in administering this industry or any industry. There might be a profit for the merchant but the government completely lost out.

By the late 1920s it can be concluded that the Guangdong cement business was far more complicated than it seemed and 20 years after the cement works was built, it was still in the doldrums. Neither *shangban* nor *guandu shangban* could produce the profit needed for the industrial expansion. In fact, these arrangements were major failures in their own right. There was no perfect fit but it was just natural to revert back to an official-management (*guanban*) enterprise. In this way, after a round trip of a decade, the government once again became the driver after 1928 in what was Guangdong's "only heavy industrial enterprise" during its latest provincial nationalisation effort. Thus, in order to resurrect state power in the province, Chinese League members in reality employed an incorporated government to gain economic power.

Sun Yat-sen in Business: A Reflection

Sun Yat-sen was a failed leader between 1912 and 1921. Little has been written about how he came back from the brink to organise the military in Guangdong. It was the creation of the Guangzhou City Council in 1921 that gave him borrowing powers for the military in the name of city development. In Guangdong, Sun Yat-sen's persistent revolutionary spirit extended beyond his grave because he laid the foundation for state power reconsolidation: he created a city corporate for regaining political power and he took over an industry for recapturing economic power. After his death, these legacies were both in the hands of his ex-secretary Lin Yungai. Lin dutifully pressed on with the unfinished quest and carried out the idealism that Sun had set out. Unfortunately, this chapter shows that the use of the city corporate to manage a cement business is problematic. Attempts to control the market through legislation were fraught with complex unforeseen difficulties. In the end, the industrial optimism of Sun Yat-sen as executed by the stoic effort of Lin Yungai after Sun's death only had limited success. Still the province staggered along without using private incorporated companies or corporations for developing a major industry but subsuming it under the city corporate. While Chiang Kai-shek was setting up the National Resource Commission secretly in Nanjing and was pondering how to industrialise China,[112] these ex-revolutionaries in Guangdong already had a head start in industrialisation. It was their good fortune that soon after they ventured into this treacherous cement business they stumbled upon a model of urban development. This sparked a big foreign investment boom. When this *market expansion* was combined with Lin Yungai's *market control* effort, cement sales went through the roof. This boom was started by the construction of a symbolic icon of modernity in 1932: The Pearl River Bridge.

Notes

1. The municipality was explicitly defined as a "legal person" by "*Shi zizhi ji* (The system of municipal (city) self-government)" promulgated by President Xu Shichang in 1921. This was the only reference showing that a city was denoted as such until the Municipal Organisation Law of 1930: Yang Hongnian and Ouyang Xin, *Zhongguo zhengzhi shi*, p. 516.

2. The *Tongmenghui*, also known as the United Allegiance Society, United League or the Revolutionary Alliance, was a secret society and underground resistance movement established in Tokyo on 20 August 1905 by Song Jiaoren and Sun Yat-sen. This was created through the merging of Sun Yat-sen's Revive China Society (*Xingzhonghui*), the Restoration Society (*Guangfuhui*) and other Chinese revolutionary groups. After the establishment of the Republic of China, the Tongmenghui formed the core of the Nationalist Party (*Guomindang*).
3. Green Island Cement Holdings Limited, "Introduction: Company Profile".
4. Shi Changjun, "Qingzhou, Qixin: shui shi zhongguo shuini gongye de faxiang di?".
5. In the Japanese colony of Taiwan in 1913, Asano Cement of Japan established the first cement company in Kaohsiung (*Gaoxiong*), southern Taiwan, and production began in 1918. Therefore, at the beginning of the Republican era, the beginnings of the modern-day Chinese cement industry can be seen: two Chinese plants on the mainland, one British plant in Hong Kong and one Japanese plant in Taiwan.
6. A brief description of memorials to the imperial court for the establishment of the Guangdong Cement Works (GCW) in *ZJGS3*, pp. 332–333.
7. A brief description of memorials to the imperial court for the establishment of the Guangdong Cement Works in *ZJGS3*, pp. 332–333.
8. A brief account of the financing arrangement for the establishment of the Guangdong Cement Works in *ZJGS3*, p. 325.
9. Financing the GCW in *ZJGS3*, p. 328.
10. Establishing the GCW in *ZJGS3*, p. 332.
11. Albert Feuerwerker, "Industrial Enterprise in Twentieth-Century China: The Chee Hsin Cement Co.", pp. 273–308.
12. Financing the GCW in *ZJGS3*, p. 326.
13. Establishing the GCW in *ZJGS3*, p. 333.
14. Financing the GCW in *ZJGS3*, p. 329.
15. Construction in Guangdong in the last five years, in *ZJGS3*; Historical Materials of Industrial Enterprises in China's Modern History: Industries Established and Monopolised by Bureaucratic Capital of the Beijing Government and the Nationalist Party in *ZJGS3*, pp. 325–326.

16. Guangdong Sheng Jiansheting, “Wu nian lai zhi guangdong jianshe”.
17. Yin Shouhua, Liang Fuliu and Yang Tinggang. “Haijun nan xia hufa shimo”, p. 46.
18. Ruixiang Tang, “Dayuanshuai chanjun chu zhi shimintu chang Sun zong ban han”.
19. Sun Zhongshan, *Jian guo fang lüe* 10th ed.
20. Duan Yunzhang and Shen Xiaomin, *Sun Wen yu Chen Jiongming*, p. 295.
21. Duan Yunzhang and Shen Xiaomin, *Sun Wen yu Chen Jiongming*, p. 295.
22. Cheng Tiangu, *Cheng Tiangu huiyilu*, p. 162.
23. Sun Yat-sen was often addressed as Premier by his followers. This refers to his title in the Nationalist Party.
24. Cheng Tiangu, *Cheng Tiangu huiyilu*, p. 137.
25. Yin Shouhua, Liang Fuliu and Yang Tinggang, “Haijun nan xia hufa shimo”, p. 232.
26. Zhang Yufa, *Zhongguo xiandai shi.*
27. *RCC4*, pp. 1509–1511.
28. Sun Yat-sen: The General Unified Financial Order dated 3 February 1924 in *SZWBB*; Sun Yat-sen: General order to establish the command bureau for military food supply in *SZWBB*, p. 377.
29. Fan Shisheng was the Commander, the Central Government Direct-Controlled Second Yunnan Army.
30. Letter from Fan Shisheng to the Generalissimo dated 1 July 1924 in *RCC4*, pp. 1509–1511.
31. Green Island Cement Company Limited.
32. Letter from Fan Shisheng to the Generalissimo dated 1 July 1924 in *RCC4*, pp. 1509–1511.
33. Letter from the Finance Committee dated 8 July 1924 in *RCC4*, pp. 1509–1511.
34. Beijing was renamed Beiping in the Republican period.
35. Guangdong dadoudu, “Ling heji yuan he ming shimintu chang dinggou dianji yi an wen”. Also see David Faure, *China and Capitalism*, p. 29 for a discussion on metal technology in late imperial China.
36. Liu Linrui: Financing the GCW in *ZJGS3*, p. 329.
37. Philip Alsop and James Post, *Cement Plant Operations Handbook.*
38. Jiansheting, in *ZJGS3*, pp. 325–326.

39. The monthly rent was 15,000 yuan per month for the first six months and 20,000 yuan per month from the seventh month onwards. The term of the lease was ten years. Sun Ke, "Shun ling Gongwu Ju zhun shimintu song lai xin tu yang shiyan you".
40. Letter from Fan Shisheng to the Generalissimo dated 1 July 1924 in *RCC4*, pp. 1509–1511.
41. Qixin Cement Company Limited and Shanghai Portland Cement Company Limited maintained such a cartel and oligopoly; see Chap. 7.
42. *LHS* v.1, p. 218; see Chap. 7.
43. Zeng Qingliu, *Guangzhou guomin zhengfu*, p. 135.
44. Jiansheting, *ZJGS3*, pp. 325–326.
45. Madeleine Zelin, "A Critique of Rights of Property in Prewar China," in M. Zelin, J. Ocko, and R. Gardella, eds., *Contract and Property in Early Modern China*, p. 28.
46. Zeng Qingliu, *Guangzhou guomin zhengfu*, pp. 143–144.
47. GZCG, "Guangzhou Shi qudi fanmai shimintu guize"; Guangzhou City Council, "Gongwuju qudi chan za shimintu guize an".
48. Article 1.
49. Article 2.
50. Article 3.
51. Article 4.
52. Article 5.
53. Article 6.
54. GZCG, "Han fu Jiancha Yuan jiang cha ban fanmai wei lie tu diau qingying ji jiang ni fa ge dian shumu fenbie he qing shimintu dian".
55. Michael Tsin, *Nation, Governance, and Modernity*, p. 163.
56. Zeng Qingliu, *Guangzhou guomin zhengfu*, p. 143.
57. Cheng Tiangu, *Cheng Tiangu huiyilu*, p. 145.
58. Sun Ke as mayor: 15 February 1921, 26 February 1923, and June 1926; Lin Yungai as mayor: February 1926, May 1927, and May 1928.
59. Zhang Yufa, *Zhongguo xian dai shi*, p. 199.
60. Parks M. Coble Jr, "The Kuomintang Regime and the Shanghai Capitalists, 1927–1929".
61. *GZSZ*; http://www.gzsdfz.org.cn/gzsz/20/rw/gz20rw030201.htm; last accessed 1 September 2007.
62. Ma Chaojun, "Chou she xinshi shimintu chang".

63. Lin Yungai, "Weichi zhengfu zhi shimintu chang yingye an".
64. GZCG, "Shi Xingzheng Huiyi tiyi qudi fanmai shimintu buchong banfa yijian shu. Fu buchong qudi shimintu banfa".
65. GZCG, "Qudi shimintu buchong banfa an".
66. GZCG, "Guangzhou Shi gongwuju qudi shimintu zhangcheng".
67. Elisabeth Köll, *From Cotton Mill to Business Empire*.
68. GZCG, "Lunshuo: shiying shiye gailun".
69. Lin Yungai, "Weichi zhengfu zhi shimintu chang yingye an".
70. GZCG, "Jishi: Gongwuju shiyan shimintu lali zhi baogao".
71. For a definition of "national product" and a general discussion of "national products" see Karl Gerth, *China Made*, p. 7.
72. GZCG, "Guanyu jin shou long mai shimintu an".
73. GZCG, "Chufa dayi dian weijin fanmai shimintu".
74. GZCG, "Guanyu long mai shimintu an".
75. Under the "promotion of self-government" policy, the mayoral system of the Guangzhou City Government was reinstated and correspondingly the executive committee system was abolished on 1 August 1929. The establishment of the provincial assembly, however, was delayed until October 1932. *GZSZ*, 1 August 1929; GZCG, "Guanyu jinshou long mai shimintu an".
76. GZCG, "Long mai shimintu zan zhun yunxiao an".
77. GZCG, "Guanyu shiyan long mai shimintu an".
78. GZCG, "Guanyu fanmai long mai shimintu".
79. GZCG, "Chufa Dalong hao fanmai wei shimintu".
80. GZCG, "Yanjin fanmai wei shimintu"; GZCG, "Yanfa Dadelong hao deng dian mai wei shimintu an"; GZCG, "Guyanyu chufa shimintu shangren Tongde gongsi"; GZCG, "Guanyu Chufa Dade dian fanmai wei tu"; GZCG, "Yancheng fanmai wei shimintu shangren"; GZCG, "Juya si fan wei tu jianshang".
81. In June 1930, Guangzhou's administrative status was changed from Special city (*Tebie Shi*) to Provincial city (*Shenghe Shi*). Cheng Tiangu was officially re-appointed as the Director of the Public Works Bureau after being its Acting Director and at the same time he was appointed as the Chairman of the City Construction Committee (*Chengshi jianshe weiyuanhui zhuxi*); *GZSZ* June 1930.
82. GZCG, "Gongwuju shiyan shiqiupai shimintu zhi jieguo".
83. GZCG, "Guanyu shiyan shiqiupai shimintu an".
84. GDPG, "Chexiao Guangdong shimintu chang Puyi gongsi cheng an"; GDPG, "Guifu Guangdong shimintu chang".
85. Lin Yungai, "Weichi zhengfu zhi shimintu chang yingye an".
86. See Chap. 6.

87. Lin Yungai, "Weichi zhengfu zhi shimintu chang ying ye an".
88. GXGZ June 1928.
89. *Quanguo wenhua xinxi ziyuan gongxiang gongcheng.*
90. GZCG "Qudi shimintu buchong banfa an".
91. Jiansheting, "Chou ban xinshi shimintu chang jiekuan hetong,"; GDPG, "Biantong shou yong xinshi shimintu chang changzhi tudi banfa an"; GDPG, "Ling caizhengting she zai Xicun xuanze Xicun shimintu chang chang zhi an".
92. Jiansheting, *ZJGS3*, p. 324.
93. GDQXX; http://www.gd-info.gov.cn:8080/was40/outline?page=3&channelid=12084; last accessed 1st September 2007.
94. GDPG, "Ling Jiansheting xuan shang cheng zhu xicun shimintu chang".
95. Cheng Tiangu, *Cheng Tiangu huiyilu,* p. 162.
96. GDQXX; http://www.gd-info.gov.cn:8080/was40/detail?record=2&channelid=58844&searchword =%B3%CC%CC%EC%B9%CC; last accessed 1 September 2007.
97. GDPG, "Ling Jiansheting xuan shang cheng zhu xicun shimintu chang".
98. GDPG, "Hezhun Xicun shimintu chang zeng shou tudi"; GDPG, "Hezhun zhui jia xinshi shimintu chang buchong jixie fei".
99. See Chap. 6.
100. GDPG, "Chi shu caimai shiqiupai shimintu an".
101. GDPG, "Chi shu caimai shiqiupai shimintu an".
102. GDPG, "Chi shu caimai shiqiupai shimintu an".
103. Zhang Yufa, *Zhongguo xian dai shi*, p. 202.
104. GDPG, "Chexiao Guangdong shimintu chang Puyi gongsi cheng an".
105. GDPG, "Guifu Guangdong shimintu chang".
106. Jiansheting, in *ZJGS3*, pp. 325–326.
107. Ma Chaojun, "Chou she xinshi shimintu chang".
108. GDPG, "Chexiao Guangdong shimintu chang Puyi gongsi cheng an".
109. GZCG, "Gongwuju shiyan shiqiupai shimintu zhi jieguo".
110. Lin Yungai, "Weichi zhengfu zhi shimintu chang yingye an"; GZCG, "Guanyu shiyan shiqiupai shimintuan"; GDPG, "Chi shu caimai shiqiupai shimintu an".
111. GDPG, "Hezhun Guangdong shimintu chang yuangong fuwu guicheng".
112. See Chap. 7.

CHAPTER 6

The Pearl River Bridge: Recovering State Power

In stark contrast to Qixin Cement Company in the north, the Guangdong Cement Works in the south was an abject failure between 1909 until 1932. So, how did cement suddenly become an enormously profitable business in Guangdong from 1932 onwards? The answer lies with the foreign investment hype following the construction of the symbolic Pearl River Bridge by officials who were ex-revolutionaries inside a city government that foreign banks can legally provide loans. In 1930s, this is arguably the most iconic symbol of modernity for Guangzhou, the proud capital of southern China. To the Cantonese-speaking southern Chinese, the Pearl River Bridge is comparable to the Eiffel Tower for Paris or the Golden Gate Bridge for San Francisco. The influx of investment from mainly Cantonese-speaking overseas Chinese propelled the economy forward and empowered the city government. Hence, the contextual economic circumstance is the cause of success. Even without any marketing effort, the cement was selling under overheating economic conditions. The ex-revolutionaries in Guangdong stumbled upon this model of development that attracted huge investments directly from the overseas Chinese while they relentlessly used the city corporate to resurrect state power lost after the imperial collapse.

In the early 1930s, Guangdong Province, the old revolutionary base of Sun Yat-sen and his followers, was under the stewardship of Sun's protégé Hu Hanmin and military strongman Chen Jitang. They rebelled against Chiang Kai-shek's rule from Nanjing, following a dispute over the

H. Ko, *The Making of the Modern Chinese State*,
DOI 10.1007/978-981-10-2660-7_6

drafting of the national Provisional Constitution. This led to the arrest of Hu Hanmin by Chiang Kai-shek in 1931. Even though Hu was released after the Japanese occupied Manchuria, the state of semi-independence in Guangdong remained. This status quo maintained until a *coup d'état* in the provincial government gave Chiang Kai-shek's Nanjing Government control of this renegade province in 1936. During this period 1931–1936, Guangdong province struggled to build up a powerful provincial "state" by means of a healthy economy to sustain its independence.

Wealth and power were created relying not only by a simple wish to build industries but also by political takeovers of local wealth in the name of Guangzhou city. Even more wealth and power were generated by attracting vast amounts of foreign direct investment into town. Our story now turns to how the ex-members of Sun Yat-sen's Chinese League in collaboration with the "warlord" Chen Jitang used the Guangzhou City Government within the province as the corporate vehicle to resurrect central state power. In the process, hearts and minds were discovered to unite not under Sun Yat-sen's nationalist ideals but by the technologically advanced electric-driven double leafbascule Pearl River Bridge that can automatically open up to let ships through. This was a powerful symbol of Chinese modernity in the 1930s built by a modern institution, the Guangzhou City Government.

The merchants dominated the economy of the provincial capital Guangzhou. The idea that the provincial government should start a heavy industrial enterprise began with the Qing-built cement works which carried on business in the 1920s. However, there was neither any coherent plan nor any intention of its incorporation under the new company law of 1904.[1] A systematic and coherent approach to constructing municipal or city industries did arrive in 1928: a policy essay was published in the Guangzhou City Government Gazette by the ex-Chinese League revolutionaries who dominated the City Government. This was a conceptual model imported from the West and promoted the idea that city businesses should be owned and managed by city governments. This promoted a diminishing role for the merchants. The apparent initial success of this model when applied to the cement industry to tap wealth from the market led to the belief that it could be emulated across all industries. Thus, it spurred investment from the government for rapid industrialisation but without incorporated companies. Was this really such a powerful model in tapping the market? Was this different from the previous form of government control of the cement industry? Mercantile practices in the market and how government policies between 1909 and 1928 responded to them have been explained in the previous chapter. The following will show the outcome of the policies of the Chinese League-controlled Guangzhou City Government after Mayor Lin Yungai took office.

The general market for a commodity like cement has to be driven by increased demand to expand. This chapter will show that no matter how much positive effort was undertaken by the city or provincial authorities to promote sales by regulating merchants and controlling trading imports, it was dwarfed by market demand created by a general economic boom. Ironically the cause of this boom was not a result of a successful control mechanism installed by the government and executed by the Public Works Bureau. Instead, it was down to the determination and effort of the Director of the Public Works Bureau Cheng Tiangu to do nothing else but undertake public works. It will be shown that, for the cement industry, there was no need to worry about industrial management, technology, or sales and distribution networks to achieve high sales and profits. These performed smoothly once the government effectively manipulated the market by control and stimulus.

To recapitulate, Cheng Tiangu was appointed by Lin Yungai to head the Public Works Bureau again from May 1929 to June 1932. After merely three years in office, he had already single-handedly created a boom in Guangdong's economy which unintentionally also drove up demand for cement. Thus, Lin indirectly and unintentionally created a booming economy and expanded the general market demand for cement. The weakness in Lin Yungai's single-minded attempt to control and direct the cement market was that he failed to investigate the details of the problems of the cement works. The questions of industrial management, the state of the cement works' non-automated machinery and technology, or sales and distribution networks were not considered by Lin to have any relation to the miserable performance of this industrial enterprise. He believed that the poor sales were due solely to the market presence of imported cement. He also believed that sales of the local Lion & Globe brand cement could be increased. He attempted this through the issuing of laws regulating the merchants and arbitrarily banning certain brands of cement by failing them in quality tests performed by the Public Works Bureau. His idea was to gradually eliminate imported cement. He believed that this would allow the locally produced cement to build up strength and volume from the 400 barrels per day capacity. Hence, Lin, in collaboration with the Provincial Construction Department Director, Ma Chaojun, quickly planned to build a new modern, fuel-efficient rotary kiln cement plant. This idea came after they separately took offices in 1928. Lin hoped his scheme would allow increased local production to eventually mop up the 3000 barrels per day market share, which was at that time held by imported cement.[2]

As shown in Chap. 5, Lin Yungai's seemingly flawless control mechanism from 1928 to 1931 only benefited the shadowy trading and speculating activities of the merchants in the merchant-managed Guangdong Cement Works. This enterprise was under the guise of *guandu shangban* arrangement but Lin did not recognise the problem until August 1931.[3] The construction of the new cement works, given the go-ahead in July 1929,[4] was also stalled until June 1930.[5] This was because the construction of the new plant was controlled by Liu Yanhua who was clearly only interested in keeping the old plant's monopoly on the Lion & Globe brand for as long as possible. Thus, Lin's determined attempt to control the cement market from 1928 to 1931 in reality failed to help the development of this industry. However, the provincial government did complete construction of the new 1000 barrels per day modern cement works in April 1932 and it achieved great commercial success. The cement works went on to two immediate expansions, completing in April 1935 and July 1937.[6]

There was a mistaken belief that the market success was due to the construction of the Guangdong-Hankou Railway, which required large amounts of cement. It was not logical to build a cement plant based solely upon one potential customer or, as previously shown, a market control mechanism. Arguably, it follows that an increase in general market demand was the only sound criteria for such a large capital investment. The rate of return accompanying such expansion was slow because of the lengthy construction period of up to two years each time.[7] So how was a general market demand generated to make the cement industry such a success? This relied on the consolidation of state power by the ex-Chinese League revolutionaries in the city and provincial governments.

Recovering State Power I: The City is the Corporation

The Theoretical Debate

As pointed out previously, the city was declared to be a *legal person* (i.e., *corporate person*) by the policy of the Municipal Autonomy System (*Shi zizhi zhi*) in July 1921 and defined as such by the Municipal Organisation Law (*Shi zizhi fa*) of 1930.[8] Guangzhou City was thus legally recognised under constitutional law as a corporation in the Republic of China. Within this city in 1928, Mayor Lin Yungai, together with the revolutionaries in the local government, took a three-pronged approach. Firstly, he wanted to maintain the operation of the old Qing dynasty cement works from 1909 to meet the demand created by the reduction in imports. Secondly, he began using the law to launch attacks on imported cement to secure the market for the *guandu shangban* production. Thirdly, he commissioned a feasibility study on building a new cement works to take over as much demand as possible from imports.

On the one hand, Lin Yungai was attempting to develop Guangdong's industries by the practical methods described above beginning with a new cement plant. On the other, an interesting theoretical model of organising government-operated enterprises was published. In 1928, Lin and his executive government could not have foreseen the great boom which Cheng Tiangu would eventually bring about. Nonetheless, the model did form the backbone of the administrative policies of the Construction Department which Lin led until 1936. The new cement plant gave the government a device to channel some of the market wealth into its coffers and with this initial capital it expanded into other industries to further tap the market.

In 1928, after Lin Yungai became Chairman of the City Government Executive Committee, the Guangzhou City Government published a discussion "essay" (*lunshuo*) in the City Government Bulletin (*Shizheng gongbao*) titled *A General Survey of Municipal Enterprises*.[9] The author Qian Jinghui was an Executive Committee member and would subsequently become the Chairman of the Municipal Bank of Guangzhou a year later in June 1929. This was in reality a policy paper setting out the City Government's municipal nationalisation agenda masked as an intellectual treatise. It was an important "essay" because it provided a theoretical basis supporting the City Government's impending business and industrial ventures. Qian's conclusions, interpreting experiences in the West, came to define when and how this Chinese city government should absorb the public sector's privately managed enterprises and the succeeding apposite holding and management structures. By this discussion of "neo-*guanban*" enterprises, the city of Guangzhou and the Chinese Republic were led to espouse, for the first time, the process of municipal nationalisation where a *city* government moves into commercial enterprises.

Municipal Enterprises: Shiban

A General Survey of Municipal Enterprises (GSME) was published in the City Government Gazette immediately upon Lin Yungai taking office again as Mayor in 1928. It sets out to describe the methodologies of municipal nationalisation by incorporated cities in Europe and the USA, and to lay out the model alternatives which Guangzhou could adopt. Its contents presented the Guangzhou City Government's more modern version of *guanban* enterprises.[10]

The essay started off by explaining that in the Western world municipal nationalisation began in the mid-nineteenth century and underwent considerable expansion in the twentieth. Most of the municipal enterprises in the European and American incorporated cities were in water supply, electricity, tramways, telephone and gas and so on . Furthermore, the concept of "municipal nationalisation" has two components of "ownership" and "operation". For example, the gas supply in Philadelphia was owned by the city but supply was operated by a private company. However, if it was like Boston where the tramways were owned by a private consortium but operated by the city, it cannot be classified as a municipal enterprise.[11]

The essay explained that municipal nationalisation was more common in European countries. In the majority of US cities, save for the water supply that was government-owned, gas, electricity and transportation et cetera were in private ownership. Although conceding that there were other factors at work, it identified two main reasons for this. First, constitutionally the city was a subsidiary of the state it was located in and there was no policy freedom. The city government could not own public utilities unless it had approval from the state government. Secondly, the "*laissez faire* policy", the belief in self-help and the conviction of independent commercial management, made government or officially operated ("*guanban*") enterprises irksome to the American people. However, these "obstacles" did not exist in European countries. It was for these reasons that municipal enterprises were blossoming across Europe.[12] The discussion then went on to survey tramways in the UK and the USA[13]; electricity in the UK, Germany and the US cities Cleveland, Birmingham and Cincinnati[14]; coal gas of Glasgow, Manchester and Birmingham; and then a general survey of the situation in Germany, Italy and France before World War I.[15] It concluded after the above survey of municipal nationalisation advancements, that the UK, France and Germany were superior to the USA. In particular, the municipal enterprises of the UK were not only expanding but results were promising. Not only were they self-funded but there was even substantial surplus enough to alleviate the tax burden of their citizens.[16]

The GSME then turns to examining the different methods of constitution of these municipal enterprises in relation to their city governments. Firstly, the "Council Committee System": this was the most popular in the first wave of municipal nationalisation. A committee would be appointed by the city council to take charge of the enterprises. Yet committee members were frequently found to promote their own political purposes and thus it had gone out of fashion in the USA. However, this was still popular in the UK. In the UK system the city executive and legislative powers reside in the elected council and its appointed committee. Below the committee were "professional officers" who executed the decisions for the non-professional committee.[17] Secondly, because the Committee system was unpopular in the USA, it developed the "Board System". Responsibility for the municipal enterprises lay not with the city council but with a management board consisting of three to five members. The members of the board were either appointed by the Mayor or directly elected by the people. Unfortunately, the Board System did not completely eliminate the old problems and bad practices which existed in the Committee System. Thus, it claimed that academics could only recommend this system to small municipalities or towns because it was economical to do so.[18] The discussion then concluded that all big cities adopt the "Single Commission System":

> In "The Single Commissioner System", those city executive authorities which do not establish a Public Utility Bureau would usually establish separate Bureaus for water supply, coal gas and electricity, with all of them administrated by a single department under a "single Commissioner". This is the case for the water supply, coal gas and electricity of New York. This city has three bureaus but administered by a single Commissioner *appointed by the Mayor*. Alternatively, other cities administer these bureaus under the *Public Works Bureau* or *some other related government division*. For example, Boston's water supply is administered by that city's *Public Works Bureau* which manages the sewers, roads and bridges. Any newly-created public utility bureaus will be established under that *Public Works Bureau*.[19]…According to the present trend, US cities mostly adopt the Single Commissioner system for professional and responsible governing. Moreover, Multi-Commissioner Systems also exist with three to five commissioners. There is no rigid requirement for the numbers but are all

> *appointed by the Mayor*; or *appointed by the Mayor with the support of the Council* or elected by the people.[20]

Although election of the Commissioner by the people was discussed as an alternative, in 1928 Guangzhou the chances of this being adopted were small. The essay basically confirmed that the Guangzhou Public Works Bureau (or "some other related government division") like its counterparts in the rest of the world would assume an even more important role in the municipal nationalisation process than that it had already assumed in this old city's modernisation. Finally, the essay did not determine the sensitive issue of the merits of municipal and private enterprise structures but admitted that there were pros and cons in these economic forms. Yet it declared some criteria for municipal nationalisation. Firstly, if a privately operated public enterprise "cannot satisfy the needs of citizens" and was "sacrificing public interest", then it must be a suitable case for municipal nationalisation. Secondly, when there existed a "good city government and a faultless organisation structure", then public enterprises should be transferred to be city-operated (*shiban*).[21]

However, the author was careful to place limitations on the criteria for municipal nationalisation by insisting that the accounts of these enterprises should be independent of the city coffers as well as independent of each other. This effectively denied failing enterprises the chance of municipal nationalisation by barring subsidies. Lastly, it urged that professional managers should be employed, that formal employment protection should be put in place, and that institutional safeguards should be constructed for the management. These should be implemented to ensure independence from the occasional change in the "political tides".[22] It will be seen that the important ideas expounded in this essay by Qian Jinghui were mostly adhered to in the subsequent municipal nationalisation and development of the cement industry, particularly its support for the Mayor's (i.e., the executive's) power of appointment.[23]

It is interesting to note that the *guanban* enterprises in Guangdong in the late 1920s were no longer opportunistic trial-and-error types of establishment like the original Guangdong Cement Works in the 1910s. Though still dictatorial, the publication of the essay at least demonstrated that there was serious comparative research into the form of industrial policy that would be adopted by the city government headed now by the members of the revolutionary Chinese League. It can be seen that the Guangzhou City Government, now completely dominated by foreign-educated followers of Sun Yat-sen, was digging in at their stronghold of Guangzhou and were doing all they could to consolidate their power. They were trying to enrich their home base of Guangdong and stabilising their income. It is entirely clear what Lin Yungai was aiming to do with the Guangzhou City Government. He was aiming to develop new sources of revenue, widening its income base and directing wealth and power from the mighty Guangzhou merchants into the hands of the revolutionaries. Whereas Yuan Shikai used commercial corporations to accure economic power, Lin Yungai used a city government as the corporation.

Lin Yungai's government was quick to implement their industrial policies. In May 1928 the government announced that a coal gas system would be built in the city to support the electric system. However, it was to be operated and built by merchant investors and not the neo-*guanban* enterprises discussed above.[24] The ideas expressed in the "General Survey" could only be implemented slowly and the Government remained financially poor. Furthermore, the announcement of this "essay" also coincided with Lin Yungai's employment of the new legal power conferred on the Public Works Bureau to launch attacks on the cement merchants in June 1928.[25]

Recovering State Power II: Urban Modernisation

After Sun Yat-sen's death in 1925 and the Northern Expedition of 1927, Lin Yungai's main concern in Guangzhou even in these early days was not the building of a single cement plant. Of course, the industrialisation of China was a wider issue which concerned him and other members of the Chinese League such as Ma Chaojun. The immediate concern, however, was the development of their revolutionary base, the city of Guangzhou. The members of the Chinese League were mostly educated in the West and understood the urgency of rebuilding Guangzhou from a city of narrow alleyways and waterways into a modern metropolis. They were bogged down, however, by lack of funds and insurmountable established vested interests within this ancient imperial trading city. Lin was conscious of this difficulty, but his plans were obstructed since he became Mayor of the City Government. His Director of Public Works at the time faced a boycott by contractors, and public works were suspended in early 1929.[26]

In mid-1929, Lin Yungai urgently recruited to the directorship the first Director of Public Works, Cheng Tiangu, who had the support of Lin Yungai's backer, ex-Chinese League and Nationalists Party (KMT) revolutionary veteran Gu Yingfen. Cheng Tiangu had just arrived back in

Guangzhou after a European tour, after working for the national government in Nanjing.[27] Cheng's return around May 1929 was very important because Lin was running out of ideas and all his general public works projects were stalled. The Provincial Governor Chen Mingshu (an ex-Chinese League member) was already dismayed by the situation and Lin had no other option but to depend on Cheng Tiangu's previous experience in public works to get the job done.[28]

When Cheng Tiangu returned as the Director, the City Government was financially stretched and had no extra money for city development.[29] Yet surprisingly, he lived up to his reputation and jumpstarted road building and other works to improve the city. He thus inadvertently brought about Guangzhou's historic economic boom of the 1930s. During his tenure as the Director of Public Works, he initiated his *Guangzhou Pubic Works Two-Year Plan* which contained all kinds of public works projects. The jewel of the planned projects was the construction of the bascule Pearl River Bridge which began in December 1929.[30] Indeed with the construction of this bridge, Guangzhou began to acquire a potent symbol of modernity. Its citizens were filled with pride and confidence and perhaps with a sense that the 1911 revolution was worthwhile after all.

Most surprisingly, Cheng Tiangu managed all these projects *without government funding*. He succeeded through the manipulation of the Public Bureau's power (perhaps to the point of abuse) and clever use of idle City Government resources at his disposal. In other words, he used his power to enrich the Public Works Bureau, and when he became Mayor in June 1931, the City Government was flush with money. The economic boom created by him naturally created a high demand for cement since he started his projects in May 1929.[31] Cheng Tiangu became increasingly powerful and would not cooperate easily with Lin Yungai's market control methods.[32] He also began to financially support the air force in the fight against the Japanese after September 1931, an unwise move which made him threatening in the eyes of the local "warlord" Chen Jitang.[33]

From the perspectives of Lin Yungai and Chen Jitang, it was not difficult for them to see that Cheng Tiangu had discovered the path to modernisation through his methods and in his *Guangzhou Public Works Two-Year Plan*. Furthermore, this effort in modernisation in turn drove up cement demand which, after 20 years of struggling, at last appeared to be the pathway to industrialisation as Sun Yat-sen had hoped. Cheng Tiangu's scheme seemed easy to understand: firstly, publish a clear plan for general development; then, finish constructing the Pearl River Bridge as a symbol of modernisation to attract direct investment from excited overseas Chinese[34]; lastly, build up government-owned industries to supply industrial products such as cement to this rapidly growing market. Lin quickly appropriated and renewed all the ideas from Cheng's *Two-Year Plan*[35] in the City Government's own *Guangzhou City Public Works Execution Plan* of December 1930. In October 1931, Cheng's staunch backer, party elder Gu Yingfen died in a dental operation and Cheng Tiangu was pushed out of office in February 1932 before the opening of the Pearl River Bridge.[36] Lin Yungai and Chen Jitang then simulated Cheng Tiangu's scheme of development and industrialisation for the province in September 1932 by jointly announcing the *Guangdong Province Three-Year Plan*.[37]

Recovering State Power III: Mayor Cheng Tiangu's Tactics

Cheng Tiangu's success did make him powerful but also attracted suspicion from the "warlord" Chen Jitang. Chen wanted a role for his military in the apparently lucrative industrialisation process. Lin Yungai's lone success of the cement industry led to the province's massive drive towards industrial development in the following few years. So what exactly did Cheng Tiangu do to create this economic boom which caused not only the rapid development of the *un*incorporated cement industry but also a rapid general industrialisation in the "corporate" province? Furthermore, how was the market driven by what he did? The explanation must begin with an examination of the Public Works Bureau.

The Public Works Bureau headed by Cheng Tiangu was the institution that spearheaded the destruction of the old local power structure and the installation of the new. Lin Yungai's problem was that the Bureau was given wide power to control but lacked the brains to instigate change. Cheng Tiangu was about to change all that when he returned to "finish off personally" what he had started while in office in 1921.[38] When the Guangzhou City Council was established in 1921, the Public Works Bureau was its core frontline department. As the first Director Cheng Tiangu said,

> The only work available for the city administration after its establishment was to focus on public works. I had courage to do my work and I had some intelligence too but the city administration had absolutely no idea where income could be found...It was like riding a tiger and I could not get off,

> there was no escape...My answer to this predicament had only two words: work hard.[39]

Indeed, Cheng Tiangu worked extremely hard. He was a city-planning fanatic and dedicated wholeheartedly to Guangzhou's public works. He devised all kinds of ways to find income for the Public Works Bureau and thus the City Council. A few months into his first office in 1921, he strongly objected to Sun Ke's plan to borrow 10 million US dollars "for city development". The American lenders required the signature of the Director of Public Works as well as submitting it to the Provincial Government for the record. Believing that this would fundamentally affect his personal reputation, he debated his position fervently with Sun Ke three times directly in front of Chen Jiongming at the Provincial Government. He believed that the meagre yearly income of approximately 2 million yuan could not support such a huge loan and this loan would bankrupt the city. He would not budge even after backer and party elder Gu Yingfen came to urge him to allow the loan with some amendments to the agreement. Instead he suggested that Sun Ke should "pick another Director who would agree to the borrowing". Cheng wrote a long letter detailing his dissatisfaction, criticising each term of the loan agreement, handed in his resignation to Sun Ke and left for Hong Kong. A few days later, however, Sun Ke abandoned the loan plan and sent messengers to Hong Kong ask Cheng to resume his office in Guangzhou.[40]

Cheng Tiangu clearly did not look beyond the daily perspective of the City Council and was insensitive to the wider political landscape. He was obsessed with turning Guangzhou into a modern Chinese city. Nothing could stand in his way. He cleared the rubble of the demolished city walls for free by exchanging with the building contractor the roadside interests after the new roads were created from them.[41] Similarly harnessing the merchants' greed and self-interest, he persuaded many neighbourhoods to put up their own money for road building because they themselves wanted wider roads. He intimidated the shop owners who were obstructing his road-building project by removing all their roof canopies on Chinese New Year's day while they were closed for celebration.[42] He deliberately made a false announcement that he would fill up a dyke by the railway terminus which was important to the British merchants. Then he tricked the British into giving up a piece of waterfront land which they had been unlawfully occupying since the Qing Dynasty by agreeing not to carry out the filling.[43] Cheng Tiangu was a clever and determined Director and he took great pride in his own astuteness which steered the city's reconstruction.[44]

Lin Yungai's Public Works Bureau in 1928 remained the core department and the vanguard of the City Government just as it was earlier in 1921. This structural relationship between the administration and the Bureau did not change but it needed a strong personality to instigate changes in an old city. Many of the projects that were started by Cheng Tiangu before Chen Jiongming's 1923 rebellion remained incomplete at the time Lin became Mayor in 1928. In the six years since Cheng left office owing to the coup, the successive Bureau chiefs only managed to build two roads.[45] In 1928, Lin had a grand plan for development, and, within this grand plan, the building up of the cement industry became the principal industry in the plan.[46] It was, however, Cheng Tiangu who made the critical contributions which would affect its twisted development.[47]

As we have seen, Lin Yungai also wanted the cement industry to thrive by banning imports and forcing the wholesalers to sell the locally manufactured Lion & Globe brand cement. He also set out to build a new cement-manufacturing facility to substitute the new local supply in place of the banned foreign imported cement.[48] Apparently irritated by poor market response to the Lion & Globe brand cement,[49] he made emotional pleas to the public to buy local products. He also attempted to revolutionise the system in the name of nationalism and was angry when his intentions were frustrated.[50] In contrast, Cheng Tiangu, acting quite independently, was dedicated to public works projects. These projects were large, requiring greater quantities of cement, and were staunchly carried out systematically under the *Two-Year Plan*. It was this *Two-Year Plan*, which was not conceived by Lin, that naturally drove Guangzhou to unprecedented levels of development. The ultimate effect was that this created a huge demand for the Five Rams brand (*Wuyangpai*) cement from the new Xicun Cement Works that was central to Lin's grand plan.

Executing the Two-Year Plan

The predicament in 1929 was the same as before: there was no funding from the City Government for public works.[51] Thus, Cheng Tiangu resorted to what he described as "revolutionary tactics" to get his funds for development.[52] In order to demonstrate what he wanted to do and how he would be self-funding his projects, he even sold copies of his *Guangzhou City Public Works Two-Year Plan* at one yuan per copy and made a tiny profit of 2000 yuan. This test, Cheng claimed, showed that there was genuine public interest in his plans to modernise Guangzhou. He boasted that he would be turning such interest in these projects into funding for Guangzhou's development. This *Two-Year Plan* contained many construction projects but the most important was the planned construction of the Pearl River Bridge. All these however, had no funding from the City Government because this government could only just support itself and could not spare any money for large-scale construction projects. Cheng's *Two-Year Plan* was no more than "cheap talk" at the stage of announcement.[53] When Sun Ke was the Mayor of Guangzhou, that is, heading the City Council in February 1923, he had to confiscate and sell most of the public property which the City Council theoretically inherited from the Qing Dynasty government. The injustice of confiscation caused uproar in the city and led to Sun Ke's resignation in September 1924.[54] Cheng had to find initial capital to fund his *Two-Year Plan* but almost everything valuable had been sold by Sun Ke.[55] One of the major places Cheng turned to was the Wenlan College which was the only establishment with significant assets remaining in Guangzhou and it was an *un*incorporated entity, making it unprotected under Republican law.

The Wenlan College had been established in 1810 in the Qing Dynasty. It was a charitable organisation established by donations from the richest four compradors residing in the western suburbs.[56] The aims of the college were the cleaning of the myriad of dykes in old Guangzhou city and to provide scholarships for outstanding scholars taking the imperial examinations. It was estimated by Cheng to have assets worth over a million yuan in 1928. After the abolition of the imperial examinations, the rules were changed to divide the payout into two. On the one hand, it continued handing out scholarships and on the other it contributed to the maintenance of the public dykes and sewers of Guangzhou.[57] However, from the beginning of the Republic, hardly any maintenance work was carried out. The *Guangzhou Minguo Daily* was the first to reveal in several articles that there were problems with the maintenance fund accounts.[58] Furthermore, traditionally, this was the headquarters of powerful local gentry and elites for a whole century and all new imperial mandarins stationed in Guangzhou would respect their power and steered clear of the college. Even when Sun Ke was liquidating assets in 1924, he did not dare to touch this college for fear of the possible consequences. The principal of the Wenlan College thus wielded great power and neither Sun Ke nor Wu Chaoshu was able to do much more when they were city chiefs.[59]

The principal was a man named Luo Songfan, nicknamed "Red-faced Pluto" (*Hongmian yanluo*), and he had two sons; one was an investigating officer in the Public Security Bureau and the other was a street thug. There were elections each year for the position of principal but for over a decade Luo's sons would come armed with weapons to threaten the members and made absolutely sure that their father was always elected. By controlling the Wenlan College, Luo controlled valuable real estate such as the best restaurant in Guangzhou, the Wenyuan Restaurant, and the Sun Yat-sen ("Sun Zhongshan") Cinema. However, Cheng Tiangu discovered that the monthly rents for these were only 50 and 100 yuan respectively, a fraction of what they should have been at that time. He concluded that Luo and his family must have pocketed the difference.[60]

It was because the maintenance of dykes and sewers in Republican Guangzhou fell within the jurisdiction of the Public Works Bureau and the historic purpose of the Wenlan College was to fund sewer maintenance; however, it was unwilling to put up the money for the performance of its "duties". This caused friction between the Bureau and the college when Cheng Tiangu returned as Acting Director.[61] Since Cheng was well aware of the power and influence of Luo Songfan, he was thus extremely careful when he wanted to arrest Luo for his corruption. While the college was holding its annual dinner at Wenyuan Restaurant, Cheng had both Luo and his chief accountant Li arrested. Instead of bringing them back to the Bureau, Cheng arranged for him to be kept in a secret hideaway somewhere on Henan Island across the river on the south bank of the Pearl River. During initial detention, Luo attempted to bribe his way out but after seven days of custody Cheng finally broke him and Luo forfeited all deeds and accounts to the City Government. The money was used for the construction of a school, cleaning the dykes and, most importantly, contributed substantially to the furthering of Cheng Tiangu's *Two-Year Plan*. This was possible because Wenlan College was not incorporated as a legal person and therefore had no legal protection as a corporation.[62]

The assets of Wenlan College provided the direct funding for the commencement of the *Two-Year Plan* but were still insufficient to fund any large-scale capital project such as the Pearl River Bridge. Nonetheless, construction of the bridge began just the same in December 1929.[63] When the project was announced in Cheng Tiangu's *Two-Year Plan* he had no money for it. Cheng and his engineers decided that one way of funding was to reclaim the bay of the Pearl River along the northern bank. Eventually, the reclamation engulfed the "Sea Pearl", the island in the middle of the bay next to the bridge and they sold the newly created land to finance the bridge's construction. This reclamation plan was carried out when piling work began for the bridge foundation. The reclaimed land next to the bridge became very expensive real estate and was auctioned off in stages by the Public Works Bureau. In the end, the final amount obtained far exceeded the cost of construction and they had a surplus of approximately 500,000 yuan.[64] Thus, the Pearl River Bridge was completed without support from other departments or the budget of the Guangzhou City Government.

The *Two-Year Plan* ended in May 1931 and Cheng had spent over 10 million yuan but still had 30,000 yuan in surplus.[65] He became Guangzhou's Mayor the following month when Lin became Provincial Governor. Meanwhile, he remained as Director to the Bureau despite the promotion.[66] As Mayor, he controlled not only the Public Works Bureau but also the police and the Guangzhou Municipal Bank. Unwisely, he meddled in military affairs by asking the bank to lend 300,000 yuan in September 1931 to Chen Jitang's cash-strapped opponent: the air force. Cheng Tiangu and the City Government were deemed to have become too powerful and wayward for all parties. In February 1932, following the sudden death of his backer Gu Yingfen and owing to increasing interference from Chen Jitang, Cheng Tiangu was forced to resign as Mayor and Director of Public Works.[67] He was offered the powerless directorship of the Provincial Construction Department. Taking the advice of Hu Hanmin, he half-heartedly took office for a couple of months before resigning and left for Hong Kong.[68] A year later the Pearl River Bridge had its grand opening on 15 February 1933 but it was Lin Yungai, Chen Jitang and the new Mayor of Guangzhou Liu Jiwen who threw the big celebration party.[69]

Recovering State Power IV: The Symbol of a Modern State

The Completion of the Pearl River Bridge in February 1933 signified to ordinary people the arrival of modern times for both the city of Guangzhou and for Guangdong Province. Cheng Tiangu's legacy was that his wits and intelligence had created a lasting symbol of modernisation. From this time onwards both the civil and military administrations jumped onto the development bandwagon. It legitimatised all modern developments in everything from urban renewal to industrial developments.

Lin Yungai was the first to jump on, well before the completion of the iconic bridge. Although it could of course be argued that he was in fact the person who started all the development. When Cheng Tiangu's *Two-Year Plan* was proceeding smoothly, Lin endorsed it with the City Government's own *Guangzhou City Public Works Execution Plan* in December 1930. He acknowledged in the preamble of this plan that the core of this plan came from Cheng Tiangu.[70] Significantly, it showed that Lin was adopting Cheng's popular and successful development model for the City Government. The *Two-Year Plan* was also a direct predecessor to yet another plan, the *Guangdong Province Three-Year Plan*. This is because when Lin took over the Provincial Government in June 1931, he took with him Cheng Tiangu's development plan approach to the provincial government level.[71] This *Three-Year Plan* was announced in September 1932 in partnership with Chen Jitang because Chen also jumped on to the bandwagon after he forced out Cheng Tiangu.

The *Guangdong Province Three-Year Plan* was a collaboration between Lin Yungai and Chen Jitang or, more precisely, between the civil administration controlled by the faction of "elders" who were members of the Chinese League and the military in Guangdong, controlled by the "military" faction. It was announced to all the heads of the Provincial Government on 14 September 1932 over a dinner party jointly organised by Lin Yungai and Chen Jitang and to be officially implemented on 1 January 1933.

The construction of the Pearl River Bridge attracted the attention of Chinese from all over the world. Its grand opening ceremony and the celebrations in February 1933 were used as an occasion by Lin Yungai and Chen Jitang, now in partnership, to host a Guangzhou City Exhibition. The exhibition was located at the foot of Yuexiu hills (*Yuexiushan*) which is in an area outside the Great Northern Gate (*Dabeimen*) of the old walled city. The gate area had been opened up by the demolishing of the city walls. The exhibition was used as a showcase of Guangdong Province's investment potential to Chinese investors from Hong Kong, Macao and other countries.[72] This exhibition was a great success in attracting investors, partly because of the hype over the bridge and partly because of the appearance of unity and hospitality by the military leader Chen Jitang, the Provincial Governor Lin Yungai and the City Mayor Liu Jiwen. This dispelled fears and misunderstanding as well as actual promises of protection of investments.[73] Another reason was because of the economic downturn outside China at this time which made investing in the province attractive.[74] The success of this exhibition was already apparent within a year:

> In the year of 1933, 253.8 million yuan entered the province via banks which amounted to 84.26% of the national total of overseas investment (and this excluded private transfers which were not recorded); and also external trade for the province reached 174.71 million yuan. In 1935, overseas Chinese investment reached 550 million yuan. This definitely had important contributions toward the development of industry and commerce and toward to increasing prosperity in Guangdong Province.[75]

That these events in Guangdong directly related to the symbolic power of a modern bridge confirm the views of scholars such as Chi-ming Hou, who posited the view that foreign investment essentially financed a large share of the modern sector of the Chinese economy.[76]

Recovering State Power V: Provincial Industrialisation

Back in June 1931, Li Yungai was appointed to the Provincial Governorship and his fortunes had changed enormously. This was exactly two years after he launched attacks on the cement merchants. His frustration was solved by the appointment of Cheng Tiangu to the Public Works Bureau and the fact that he was now at the helm of the Provincial Government.[77] At this moment in time, he was able to tackle the problems facing the local cement industry with greater power. This was the rebirth of state industry in its neo-*guanban* form.

As shown previously, the *guandu shangban* Guangdong Cement Works was a disaster and this arrangement was abolished on 11 August 1931.[78] Two months later, Lin Yungai, who was by now heading the Provincial Government, ordered the then Mayor of Guangzhou Cheng Tiangu to make a loan of 150,000 yuan from the Public Works Bureau to restart the old cement works under a new joint management by the City Government and the Provincial Construction Department. The loan would be paid back in three years at a yearly interest of 8 %.[79] Furthermore, using his new power, he legislated for the old cement works to provide formal employment protection for professional managers and specialised technicians. The legislation also included the construction of institutional safeguards for the management to protect its independence.[80] On the whole, he followed closely the recommendations in *A General Survey of Municipal Enterprises* to set up the cement industry, but now at the provincial rather than the municipal level.

The new automated Xicun Cement Works plant was completed in April 1932 and its Five Rams brand cement reached the market in July 1932.[81] However, one month before the new cement arrived in the market, Cheng Tiangu had already resigned from his at the Provincial Construction Department post on 2 June 1932 and departed for Hong Kong.[82] By this time Lin had firm control over the cement retail market[83] and a new and fully automatic cement plant under his control. In the meantime, another Chinese League member Liu Jiwen was installed as Mayor of Guangzhou City Government. He was a graduate of Waseda University in Tokyo, London School of Economics and Cambridge University. He joined the Chinese League in 1909.[84] Lin Yungai then abandoned the Finance Department which he concurrently headed as Mayor to become Director of the Construction Department. The construction department was responsible for the day-to-day administration of the new cement plant. In August 1932 when the new Xicun Cement Works began production, the Construction Department with Lin Yungai now as the Director (instead of Chen Tiangu) took over the sales and marketing functions.[85] Six months later, the management arrangement with the City Government was terminated and the Construction Department took complete control of the old cement works in Henan.[86] Finally, it was merged with the new Xicun Cement works in May 1933 and ceased to exist as an independent entity.[87]

The new Xicun Cement Works in the northern outskirts of the city belonged to the provincial government and was administered by its Construction Department. Again the recommendations of the GSME were followed faithfully. There were formal employment protections as well as institutional safeguards for the management.[88] Sun Yat-sen's Chinese-language secretary in San Francisco Liu Juke was appointed as the plant General Manager and Sun's English-language secretary in America who was a member of the Revive China Society (*xingzhonghui*)[89] was appointed as the Director.[90] Lin Yungai continued to apply the same methods of control to the cement market but now, armed with a modern Danish F. L. Smidth-designed automated cement plant, there was little need to worry about the quality of cement.

This new plant was an instant success during the economic expansion generated by Cheng Tiangu's *Two-Year Plan*. From 16 April 1932 when production began until 30 June 1933, it made a profit of 1,236,000 yuan. In two years and two months (from June 1932 to August 1934) it made a profit of over 5 million yuan.[91] At the same time, the value of imported cement into Guangdong dropped from 24.3 million yuan to 6.3 million yuan. By the time of the addition of another kiln in 1935,[92] imported cement had been almost eliminated by Lin Yungai's market control mechanism and Green Island Cement in Hong Kong had to stop production.[93] Originally all the cement from both the old cement works and the new cement works were assigned to an Anxing Company for wholesaling.[94] However, the Construction Department soon repossessed this selling right and set up a Cement Sales Office and Liu Juke was appointed to head this office.[95] Not only was Lin heavily regulating the wholesalers and slamming taxes on imports,[96] he gained control of the sales and marketing of the cement via this newly established institution.[97] From 1933 it became the National Product Sales Office.[98] The Government was creating a monopoly by its control mechanism and by producing the high-quality Five Rams brand cement it had eliminated the appetite for high-quality Hong Kong cement.

Cheng Tiangu's departure after three years in office from May 1929 to June 1932 might have been a loss to Guangzhou's city development. Nonetheless, before his departure he had already created a boom in Guangdong's economy which *unintentionally* also drove up demand for cement. In the summer of 1932, Provincial Governor Lin Yungai was enjoying the fruits of his very wise choice of Cheng Tiangu as Director of Public Works. The beauty of this outcome lay in the effortless ease in which Lin created genuine growth for the cement works business. It shows that there was no need to worry about industrial management, technology, or sales and distribution networks to achieve high sales and profits. These performed smoothly without a glitch once the government successfully intervened in the market by *control* and *stimulus*. This worked for Yuan Shikai in 1906 and also worked for Lin Yungai in 1932. It did not matter even if the stimulus was an accident or a stroke of luck in creating demand for the cement. Supply can easily follow demand with automated manufacturing. This has always been the unique nature of relatively trouble-free cement industry. It can always be a successful investment if the state has the power to manipulate the market mechanisms to protect that investment.

In fact, it was the success of the new Xicun Cement Works from April 1932 that prompted Lin Yungai to collaborate with Chen Jitang to announce a new large-scale *Guangdong Province Three-Year Plan* which presented a detailed plan for the development and industrialisation for the whole province. The unexpected hype surrounded the construction of the Pearl River Bridge by Cheng Tiangu also emboldened these ex-revolutionaries and Chen Jitang. In Guangzhou, the Xicun Cement Works would soon have its north side sliced off for the construction of the nitrate fertilizer plant.[99] Soon a whole host of industrial plants and factories were built around the cement works and Lin Yungai renamed the area the Xicun Industrial Park.[100] This industrial park had the greatest concentration of industries in Guangzhou.[101]

Then, in 1935, the *National* Product Sales Office became the Guangdong *Provincial* Products Managing Office. This was responsible for selling products and purchasing equipment for the new industries administered by Lin Yungai's Construction Department. At the same time, a Provincial Industrial Audit Committee was established to scrutinise the investment, budget, income and expenses of the industries. A Guangdong Province Industrial Bank was established to finance these industries.[102] Under the watchful eye of the Construction Department, all the factories were responsible for production; the Managing Office was responsible for sales and purchase; the Audit Committee responsible for auditing; and the Bank responsible for the financing. In this way Lin Yungai cooperating with the "warlord" Chen Jitang rapidly industrialised Guangdong Province by way of provincial nationalisation adhering to the Neo-*guanban* way as discussed in the theoretical essay of 1928.

Under the *Guangdong Province Three-Year Plan*, chemical plants were concentrated in the Xicun Industrial District (officially the No. 1 Provincial Industrial District in the northern-western outskirts of the city) and textile factories were in the Henan Industrial District (officially the No. 2 Provincial Industrial District located south of the Pearl River on Henan Island where the old cement works was built). In Xicun, the industrial plants established were: the cement plant, sulphuric plant, the anodising plant, the fertilizer plant, the beverage plant and the fuel plant. In Henan the industries established were: the cotton-weaving factory, the silk-weaving factory, the wool-spinning factory, the linen factory and the dying factory. Other factories located elsewhere included a paper factory, iron and steel works (planned) and six major sugar refineries around the delta.[103] Interestingly all the manufactured products from these various industries were sold under the unified brand of "Five Rams". Lin Yungai and his collaborators were not industrialists and clearly they were neither sensitive to the subtleties of different manufacturing and market logistics of each industry, nor did they make an effort to understand the market place for different products. They were just eager to recreate the huge profit produced by the Xicun Cement Works as quickly as possible. Therefore, by 1935, just like a business corporation, they sold everything under a single brand. By now, even the Guangdong *provincial* government was operating as a single commercial corporation.

Unfortunately, the great success of the cement industry could not be replicated in these other industries. Even under the elaborate Neo-*guanban* arrangements, only the cement and sugar industries made any profit. Nevertheless, the sugar industry, where six large sugar-processing plants were established, was fraught with problems. This industry relied on agricultural raw material, and the manufacturing facilities were concentrated in the Pearl River Delta region, causing intense competition around the supply of sugar cane and stoppages at the factories were frequent.[104] The sugar industry made a profit only because Chen Jitang was selling "smokeless sugar", meaning sugar that was not manufactured but imported.[105] He was illegally importing by smuggling sugar from Hong Kong (because China's customs was still under foreign control) and then selling them as Five Rams brand sugar. The sugar barges were towed into Guangzhou protected by Chen's "anti-smuggling patrol boats".[106] In other words, Chen was carrying on a sugar (smuggling) trade for quick profit and was not wholeheartedly dedicated to Guangdong's industrialisation. Furthermore, the Guangdong Provincial Products Managing Office which controlled sales and purchases was a haven for corruption.[107] Subsequently, when reviewing the *Three-Year Plan*, Chen Jitang lamented the poor results and blamed them on those responsible for the factories "not following the original plans and getting involved in corrupt practices to reap benefits".[108]

A Chaotic End

The industries were built to tap the wealth of the expanding general market sparked by Chen Tiangu's *Two-Year Plan*. Lin Yungai, who was quickly joined by the "warlord" Chen Jitang, was attempting to replicate the immensely successful formula of an official or government-managed (*guanban*) cement industry. However, the unique simplicity of a fully automated manufacturing industry that could add value to raw materials without the need to rely on an agricultural surplus in the countryside, and which could function with minimal industrial management and marketing effort, did not exist in other Guangdong industries. Therefore, the Xicun Cement Works was the *only* profitable government-operated heavy industry until the mid-1930s because this was an *automated* plant operating in a government-regulated market which was riding high in a general economic boom.

The leader of the ex-Chinese League and the party elders, Hu Hanmin, died on 12 May 1936[109] and there was a major provincial financial meltdown in July 1936.[110] Chen Jitang and Lin Yungai's collaborative rule of Guangdong Province ended in July 1936. This is because Chen Jitang was forced to step down on 17 July 1936 after all of Guangdong's airplanes flew away following the local air force's defection to Chiang Kai-shek's Nanjing Government.[111] Under the new Provincial Government which switched loyalty to Nanjing, the industrial policies of the previous government were reversed. In November 1936, the succeeding Provincial Government made modifications to all provincial holdings and enterprises' administrative frameworks that was installed by Lin Yungai. They adjusted the operations but keeping the basic structure. The major change was the consent given to allow commercial investment in the "nationalised" *guanban* (government-managed) enterprises within the province. The *shangban* (merchant-managed) enterprises were also allowed commercial investment under special permission from the Guangdong Provincial Government.[112] However, this stopped short of adopting independent commercial corporations with legal personality.

The Power of the Pearl River Bridge

In recapitulation, Guangdong province did not support independent industrial corporations (i.e., incorporated companies). It employed the City Government to directly hold or own large industrial firms. Part Two reinforces the argument concerning incorporation in Part One, that is, without the shield of incorporation, the enterprises within the government structure were left exposed to takeovers by the politically powerful. Hence, the history of Guangdong provincial industrial organisation in the 1930s was very similar to the history of late Qing imperial industrial organisation when commercial corporations with legal personality played no part.

Indeed, the developments in the city itself were conspicuous enough to attract the interest of the local "warlord" Chen Jitang. Alas, without incorporated private enterprises, everything was decisively taken over by the Nanjing government in one fell swoop once the government was taken over. This resonates well with the story in northern China. City developments such as the widening of streets, building new kinds of housing, installing a modern sewage system, reconstructing the waterfront and the construction of a modern mechanical bridge all attracted attention for the power-hungry and income-craving political players. Without the shelter of incorporated companies to individually protect these lucrative city developments projects by law, Chen Jitang could interfere easily and this led to the ousting of the Mayor and Public Works Bureau chief Cheng Tiangu. This also illustrates the vulnerability of profitable but *un*incorporated concerns to political takeovers similar to the wrangle between Yuan Shikai and Sheng Xuanhai. Nevertheless, the local government as an entity did gain power. It consolidated economic power and kept it to itself. Unlike the story of the Imperial Government, there were no private industrial corporations to chip away its power. The economic power situation of Guangdong in the 1930s was the exact opposite of the late Qing situation when commercial corporations contributed to the structural disintegration of the empire. In Guangdong, all industries were inside the governmental structure and economic power was centralised.

Despite the complexity and chaotic politics in Guangdong Province, one thing did begin to emerge from the ruin of the imperial dynasty: the clear symbolic power of constructing a technologically advanced modern bridge. The City Government became a corporation and thus achieved a measure of financial independence because banks could legally lend to the city. It was, however, the modern bridge that was the mobilising force for the people, the icon for attracting investments and a legitimating sign for the government. The ruthless market control or the "central planning" employed by Lin Yungai's governments may have eliminated irritating market competition but it is clear that it was the construction of the Pearl River Bridge (a symbol of modernity) by Sun Yat-sen's diehard followers inside an incorporated city (a vehicle of modernity) that in fact propelled the economy forward and empowered this corporate entity: the Guangzhou City Government, thereby taking the first successful steps to resurrect the power of the state that was lost in the imperial collapse.

Epilogue: Sun Yat-sen's Legacy

The final expansion of the Xicun Cement Works was completed in July 1937. In October 1938, however, the Xicun Industrial District was heavily bombed by the Japanese air force before the land invasion. During the war, the works were taken over by Asano Cement of Japan and, of the three rotary kilns, one remained in production, one was destroyed by the bombings during the air attacks and the other one was dismantled by the occupying forces and shipped to northern China.[113] After the war, the economy collapsed and the Xicun Cement Plant was crippled by war destruction. In the end, the Japanese invasion ruined the cement works, the Xicun Industrial District and almost completely wiped out the fragile industrial base in Guangdong that had conscientiously been built up by Lin Yungai, the surviving ex-members of the Chinese League and "warlord" Chen Jitang over the previous decade. It was an end to a project that was started by Sun Yat-sen.

To sum up, in Guangdong province at least, private industrial corporations were not allowed. By 1938, the Republican Chinese state in this province was thus reversing a trend started since Yuan Shikai's takeover of Qixin Cement. The state here was successful in the recentralisation of economic power. The Japanese invasion halted this process but the process resumed for the entire country after the war under communism. This resulted in the recentralisation of Chinese state power into the central government of the People's Republic of China. Once again, it was achieved by disallowing private corporate bodies in society and completely controlling the goods market by the state. What is important to note is that the rapid but unprofitable industrialisation of Guangdong province is a precursor to what was about to happen after the communist victory in 1949. This part showed how Guangdong became the first part of China that developed a command economy before the communist People's Republic was founded. For better or worse, it was the old revolutionaries that Sun Yat-sen led, and not Mao Zedong or his communist comrades, who first laid the foundation in Guangdong province of a state-led command economy in China (Fig. 6.1).[114]

Fig. 6.1 The Pearl River Bridge, circa 2010

Notes

1. For a discussion of the important implications of incorporation, see David Faure, *China and Capitalism*, p. 45.
2. Ma Chaojun, "Chou ban xinshi shimintu chang".
3. GDPG, "Chexiao Guangdong shimintu chang Puyi gongsi cheng an".
4. Jiansheting, "Chou ban xinshi shimintu chang jie kuan hetong,"; GDPG, "Biantong shou yong xinshi shimintu chang changzhi tudi banfa an"; GDPG, "Ling caizheng ting she zai Xicun xuanze Xicun shimintu chang zhi an".
5. GDPG, "Ling Jiansheting xuan shang cheng zhu Xicun shimintu chang".
6. Xiao Zili, *Chen Jitang*.
7. Xie Yingming, "Shengying gongye gaikuang ji yishu".
8. Yang Hongnian and Ouyang Xin, *Zhongguo zhengzhi shi*, p. 516.
9. GZCG, "Lunshuo: shiying shiye gailun".
10. GZCG, "Lunshuo: shiying shiye gailun".
11. Introduction, GSME.
12. Heading 1. GSME.
13. Heading 1, subsection (1), GSME.
14. Heading 1, subsection (2), GSME.
15. Heading 1, subsection (3), GSME.
16. *GSME.*
17. Heading 2, subsection (1), GSME.
18. Heading 2, subsection (2), GSME.

19. Heading 2, subsection (3), GSME.
20. GSME, p. 3.
21. GSME, p. 4.
22. GSME, p. 4.
23. GDPG, "Guangdong simintu chang jiang gong fuwu daiyu tiaoli"; GDPG, "Guangdong shimintu chang zushi zhangcheng"; GDPG, "Guangzhou Shi zhengfu Guangdong jiansheting heban Guangdong Henan shimintu chang zhangcheng"; GDPG, "Hezhun Guangdong shimintu chang yuangong fuwu guicheng,"; GDPG, "Guangdong Xicun shimintu chang zuzhi zhangcheng"; GDPG, "Guangdong Xicun Henan shimintu chang jianli banshi guize"; GDPG, "Hezhun Xicun shimintu chang yuangong qingjia guize"; GDPG, "Hezhun Guangdong Xicun shimintu chang yuangong fuwu guicheng"; GDPG, "Guangdong Xicun shimintu chang dongshihui zuzhi zhangcheng"; GDPG, "Guangdong Xicun shimintu chang dongshi hui zushi zhangcheng", "Guangdong Xicun shimintu chang zu zhi zhang cheng", "Guangdong Xicun shimintu chang, Henan fen chang zhuzhi zhangcheng, jianli banshi guize".
24. GZCG, "Jishi: Gongwu Ju shiyan shimintu lali zhi baogao".
25. See Chap. 5.
26. Cheng Tiangu, *Cheng Tiangu huiyilu*, p. 160.
27. Cheng Tiangu, *Cheng Tiangu huiyilu*, p. 160.
28. Cheng Tiangu, *Cheng Tiangu huiyilu*, p. 162.
29. Cheng Tiangu, *Cheng Tiangu huiyilu*, p. 163.
30. Lin Keming, *Nan tian sui yue*, p. 215.
31. GDPG, "Chi shu caimai shiqiupai shimintu an".
32. GZCG, "Gongwuju shiyan shiqiupai shimintu zhi jieguo".
33. Cheng Tiangu, *Cheng Tiangu hui yi lu*, p. 262.
34. c.f. Sun Ke established a Whampoa Development Company (*Huangpu fazhan gongsi*) in 1924 in the hope of developing Guangzhou. He called for the participation of overseas Chinese but had to abandon this ambitious scheme due to financial difficulties caused by the lack of response. *GZSZ*, June 1924.
35. This would end in May 1931 except for the Pearl River Bridge, which would not be completed until February 1932.
36. Cheng Tiangu, *Cheng Tiangu hui yi lu*, pp. 265–267.
37. Xiao Zili, *Chen Jitang*, p. 529.
38. Cheng Tiangu, *Cheng Tiangu hui yi lu*, p. 164.

39. Cheng Tiangu, *Cheng Tiangu hui yi lu*, p. 112.
40. Cheng Tiangu, *Cheng Tiangu hui yi lu*, p. 114.
41. Cheng Tiangu, *Cheng Tiangu hui yi lu*, p. 112.
42. Cheng Tiangu, *Cheng Tiangu hui yi lu*, pp. 119–120.
43. Cheng Tiangu, *Cheng Tiangu hui yi lu*, p. 125.
44. Cheng Tiangu, *Cheng Tiangu hui yi lu*, p. 185.
45. The Mayor was designated as the "Chairman" of the City Council in 1923.
46. Ma Chaojun, "Chou she xinshi shimintu chang".
47. GDPG, "Guangzhou Shi zhengfu Guangdong jiansheting heban Guangdong Henan shimintu chang zhangcheng".
48. Lin Yungai, "Weichi zhengfu zhi shimintu chang yingye an".
49. GZCG, "Guanyu shiyan shiqiupai shimintuan," *GZGB* 5 December 1930, GZCA, pp. 57–59.
50. Lin Yungai, "Weichi zhengfu zhi shimintu chang yingye an".
51. Cheng Tiangu, *Cheng Tiangu hui yi lu*, p. 153.
52. Cheng Tiangu, *Cheng Tiangu hui yi lu*, p. 182.
53. Todd Sandler, *Economic Concepts for the Social Sciences*, p. 45.
54. Cheng Tiangu, *Cheng Tiangu hui yi lu*, p. 163.
55. Cheng Tiangu, *Cheng Tiangu hui yi lu*, p. 171.
56. Li Lushan, "An Account of the Wenlan College of Xiguan".
57. GZCG, "Buchong qudi shimintu banfa an Wenlan shuyuan qinghao kuan an".
58. Li Lushan, "An Account of the Wenlan College of Xiguan".
59. Cheng Tiangu, *Cheng Tiangu hui yi lu*, p. 171.
60. *Cheng Tiangu, Cheng Tiangu hui yi lu*, p. 173.
61. GZCG, "Wenlan shuyuan qinghao kuan an".
62. Cheng Tiangu, *Cheng Tiangu hui yi lu*, pp. 172 and 174.
63. Lin Keming, *Nan tian sui yue*, p. 215. Also note that in June 1930 the Director of the Construction Department was cross-examined by Cheng Tiangu as Chairman of the City Construction Committee regarding the delay to the construction of the new Xicun Cement Works: GDPG, "Ling Jiansheting xuan shang cheng zhu Xicun shimintu chang".
64. Cheng Tiangu, *Cheng Tiangu huiyilu* , p. 68.
65. Cheng Tiangu, *Cheng Tiangu huiyilu* , p. 68, p. 185.
66. Zhong Zhuo'an, *Chen Jitang*.
67. Cheng Tiangu, *Cheng Tiangu huiyi lu*, p. 262–263.
68. *GZSZ*; http://www.gzsdfz.org.cn/gzsz/02/dsj/sz02dsj0222.htm; last accessed 1 September 2007.

69. Mo Yinggui "Yinjin qiao zi suo yi," in *Nan tian sui yue*, p. 306.
70. *GZSZ*; http://www.gzsdfz.org.cn/gzsz/21/fl/sz21fl0301.htm; last accessed 1 September 2007.
71. Lin Yungai was appointed Provincial Governor to replace the previous Governor Chen Mingshu by the South West Government which was formed on 27 May 1931.
72. Mo Yinggui, "Yinjin qiao zi suo yi (Fragmented recollections of measures in attracting overseas Chinese investments)" in *Nan tian sui yue*, p. 306.
73. Mayor of the GZCG Lin Yungai, "Baohu huaqiao hui guo yu ban shiye an" (The protection of returning Overseas Chinese and their investment in industries), *GZGB* 16 November 1929, GZCA *zhi/zheng* 585:347, pp. 120–121.
74. Mo Yinggui, "Yinjin qiao zi suo yi" in *Nan tian sui yue*, p. 308.
75. Mo Yinggui, "Yinjin qiao zi suo yi" in *Nan tian sui yue*, p. 309.
76. Chi-ming Hou, *Foreign Investment and Economic Development in China*, pp. 125–164.
77. The Standing Committee of the Guomin zhengfu (Nationalist Government) resolved to appoint Lin Yungai as the Chairman of the provincial government; Zhong Zhuoan, *Chen Jitang*.
78. GDPG, "Chexiao Guangdong shimintu chang Puyi gongsi cheng an".
79. GDPG, "Guifu Guangdong shimintu chang".
80. GDPG, "Guangdong simintu chang jiang gong fuwu daiyu tiaoli"; GDPG, "Guangdong shimintu chang zushi zhangcheng"; GDPG, "Guangzhou Shi zhengfu Guangdong jiansheting heban Guangdong Henan shimintu chang zhangcheng".
81. Ding Shenzun, Xia Zhuoqiong eds, *Guangdong minguo shi*, p. 739.
82. *GZSZ*; http://www.gzsdfz.org.cn/gzsz/02/dsj/sz02dsj0222.htm; last accessed 1 September 2007.
83. GZCG, "Guangzhou Shi gongwuju qudi shimintu buchong banfa an".
84. Betty Peh Ti Wei, *Liu Chi-Wen*.
85. GDPG, "Henan Xicun shimintu chang yinye shiwu you jianting she chu banli".
86. GDPG, "Henan shimintu chang you jiansheting shou hui zi ban".
87. GDPG, "Yijue heping Henan ji Xicun shimintu chang".

88. GDPG, "Hezhun Guangdong shimintu chang yuangong fuwu guicheng"; GDPG, "Guangdong Xicun shimintu chang zuzhi zhangcheng"; GDPG, "Guangdong Xicun Henan shimintu chang jianli banshi guize"; GDPG, "Hezhun Guangdong Xicun shimintu chang yuangong fuwu guicheng"; GDPG, "Guangdong Xicun shimintu chang dongshi hui zushi zhangcheng", "Guangdong Xicun shimintu chang zu zhi zhang cheng", "Guangdong Xicun shimintu chang, Henan fen chang zhuzhi zhangcheng, jianli banshi guize".
89. The Revive China Society or the Society for Regenerating China was founded on 24 November 1894 by Sun Yat-sen in Honolulu to forward the goal of establishing prosperity for China. Those admitted to the society swore the following oath: "Expel the foreigners, revive China, and establish a unified government". It was later merged into the Chinese League, which in turn became the Nationalist Party of China.
90. GDPG, "Renming Liu Juke wei Guangdong Xicun shimintu chang zhang".
91. Xiao Zili, *Chen Jitang*, p. 333.
92. *GZSZ*, "Xicun shimintu chang, di-yi ci jinxing kuojian touchan".
93. Xiao Zili, *Chen Jitang*, p. 333.
94. GDPG, "Hezhun bensheng Xicun Henan liang shimintu yu Anxing gongsi dingli quanquan tuixiao heyue".
95. GDPG, "Henan Xicun shimintu chang yinye shiwu you jianting she chu banli"; GDPG, "Guangdong shimintu yingye chu banli zhuanying shiwu zhangcheng".
96. GDPG, "Cheng ban shimitu fu jia daxue jingfei"; GDPG, "Guangdong shimintu chang chupin mian sui"; GDPG, "Zhun Dacheng gongsi yi qi xu ban quan sheng bo lai shimin tu fujia daxue jingfei"; GDPG, "Ling mian Guangdong shimintu chang chupin ge sui"; GDPG, "Guangdong shimintu yingye chu bo lai shimintu bao ling xuke zheng ji daxue fujia fei zhengshou xiji", "Zhuanying yu dai zheng daxue fujia fei banshi xiji"; GDPG, "Jia bei zhengshou bo lai shimintu fujia fei choulü"; GDPG, "Ting fa gou yun bo lai shimintu mian sui huzhao"; GZCG, "Fan gong gong jianzhu yi lü gou yong Guangdong shimintu chang zhi tu bing tingzhi fa gei gou yun bo lai shimintu mian sui zhizhao".
97. GDPG, "Guangdong shimintu chang yingye chu zuzhi zhangcheng ban shi xize".

98. GDPG, "Shouzheng tongzhi shimintu zhangze" (Genben banfa, Guangdong shimintu yingyun qudi guize, yinyun shang daili tuixiao shengying shimintu guize, yingyun shang daili tuixiao shengying shimintu jiangli guize, Guangdong Sheng guohuo tuixiao chu shimintu bu gong zuzhi zhangcheng, Guangdongsheng guohuo tuixiao chu shimintu bu fen banshichu zuzhi zhangcheng, Guangdongsheng guohuo tuixiao chun shimintu bu qi huo si shimintu bian jia ji geijiang zhangcheng, Guangdong sheng guohou tuixiao chu shimintu bu chufa bo lai shimintu si yu zhangcheng, Guangdong sheng guohuo tuixiao chu shimintu bu gonchang ji fen banshichu banshi xize).
99. GDPG, "Hezhun shou yong Xicun shimintu chang beibian diyu wei huaxue gongchang jianzhu dizhi"; GDPG, "Shouyong Xicun shimintu chang ce shan di chou ban huaxue gong ye chang"; GDPG, "Cheng Sheng fu cheng fu guanyu Xicun shimintu chang shou yong nanbian shangang"; GZCG, "Xicun shimintu chang gengzheng shouyong Zhayougang deng chu diduan".
100. Xie Yingming, *Shengying gongye gaikuan,* p. 219.
101. Xiao Zili, *Chen Jitang*, p. 334.
102. Xiao Zili, *Chen Jitang*, p. 333.
103. Xiao Zili, *Chen Jitang*, p. 330.
104. Zhang Xiaohui, *Minguo shiqi Guangdong shehui jingji shi*, p. 184.
105. For an in-depth study of the situation see, Emily M. Hill, *Smokeless Sugar.*
106. Xian Zien, "Ban tang chang jingguo ji qi zhen xiang".
107. Zhang Xiaohui, *Minguo shiqi Guangdong shehui jingji shi,* p. 185.
108. Yu Yan'guang and Chen Fulin, *Nanyue ge ju: Cong Long Jiguang dao Chen Jitang*, p. 348.
109. Xiao Zili, *Chen Jitang*, p. 531.
110. Jin-a Gang, "20 shiji 30 niandai Guangdong Sheng de huobi tongyi zhengche de bengkui guocheng" in *Shijie jingji tizhi xia de Minguo shiqi jingji*, pp. 44–56.
111. Chen Jitang stepped down. Xiao Zili, *Chen Jitang*, p. 532.
112. Zhang Xiaohui, *Minguo shiqi Guangdong shehui jingji shi*, p. 185.
113. Xie Yingming, *Shengying gongye gaikuang ji yishu.*
114. Or a "China unincorporated". See William C. Kirby, "China Unincorporated: Company Law and Business Enterprise in Twentieth-Century China," *The Journal of Asian Studies*, 54:1 (Feb. 1995): pp. 43–63.

PART 4

The Making of Modern Incorporated Companies

State and Private Corporations: Chiang Kai-shek and Cement Companies, 1931–1949

In the early Republic, corporations flourished. This facilitated both self-made men and corrupt government officials to become wealthy and powerful. But the pendulum began to swing the other way as Generalissimo Chiang Kai-shek took power. By establishing the National Resources Commission around 1932, Chiang began the long process of recapturing economic power at the national level. He reversed the trend of state power dissipation by way of incorporation of modern private commercial companies that began in 1904 but allowed the Republican Chinese state to keep legal recognition of corporations, and hence their legal personality. They also formed many state-owned corporate companies.

Chapter 7 explains that modern corporations empower individuals. Accordingly, corporations enabled a build-up of economic power in post-imperial Republican Chinese society that would command the respect, friendship and envy of the Republican state. This would ultimately lead to the state setting up the National Resource Commission (NRC) to capture more power from 1931 onwards. This was the statutory body which Chiang Kai-shek initially set up during the war to garner national resources for industrial development. In other words, from this point in time, the Chinese state began the long process of recapturing economic power at national level.

After World War II, Chiang Kai-shek gained full state power over his political rivals by winning the presidential election. He became the constitutionally recognised President of the Republic of China on 20 May

1948. He immediately appointed academic Dr. Weng Wenhao, the geologist and head of the NRC, as the new Premier of the Republic of China in 1948. This move was another attempt to consolidate the power that Chiang had accumulated since becoming the trusted protégée of Sun Yat-sen. He methodically amassed power through militarily campaigns, political manoeuvres and now industrial development. However, the industrial policy of this redefined Republic of China was a disaster. This was shown by investigating the wholly incorporated cement industry of this period.

Chiang Kai-shek did not nationalise major industries in the hands of the powerful such as the northern Qixin Cement or the Shanghai Portland Cement. In other words, the nationalisation attempt by Chiang Kai-shek's government employing the NRC as a vehicle was rather weak. It did not seek to abolish corporations completely but chose to use the NRC effectively as a governmental "holding" corporation. Therefore, power remained in the hands of the capitalists such as Liu Hongsheng who controlled the early large corporations in Shanghai. Chiang Kai-shek and his economic advisers did not achieve much before his Nationalist army lost the civil war to the Communists. He did manage to seize control of the incorporated China Merchants Shipping Company by nationalisation. Owing to its legal personality, however, he only succeeded after a big fight with the family of imperial Viceroy Li Hongzhang which was still influencing this company, almost 40 years after imperial rule. After winning the civil war in 1949, the Communists took a more brutal, ideological and legal approach. Once in government, they powered ahead with full nationalisation abolishing all companies and corporations.

CHAPTER 7

Chiang Kai-shek and Corporations: A Holistic Strategy

Modern corporations empower individuals. Accordingly, corporations enabled a build-up of economic power in post-imperial Republican Chinese society that would command the respect, friendship and envy of the Republican state. This would ultimately lead to the state setting up the National Resource Commission (NRC) to capture more power from 1931 onwards. This is the statutory body which Chiang Kai-shek initially set up during the war to garner national resources for industrial development. In other words, from this point in time, the Chinese state began the long process of recapturing economic power at national level. Private incorporated companies that were formed under the more elaborate and refined Republican Chinese company legislation which succeeded and superseded the 1904 Qing Company Law were separated into two kinds of different origins: The first kind is private competitive companies formed and incorporated under the Republican company legislations by individual entrepreneurs that grew bottom-up into scale.[1] The second kind is private competitive companies incorporated under the Qing and Republican company legislations by state bureaucrats top-down. In the Republican period, existing businesses were either taken over by government investing in their companies or new businesses were formed by government corporate investments.[2] Interestingly, just as Hallis has predicted, in terms of state power, both kinds were situated "between the state and the individual".[3]

The issue of corporate or legal personality was an important factor in the fall of the Qing Empire. The Qing self-preservatory industrialisation failed

H. Ko, *The Making of the Modern Chinese State*,
DOI 10.1007/978-981-10-2660-7_7

and corporate personality was a contributory factor, but as seen in Part One, it was the lack of it. On the one hand, the imperial Chinese government had attempted to emulate Western industrialisation since the 1860s *without* adopting Western-type corporations. Instead, as shown in Chapter 1, industrialisation was managed by the Qing imperial bureaucracy under the *guandu shangban* (official supervision and merchant management) scheme. The corporate form, however, was the backbone of Western entrepreneurial organisations during industrialisation. The effect was that Chinese industrialisation languished and was branded as "retarded".[4] On the other hand, once the imperial state ultimately sanctioned corporate personality, investment in railways boomed and enterprises took off. These corporate entities were defined by the 1904 Company Law, and a multitude of these were created.[5] The outcome of this was that the empire inadvertently damaged itself. The observation is plain: the maintenance of the old order under absolute imperial rule and the idea of rapid modern industrialisation imitating the West appear to be incompatible. The empire perished in 1911 but the Company Law remained. Naturally then, Chinese corporations in the form of incorporated commercial companies also survived into the Republic and they evolved and multiplied.[6] Therefore, in order to further appreciate the importance of corporate personality and incorporated companies in modern Chinese history, the story turns to the history of corporations in post-imperial China as manifested in its *commercial* form. Moreover, in 1912 a short piece of constitutional writing created the Republic of China and its government. This is the Organic Law of the Provisional Government.[7] Hence, as explained in the Chapter 1, it too was a corporation: this is the *governmental* form.

What Has Changed?

Since the 1950s there was an enthusiastic interest among both Western and Chinese scholars in China's initial industrialisation process. There was a voracious search for reasons for "China's retarded industrialisation" in the management and conduct of industry.[8] However, the true reason of this "retardation" lies neither with the industries nor with the management itself. It lies with the fact that industries *remained firmly within the imperial governing system*. Their very nature was to serve the interest of the Qing Empire and not to promote general industrialisation. This was changed by the arrival of corporate personality which came with the Company Law of 1904 that introduced corporate bodies as incorporated companies into China, thereby allowing industrial companies to spring up from below.

The reason can easily be overlooked even by a careful historian such as Parks M. Coble, Jr. In 1980, Coble did a thorough analysis of the origins of some of the Republican companies under the post-1927 Nanjing Government in *The Shanghai Capitalists and the Nationalist Government, 1927–1937*, but like Feuerwerker before him, he did not consider companies from the angle of their corporate or legal personality. After comparing government-directed modern enterprises in the Self-Strengthening movement of the late Qing period with those in the Nanjing period, he concluded that there was a "re-emergence of a traditional pattern of official domination". He was, however, surprised by the "degree of independence" private capitalists had gained since the late Qing period and prior to 1927.[9]

There is nothing unusual at all if Coble's analyses had made clear that, even though both were "government-directed", the Self-Strengthening enterprises did *not* have corporate personalities and that the Republic ones *did*. Hence, the "degree of independence" he observed. Such confusion is ubiquitous in historical analyses of late Qing industrialisation. Therefore, in order to ensure understanding of the role played by corporate bodies in modern states, this theoretical concept of corporate personality has to be understood. This is because without a solid understanding of this Western concept, it would neither be possible to understand the nature of the post-imperial modern Chinese state, nor the entire distribution of economic and political power in that state. After all, what are the inherent structural differences between the imperial Chinese state and the post-imperial Chinese state? One of the main differences again is the acceptance by China of corporate personality and the creation of corporations. State power no longer concentrates and emanates from one emperor but is distributed between the constitutional state governments, commercial corporate persons and masses of individuals in that descending order. How these three elements interact with industry and industrialisation gave shape to modern China.

The history of the final days of the Qing dynasty has shown that, even though corporate personality may be abstract, it was nevertheless powerful and was directly responsible for the disintegration of the old Chinese imperial state system. This was an ancient system within which the state could not be said to be a legal person but reverts to a divine person at the apex of the system—the Emperor. The system centred on the Emperor's theoretically absolute power derived from the Mandate of Heaven and was not derived from a constitution written by ordinary human beings.[10] Accordingly, the next question to ask must be how the entrance of corporate personality under the cloak of company law and the constitution altered the relationship between economic and political power within the succeeding states of the Republic of China and the People's Republic of China.

When the Republic was established by a constitution in January 1912,[11] the character of the Chinese state changed. Furthermore, local governments such as the provinces and cities were established constitutionally and similar to the old English boroughs discussed in the Introduction chapter, in that they also possessed corporate or legal personality and can be considered as corporations in their own right.[12] So what is the difference between these new provincial and municipal governments formed by Chinese constitutional law (which includes many constitutional documents after 1912) and the incorporated Chinese joint stock companies formed by the Company Law?[13] The theoretical difference is this: the province "*does not compete in business* with others of its kind: whereas the joint stock company does, even to the limit of its strength and to the destruction of other companies".[14] Furthermore, it can be argued that the short-term high-level impact of the Company Law of 1904 and the corporation created under its auspices is that it directly caused the collapse of the outmoded Qing imperial system by increasing the independent power of Yuan Shikai as seen in Chap. 4. The subtler long-term low-level consequence, however, was the effect on the commercial and industrial development of China. What the Company Law granted to companies was *the privilege of being a corporation subject to competition*. Incorporation was neither "a privilege which carries with it a *limitation of competition* to within the company" (i.e., a monopoly) nor "a market privilege" (i.e., a franchise), but "a privilege to associate in a company for the purpose of *competing with other companies*".[15]

In the Republican period of China, two types of corporations existed in society. Firstly, the state recognised explicitly in Republican constitutional law that a local government had corporate personality.[16] Secondly, the state recognises by company law that companies had corporate or legal personality[17] and these are of two kinds: (1) those constructed bottom-up by entrepreneurs with private capital, as well as (2) the top-down companies created partly by bureaucratic investments and partly by public government capital, or simply just public government investments. The previous chapters of this book considered the history of how the cement industry existed under the *governmental* form of corporate personality, and the present chapter will introduce the *commercial* form of corporate personality that was buoyantly alive in the Republic of China. Furthermore, these companies could grow so complex and so large that eventually these businesses and businessmen received the attention of the state.[18] As explained, corporations in its modern form evolved from the conceptual marriage of the joint stock company and the guild corporation.[19] They integrated business industrial competition in any modernising country and redefined competition. Therefore, there is a need to appreciate business competition in order to comprehend the relationship that corporations have with competition, that is, what corporations can do to promote (elimination of monopolies), upgrade (transformation of business scale from individual to corporate), advance (creation of competition on a corporate-to-corporate plane) and restrain (collusion of corporation in cartels) this competition.

Bottom-Up Republican Companies (Corporations)

Business is a competition. Thus, businesses compete and businessmen are competitors. What the modern *commercial* form of corporation did to modern society at the structural level is that it provided these competing businesses and businessmen with a vehicle to compete on a *larger scale* than that which was possible for them individually without corporate cover. Kai Yiu Chan provides an insight into corporate business enterprises in the city of Shanghai during the Republican period. He studied local businessman Liu Hongsheng and his corporate conglomerate in pre-War Shanghai. Incidentally, Liu also owned the Shanghai Portland Cement Works Company Limited which is the third Chinese operational cement works and an incorporated enterprise.[20]

Competing as a Corporation: Shanghai Portland Cement Works

The cement industry was different to anything Liu Hongsheng had done before. The Shanghai Cement Works Company Limited was established in the summer of 1920. From the start it required a large capital input beyond the individual means of businessman and investor Liu Hongsheng. Therefore, a company with *full corporate personality* was established instead of the *un*incorporated and *un*limited form used for his other business ventures. Investments were invited from 23 members of the Shanghai Chamber of Commerce. In February of 1921, the well-known Qing dynasty entrepreneur Zhang Jian also invested, together with his brother Zhang Cha.[21] Through the use of an incorporated company, Liu Hongsheng was able to make the company attractive to investors and raise capital. This is because the investors were able to participate in the board of directors, the decision-making "brain" of this corporation.[22]

By 1920, Liu Hongsheng as a major coal trader was not content with merely selling and delivering northern Kailuan coal to large wholesale buyers near southern Shanghai. He established his own wharfs to store the coal and sold them directly, thus acting as a wholesaler himself.[23] Furthermore, he also secretly established his own coal-retailing companies. In these businesses, large amounts of coal slack (fragments, powder or dust) were left behind and there were very few outlets for these leftovers. Liu was advised by a couple of friends to establish a cement plant because in the "modern" cement-manufacturing process of the 1910s, a large amount of pulverised coal powder was required to be injected into a horizontal rotary kiln to achieve a high temperature combustion of 1000 degrees centigrade for efficient and high-yield cement manufacturing.[24] With a view towards solving the problem of a lack of a market for coal slack as well as having an eye on the huge profit accrued to Qixin Cement during World War I,[25] Liu Hongsheng established the Shanghai Portland Cement Works Company Limited in September 1920 with authorised capital of one million yuan.[26] It was to be constructed in Shanghai because Liu had a large amount of coal slack there that could be grounded into powder as well as taking advantage of the booming Shanghai market itself. Liu and the other promoters also recognised that transporting the main raw material limestone to Shanghai was 50 % cheaper than transporting the same weight of the finished product cement. They noted that it was less risky to transport the raw material because cement leakages from barrels and the atmospheric moisture would cause the highly anhydrite cement to hydrate into lumps which would render it useless. Furthermore, they also recognised that, in the event of a ship wreck or other disaster resulting in the loss of the shipment, the loss of raw materials would be easier to bear because the cement itself was a more expensive manufactured product.[27] The manufacturing plant was speedily ordered from Germany and the capital was increased to 1.2 million yuan in February 1921. This is because the rising building cost caused a capital shortage in the company.[28]

By September 1922, however, the construction was again out of money and the board of directors decided to borrow from a traditional native bank (*qianzhuang*) by mortgaging company assets for 350,000 yuan.[29] Unfortunately, the construction costs continued to spiral out of control and Liu had to take over as General Manager. This was caused by the refusal of the original General Manager, the wealthy coal comprador Han Yungeng, to invest more money. Instead, he insisted on resigning from the position. None of the other shareholders were willing to put more money into the venture either. The company thus failed in its attempt to raise more capital by issuing further shares.[30] Consequently, Liu remained as the largest shareholder, putting up almost 60 % of the capital.[31] Owing to this failure, the board of directors, which was naturally led by Liu Hongsheng, decided in May 1923 that a further loan was required. Therefore, all the company's assets were charged to various friendly companies as collateral. This was for a 650,000 taels short-term one-year loan.[32] This loan was further guaranteed by Liu Hongsheng's coal-trading businesses. In the end, the total cost of construction overshot by over 200 % and the final figure came to 3.6 million yuan.[33] The cement works staggered along to completion after a five-month delay. Construction work was completed on 5 July 1923 and production finally began on 16 August 1923. This was three years after establishment by the promoters.[34]

Corporation Versus Corporation

The successful private self-financing and completion of the Shanghai Portland Cement Works Company Limited in 1923 transformed Liu Hongsheng from a mere *individual* comprador to the corporate chief of a heavy industry. This cement works became an instant competitor in a market which had been completely dominated by the Qixin Cement Company Limited ever since Yuan Shikai and Zhou Xuexi re-established the Tangshan Cement Works as a corporation in 1906. This nineteenth-century imperial "Self-Strengthening" state monopoly that devolved top-down into the hands of bureaucrats survived into the Republic as one of the most successful Chinese commercial corporations. It met its first domestic challenger rising from below and led by Liu Hongsheng only 11 years after the establishment of the Republic. Bottom-up, this cement corporation was created by a dozen ordinary but diligent Shanghai businessmen pooling their resources.

Qixin Cement Company Limited was the only major domestic producer in China. The opening of the Shanghai Portland Cement Works Company Limited seriously threatened the market of Qixin.[35] In bad market conditions, this triggered an immediate competitive trade war.[36] Yet the competition remained purely on a *corporation-to-corporation* level and did not involve any government intervention even at a point when Qixin was controlled by people with connections to the Beijing government. At this time, the major shareholders of the Qixin Cement Company Limited were divided into three factions. The first was the Anhui Province faction which was centred around Zhou Xuexi. The second was the Henan Province faction which was centred around the family of Yuan Shikai. Lastly, there was the faction led by the General Manager Li Ximing, which had real management power.[37] Feuerwerker believed that Zhou Xuexi's "important political connections" (the fact that many of the associates and investors in his enterprises were themselves civil or military officers) "provided a hospitable environment for the growth and prosperity of Qixin…before the demise of the Beijing government" in 1927.[38] However, when faced with serious open market competitors there was absolutely no evidence that "connections" or "patronage" was of any assistance. Liu Hongsheng explained this competition to his Hankou selling agent:

> According to market information, the selling price of Qixin's Pagoda Brand Cement at their Shanghai main warehouse is fixed at 2 taels 7 qian and 3.6 cents. Thus, this office secretly sent someone to request Qixin to deliver to Port Huanshi. By using the market price of Shanghai and subtracting all the cost for transportation from Port Huangshi to Shanghai, the price we are willing to pay was calculated. Yet, Qixin demanded we pay an additional 3 taels and 7 qian. They even blatantly declared that the sole purpose of shipping the Pagoda brand cement to Shanghai is to upset the market for their enemy: our Elephant brand cement et cetra and et cetra. Hence, you can imagine how intense the competition between Qixin and our company has become.[39]

Not to be outdone, Liu Hongsheng counter-attacked in the north. He wrote to his Tianjin agent and gave assault instructions:

> Upon investigation it is concluded that if Qixin dare to drop the price of the cement it delivered to Shanghai (whether the Pagoda brand or the Horse brand would cost at least 4.5 or 4.6 yuan), it must be subsidising its loss in the south by their profits in the north. In order to maintain the price in Shanghai, I propose a limited price reduction of our cement in Tianjin so as to cause Qixin's northern profits to drop. This should dampen and kill their southern aggression. Furthermore, we will be purchasing 10,000 bags of Qixin's bagged cement and will gradually send north to you and you have to find someone to sell them in the north at a discounted price. The selling

> price for each bag should be 20–30 cents lower than Qixin's listed price. By so doing, not only can we mess up Qixin's market price, we can also caution and stop them from further supplying Shanghai with cheap cement that might find its way back to Tianjin.[40]

Liu Hongsheng's tactics were effective, and in February 1925, the sales manager of the northern region, Yu Shouyi, through an old classmate working in the Custom Service, obtained Qixin's 1924 sales figures from the Tianjin Customs Service. The figures showed that Qixin sold less than 500,000 barrels of cement, even less than the figure of 600,000 barrels before its plant expansion.[41] The market price of cement also dropped to a ten-year low. Qixin Cement was thus forced into negotiating with Shanghai Cement for an oligopolistic alliance.[42] Liu Hongsheng and Li Bahe were authorised by the board of directors to represent the company in these talks.[43] An agreement between these two companies to establish this formal alliance was reached and signed on 30 June 1925 and took effect on 1 July 1925 to eliminate competition.[44] The fundamental condition of this deal was that Shanghai Cement was to withdraw from the market in central and northern China (which led to the closure of the Hankou sales office) and Qixin Cement was to withdraw from the Shanghai and southern market.[45] As a result, price rises were achieved through coordinated actions.[46] This was a fantastic deal for Shanghai Cement because its Elephant brand was outselling Qixin Cement in the joint-selling regions as well as in the "no man's land" areas outside the areas controlled by the agreement. Most importantly, Shanghai Cement as a Shanghai local manufacturer was invincible in Shanghai.[47] The Elephant brand of Shanghai Cement was sold mainly in Shanghai and this city alone accounted for three quarters of its output. Shanghai Cement immediately began to show a profit because of the cartel arrangement.[48] In 1927, a new cement facility, the China Cement Company, was being built near Nanjing, the new seat of the Central Government. This new cement works threatened the mini-cartel of Qixin Cement and Shanghai Cement. Thus, after negotiations, China Cement was incorporated into this cartel arrangement on 1 January 1929 and competition was likewise eliminated by controlling the market.[49]

Liu Hongsheng's ascendency was made possible by the Republican state's legal sanction of corporate personality. The various enterprises Liu created with corporate personalities, such as the Shanghai Portland Cement Works Company Limited, assumed a power position between him and the state. Legally, this is completely different to those companies seen in the last days of the Qing Dynasty. A legal recognition by the Republican state of these corporate entities had allowed an insignificant person such as Liu Hongsheng to build a local industrial conglomerate with private corporations from bottom-up. This is in sharp contrast to the large enterprises in the Qing imperial state before incorporation was possible in 1904. These were all top-down business concerns with no corporate personalities. These large enterprises were established by imperial edicts and theoretically all belonged to the Emperor. In practice, they were being controlled by imperial bureaucrats or senior political figures. In other words, Liu Hongsheng and his corporations confirmed that corporate or legal personality introduced fundamental changes to the state economic and political configuration. Its introduction to China had not only destabilised the imperial dynasty by allowing state power to escape through corporations, but it also created a powerful vehicle for any private individual with no state patronage to rise up in the state by acquiring economic power.[50]

Top-Down Republican Companies (Corporations)

Unlike the situation in the Qing dynasty's "Self-Strengthening" period before the imperial Company Law was introduced in 1904, top-down corporations *with* corporate personalities were created by the Republican Company Law. The origins of these top-down corporations were meticulously analysed by Parks M. Coble, Jr.[51] in *The Shanghai Capitalists and the Nationalist Government, 1927*–1937. This began after T. V. Soong, minister of finance, resigned and his brother-in-law H. H. Kung was appointed to replace him on 29 October 1933.[52] Coble's study found that there were numerous profitable semi-government corporations appearing in 1936 and 1937, and these were organised as joint private-public ventures. These would have half of the stock owned by the government or government banks, and half owned by private individuals who are connected to government in one way or another. Furthermore, the approval of companies, awarding of lucrative franchises and financing were all executed by a small number of close individuals in government. This rather incestuous and corrupt situation has become prevalent by the mid-1937.[53] Soong remained in government after resigning this ministerial job in 1933 and was instrumental in this movement after 1935. What Coble observed happening in the 1930s was in reality the new Nationalist government's reassertion of state economic power. This was achieved partly by way of Nanjing granting special privileges to semi-government corporations but all this was taking place in an uncoordinated way in all divisions: (1) The Ministry of Industry used its legal authority to seize control of several areas of the economy because it had less access to banking capital. This Ministry focused on working with provincial officials. (2) The Military Affairs Commission led by Chiang Kai-shek established the National Resource Commission. This is a pure governmental body that embarked on a major nationalisation program of private enterprises while establishing new ones at the same time. (3) As described above, T. V. Soong established pure private companies with government officials becoming shareholders.[54]

All this reconfirms the argument that corporations interact with a modern state. The arrival of enterprises with corporate personality played a crucial part in making the imperial system unsustainable and was an accelerator in its collapse. Once the empire was gone and the Republic was established, state economic power came to permanently reside in and was distributed among corporations that continued to exist. More directly, it means that, in the mid-1930s, a major part of China's economy and economic power (except for "warlord"-controlled provinces such as Guangdong as shown in Part Three) was in the hands of private corporations. In the areas under the control of the Nationalist Nanjing government, the state attempted to take over the economy by taking over private corporations but at the same time forming new state-owned corporations. In other words, the most important understanding is that the state was *seizing power while continuing to recognise corporations and legal personality*.

Republican Incorporated Companies: What Next?

Returning to Parks M. Coble, Jr.'s bewildered observation regarding the "unusual degree of independence" of the private capitalists prior to 1927, it can be seen now that it is not "unusual" at all. The legal recognition of corporate personality by the Republican state protected both bottom-up private incorporate companies as well as top-down incorporated "government-directed" companies. Moreover, at the end of his in-depth analysis in *The Shanghai Capitalists and the Nationalist Government, 1927–1937*, Coble concluded that: it was the political weakness of Chinese government that allowed capitalists to flourish with freedom and independence, but on the arrival of a revitalised Nationalist Central Government in Nanjing, "the old pattern of *official domination* of the merchants" began to re-emerge.[55]

"Official domination" is perhaps a true description of the intention of the Nationalist government. In practice, however, to dominate the merchants would have taken more than a "revitalized Chinese government". Rather, it would require the complete elimination of corporations in society to effect the desired "domination" of the merchants. "Official domination of the merchants" by the Communist regime was accomplished not by investing in private corporations or forming of government corporations as described by Coble; it was achieved in the 1950s by transforming the entire government of the Chinese state into a hybrid political-commercial corporate person that took over all other forms of organisation with corporate personalities. The precursor to this, however, began not after T. V. Soong pushed into the private sector in 1935 ("official domination"), but in 1931 when the NRC was secretly formed by Chiang Kai-shek to institutionalise the modern Chinese *state*'s push into the economic realm. Thus, unlike the boroughs in England, under Chiang Kai-shek's strategy, the governmental form of corporations did go into business and competed with incorporated companies.

Chiang Kai-shek and the NRC Strategy

After World War II, Chiang Kai-shek gained full state power over his political rivals by winning the presidential election and became the constitutionally recognised President of the Republic of China on 20 May 1948.[56] He immediately appointed Dr. Weng Wenhao, the Geologist and head of the NRC, as the new Premier of the Republic of China in 1948.[57] This move was another attempt to consolidate the power that Chiang had accumulated since becoming the trusted protégée of Sun Yat-sen. He methodically amassed this power through militarily campaigns, political manoeuvres and now industrial development. However, the industrial policy of this redefined Republic of China was an failure. This could easily be seen by looking at the wholly incorporated cement industry of this period.

Chiang Kai-shek did not nationalise major industries in the hands of the powerful corporations such as the northern Qixin Cement or the Shanghai Portland Cement. In other words, the nationalisation attempt by Chiang Kai-shek's government employing the NRC as a vehicle was rather weak. It did not seek to abolish corporations completely but chose to use the NRC effectively as a governmental "holding" corporation. Therefore, power remained in the hands of the capitalists such as Liu Hongsheng who controlled the early large corporations in Shanghai. Chiang Kai-shek and his economic advisers did not achieve much before his nationalist army lost the civil war to the Communists. He did manage to seize control of the incorporated China Merchants Shipping Company by nationalisation but only succeeded in doing so after a big fight.[58] After winning the civil war in 1949, the Communists took a more brutal approach. Once in government, they powered ahead with full nationalisation, abolishing all companies and corporations.

The National Resource Commission

Chiang Kai-shek's career from the early 1920s onwards was, except for a lull during the Sino-Japanese War where an external enemy had to be fought, a career in civil war. As Yang Tianshi of Peking University has reconfirmed with newer sources, it was in fact the Sino-Japanese War from 1937 to 1945 that consolidated Chiang's power.[59] Throughout his political career, Chiang attempted to unite China through military force and the building of a constitutional state with himself at the helm. However, he faced a disunited state with enormous internal problems that prevented his consolidation of power. On the one hand, separatism manifested itself in the Nationalist Party (KMT) among the old guard such as Wang Jingwei, Sun Ke and Hu Hanmin, each holding sway in his own faction. On the other hand, the militarists Feng Yuxiang, Yan Xishan and Li Zongren remained suspicious. These men had risen to prominence independently of the Central Government and descended from the old "warlord" armies; "their loyalties" were therefore "conditional and attenuated", and generally they were resentful and dreaded Chiang Kai-shek's swelling power.[60]

Furthermore, there were hostile Communists who were guided by the more powerful Soviet ideology that was not only unacceptable to Chiang Kai-shek but threatened the existence of the entire Republic. Not surprisingly then, even after Japan had taken over Manchuria in 1931, he still described the external Japanese menace as no more than a "skin problem".[61] With all these internal problems, Chiang allowed T.V. Soong and H. H. Kung to take care of economic matters and seemingly paid little attention to China's industrialisation.[62] Yet Chiang Kai-shek was well aware of the situation. In order to establish an industrial base, he used the cover of the "Campaign of Encirclement and Extermination against the Communists" to legitimately dispatch civilian personnel and military troops to the various western provinces that were controlled by the suspicious military leaders mentioned above.[63] Such a base was necessary for the anticipated long-term war of attrition planned against the Japanese by Chiang. Also, using this cover, Chiang tried to avert an early military attack or confrontation with this far more advanced and superior military force.[64]

For rapid industrialisation he established the NRC. It was created as a statutory body on 1 November 1932 known then as the National Defence Planning Commission. This was ten months after the Mukden Incident of 1931 when the Japanese occupied Manchuria. The NRC was enabled by the National Defence Planning Commission Organisation Ordinance and placed under the Military Affairs Commission in the administrative hierarchy.[65] It was a small, secret body with approximately 50 staff that served directly under Chiang Kai-shek. It attempted to supervise and plan spending for creating an industrial base in support of the military.[66] In the summer of 1932, Dr. Weng Wenhao, who produced the first colour geological map of China and was head of the Beiping Geological Survey Institute, was chosen by Chiang Kai-shek to be Secretary-General of the NRC. Weng, who some claims to be the first ever Chinese to be awarded a PhD in Geology, was appointed to find ways to tap the natural resources of the vast expanse of western China which Chiang intended to exploit in preparation for impending war with Japan.[67]

The Ministry of Economic Affairs

On 1 April 1935, the commission was renamed the National Resources Commission. The NRC remained under the Military Affairs Commission until the outbreak of the Sino-Japanese War in July 1937.[68] At this point, with Hu Hanmin dead and Guangdong Province firmly under Nanjing's control,[69] Chiang Kai-shek, as Commander-in-Chief of the armed forces, sidelined his remaining political competitor Wang Jingwei. He was able to grab for himself unchallenged political powers brought about by the mobilisation effort in the war against Japan.[70]

The war also led to the rapid reorganisation of the government administration and to a consolidation of economic power. On 22 July 1937, half a month after the Marco Polo Bridge Incident when the war started, the Nanjing Government established the National Mobilisation Planning Commission (*Guojia zhong dongyuan weiyuanhui*) and decided that central planning would be the wartime economic model. On 1 January 1938, the Central Administrative Organs Reorganisation Order (*Tiaozheng zhongyang xingzheng jigou ling*) was issued, creating the Ministry of Economic Affairs. This is achieved by reorganising the Ministry of Industry and incorporating into its administration the NRC and several commissions belonging to the Nanjing government. The several included the Construction Commission and the Economic Commission and, within these, also included their hydro businesses. Several military commissions responsible for agriculture, mineral and industry were also incorporated. Finally, Weng Wenhao was chosen as the first Minister of Economic Affairs.[71]

Two months later in March 1938, an Extraordinary Congress of the Nationalist Party was convened at Wuhan University. The congress passed the *Program of Armed Resistance and National Reconstruction* which stipulated that the nation's power would be concentrated in the Nationalist Party and its leader Chiang Kai-shek.[72] This represented the extension of the Nationalist Government's control on economic power. On 30 March, the Congress passed the *Economic Programme for the Emergency Period* (*Feichang shiqi jingji fangan*) and the next day, on 31 March, passed the *Outline Procedures for the Implementation of Industrial Policy* (*Gongye zhengce shishi tayao an*). In the closing declaration of the Congress on 1 April 1938, the relationship between private and state enterprises was specifically reiterated:[73]

> those enterprises that are suitable for state organisation should be established by the state and its capital raised by the state; those that are suitable for private organisation should be established by private individuals under the overall state plan and instructed by the state and rewarded by the state so as to achieve beneficial developments.[74]

Chiang Kai-shek had become the most powerful political, military and now economic leader in China. The industrialisation process was the responsibility of the NRC which was still functioning effectively and still under Weng Wenhao's watch, even though it had become part of the Ministry of Economic Affairs. Thus Chiang had entrusted wartime China's industrial economy to Weng Wenhao, while he dealt with the political and military situations. Their collaboration would continue until after the arrival of the new constitution in which political and economic power would theoretically be consolidated under President Chiang Kai-shek, who headed the state, and Premier Weng Wenhao, who headed the government.

Republican Corporations Versus the Republican State

Weng Wenhao declared the economic policy of the Nanjing Government six days after he took office on 31 May 1948. He clearly spelt out the policy of the new government in the treatment of the relationship between the *state* and the *corporation*. He emphasised the role of the NRC as the link:

> The NRC played an important part during the years of war and is now laying the foundation for China's industrialization...NRC is the largest industrial undertaking in China...NRC's industrialization work is now represented by 96 subsidiary production units, employing a total of 230,000 staff and workers. The subsidiaries, divided into all categories as shown in the accompanying table,[75] are in the main incorporated under Chinese law on an equal, footing with private concerns and without special rights or privileges. The corporation form of organisation is adopted to ensure initiative, enterprise and efficiency under a coordinated plan of development. NRC production units are not only self-supporting bodies, but have to fend for themselves in the open markets as well. In spite of adverse circumstances, these subsidiaries altogether made a profit of 799 billion national dollars in 1947. The fundamental policy of the Chinese Government is to lay the foundation for a modern economy with heavy and basic industries to be established and operated by the state, and at the same time to perfect and promote private undertakings in the supplementary part of basic industry.[76]

Weng Wenhao's claim in the *Economic Times* sounded impressive, but in reality, his Republican government's methodology for the *state* to accommodate *corporations* with the NRC playing a middleman role in China's industrialisation was eventually a failure. China's industrialisation never took off in the difficult post-war conditions and the Chinese cement industry faced complete collapse.[77]

It is revealing to contrast Weng Wenhao's positive account of Chinese industry in 1948 with the actual state of Chinese industries towards the end of World War II in 1944. This is revealed in a report to T. V. Soong, the then Minister of Foreign Affairs, by the industrial expert S. Trone sent by the US government. He toured the three inland provinces of Sichuan, Yunan and Guangxi where the Nationalists were holding out against the Japanese in retreat. He inspected part of the arsenal and visited nearly all the industries of the National Recourses Commission and nearly all the privately owned industries: coal mines, generating stations et cetera. Apart from the arsenals, he found that none of the industrial establishments represented manufacturing in a modern sense of the word. There was very low existing efficiency nearly everywhere: in factories, mines, power houses, et cetera. Trone compared the result of the production with the number of workers used, engineering staff, office staff employed and concluded that all these were producing very little with a big staff of men and copying more or less successful foreign machines in small numbers.[78]

If the development of Chinese industries was in such a sorry state in 1944, how could the NRC suddenly control so many *corporate* subsidiaries that were altogether making "a profit of 799 billion national dollars in 1947", only two years after World War II ended and just three years after this grim report? The answer lies in the Japanese occupation of China and the fact that, on their defeat, the NRC gained the most in the scramble for the Japanese-developed industries.[79] Parties involved in the scramble include the military under Li Zongren, the Hebei Provincial Government, the city government of Beiping (Beijing), the city government of Tianjin and the various ministries of the Central Government. The situation in the cement industry illustrates this (see Tables 7.1, 7.2, 7.3, 7.4 and 7.5). Ironically, the above 31 May 1948 pronouncement was one of the last important state policies in the final days of the Chiang Kai-shek Nanjing government. Six months after this, on 26 November, Weng Wenhao's government collapsed, Chiang Kai-shek resigned as President on 21 January 1949 and Mao Zedong declared the founding of the People's Republic of China on 1 October 1949.

Table 7.1 shows the cement enterprises in Manchuria (the Northeast) alone. It can be seen that, whereas there were only four cement plants in the rest of China in 1931, Manchuria alone had 14 and all of these were established by Japan even before the outright occupation of Manchuria in 1931. Together with the three plants in Taiwan and the two established in the occupied north between 1937 and 1945, the NRC took over 19 cement plants in 1946. Table 7.3 shows that only two plants were established by the NRC with local governments in western China during the Nationalist Government's retreat to the provisional capital Chongqing between November 1937 and May 1946. Thus, from the perspective of one major early twentieth-century industry, it can be seen that, in the end, the Japanese war effort in Taiwan and Manchuria had a major contribution to Chinese industrialisation.

Table 7.1 Japanese cement enterprises in the Northeast, 1945[a]

Name		*Founding year*	*Operating capacity (10,000 T)*	*Designed capacity (10,000 T)*
Dalian	大连	1921	25	21
Jilin	吉林	1922	28	26
Liaoyang	辽阳	1923	18	13
Fushun	抚顺	1924	30	21
Benxihu	本溪湖	1924	35	25
Haerbin	哈尔滨	1924	15	11
Quantou	泉头	1924	16	14
Anshan	鞍山	1926	15	16
Jinzhou	锦州	1927	20	15
Guanyuan	官原	1929	30	17
Miaoling	庙岭	1929	16	9
Andong	安东	1929	25	18
Mudanjiang	牡丹江	1930	15	10
Xiaotun	小屯	1931	5	–
Total			**293**	**218**

[a]Yu Guocheng, "Ribenren zai dongbei zhi shuini shiye (Japanese cement enterprises in the Northeast)", June 1946, Nanjing Archive NRC 28 (2) No. 2957

Table 7.2 Japanese cement enterprises in Taiwan, 1945

Name		*Founding year*	*Operating capacity (10,000 T)*	*Designed capacity (10,000 T)*
Gaoxiong	高雅	–	–	–
Zhudong	竹东	–	–	–
Suwo	苏沃	–	–	–

Table 7.3 NRC self-invested & directly held cement enterprises in 1946[a]

Name		*Founding year*	*NRC ownership (%)*	*No. of plants*
Guizhou[b]	贵州	1941	26.6	1
Gansu[c]	甘肃	1941	57	1

[a]"The 1948 Report of the Cement Business", Nanjing Archive NRC 28 (2) No. 3269
[b]*Guizhou shuini gufen youxian gongsi* (Guizhou Cement Joint Stock Company Limited)
[c]*Gansu shuini gufen youxian gongsi* (Gansu Cement Joint Stock Company Limited)

Table 7.4 NRC cement holding companies in 1948: formed from cement plants taken over from Japan in 1946[a]

Name		*Founding year*	*NRC ownership (%)*	*No. of plants*
Taiwan[b]	台湾	1946	60	3
Huabei[c]	华北	1946	100	2
Liaoning[d]	辽宁	1946	100	2+[f]
Huaxin[e]	华新	1946	28.6	3

[a]"The 1948 Report of the Cement Business", Nanjing Archive NRC 28 (2) No. 3269
[b]*Taiwan shuini gufen youxian gongsi* (Taiwan Cement Joint Stock Company Limited)
[c]*Huabei shuini gufen youxian gongsi* (Huabei Cement Joint Stock Company Limited)
[d]*Liaoning shuini gufen youxian gongsi* (Liaoning Cement Joint Stock Company Limited)
[e]This company is basically the holding company for the cement plants in Manchuria (Northeast) and the exact number of functioning plants is not clear. Some facilities had lost their manufacturing equipment to the retreating Soviet army which dismantled and looted the factories all across Manchuria
[f]*Huaxin shuini gufen youxian gongsi* (Huaxin Cement Joint Stock Company Limited)

Private Corporations Versus State Corporations

It is clear that the escalation of the war with Japan became the main driver of Chinese cement plant construction. Upon Japan's defeat at the end of the war, it appeared that the NRC had grown into an apparently large bureaucratic behemoth along Soviet lines, managing a large centrally controlled state-owned industrial sector and coordinating foreign trade.[80] On the one hand, US experts were sent to help in the post-war reconstruction "plan". On the other hand, internal American recommendations at the end of the war were very nervous about whether governmental help to industrialise China would turn it into another centrally planned country.[81] American concerns were well-founded because there were constant debates within the NRC regarding Soviet planning ideas and leaders such as Weng Wenhao were in favour of this kind of planned industrial policy.[82] Internally, the latest Soviet Communist planning ideas were being translated and published as references.[83] During the initial years of the NRC, Weng Wenhao openly urged the construction of a "planned" and "regulated economy" in order to achieve "strong and orderly" industrialisation. He made it lucidly clear that he believed this was the way to make China a strong nation.[84]

Advice was provided by the US government for the "industrialisation of China" but only with the utmost caution, as illustrated by the preface of a governmental industrialisation guide written to the Chinese government

Table 7.5 All cement companies in 1948[a]

	Cement firm	*Chinese name*	*No. of plants*	*NRC shareholding*
1	Huabei[b]	华北水泥公司	2	NRC 100 %
2	Xibei[c]	西北事业建设公司洋灰厂	1	–
3	Tianxiang[d]	天祥事业公司水泥厂	1	–
4	**Qixin[e]**	**启新洋灰公司**	**1**	–
5	China[f]	中国水泥公司	1	–
6	Guizhou[g]	贵州水泥公司	1	NRC 26.6 %
7	Jiahua[h]	嘉华水泥公司		–
8	Huaxin[i]	华新水泥公司	3	NRC 28.6 %
9	Taiwan[j]	台湾水泥公司	3	NRC 60 %
10	Shunchang[k]	顺昌水泥公司	1	–
11	**Xicun[l]**	**西村士敏土厂**	**2**	–
12	**Shanghai[m]**	**上海水泥公司**	**1**	–
13	Jiangnan[n]	江南水泥公司	1	–
14	Sichuan[o]	四川水泥公司	1	NRC rented
15	Liaoning[p]	辽宁水泥公司	2+	NRC 100 %
16	Gansu[q]	甘肃水泥公司	1	NRC 57 %
17	Jianya[r]	建亚水泥厂		–
18	Zhijing[s]	致敬洋灰公司	1	–
19	Jiangxi[t]	江西水泥公司	1	–

[a]"Zhiyuan weiyuanhui shuini huiyi ji shencha yijia (The opinion of the NRC meeting and survey)" 1947, Nanjing Archive NRC 28 v. 2 No. 8003; "Zhongguo shuini gongye tongyehui chensong huiyi jilu ji lijianshi ming ce (The submission of the minutes and officer register of the China Cement Industrial Business Union)" April–October 1948, Nanjing Archive NRC 28 v. 2 No. 8003; "Wo guo shuini gongye huifu jihua dagang chaoan (The draft outline plan for the reviving of our nation's cement industry)" 1949, Nanjing Archive NRC 28 v. 3 No. 17433

[b]*Huabei shuini gongsi* (Huabei Cement Company)

[c]*Xibei shiye jianshe gonsi yanhui Chang* (Xibei Business Enterprise Construction Company Cement Works)

[d]*Tianxiang shiye gongsi Shinichang* (Tianxiang Business Enterprise Company Cement Works), located in Shanghai

[e]*Qixin yanghui gongsi* (Qixin Cement Company Limited), located in Tangshan, Hebei Province

[f]*Zhongguo shuini gongsi* (China Cement Company), located in Lungtan, Jiansu Province

[g]*Guizhou shuini gongsi* (Guizhou Cement Company), located in Guiyang, Guizhou Province

[h]*Jiahua shuini gongsi* (Jiahua Cement Company)

[i]*Huaxin shuini gongsi* (Huaxin Cement Company), located in Huangshi, Hebei Province

[j]*Taiwan shuini gongsi* (Taiwan Cement Company)

[k]*Shunchang shuini gongsi* (Shunchang Cement Company), located in Shanghai

[l]*Xicun shimintu Chang* (Xicun Cement Works), located in Guangzhou, Guangdong Province

[m]*Shanghai shuini gongsi* (Shanghai Portland Cement Works Company Limited)

[n]*Jiangnan shuini gongsi* (Jiangnan Cement Company), located in Jiangsu Province

[o]*Sichuan shuini gongsi* (Sichuan Cement Company)

[p]*Liaoning shuini gongsi* (Liaoning Cement Company).

[q]*Gansu shuini gongsi* (Gansu Cement Company), located in Gansu Province

[r]*Jianya shuini gongsi* (Jianya Cement Company), located in Shanghai

[s]*Zhijing Shuini Gongsi* (Zhijing Cement Company), located in Jinan in Shangdong Province

[t]*Jiangxi Shuini Gongsi* (Jiangxi Cement Company), located in Taihe, Jianxi Province

which said that the "Industrialization Guide" did not propose "a final industrialisation pattern" that was subjected to strict government control. Moreover, the Guide should be used to "illuminate the opening stage" for "private enterprise".[85] The attitude of the US government, which was supporting Chiang Kai-shek's government, was clear: they did not support the Chinese state enlarging itself into the economic realm and they threatened to withdraw aid unless liberal economic reforms were implemented.[86] The American adviser S. Trone made the American position very clear. He believed that to produce without justifying investment is understandable as a war necessity only but will lead to nowhere in peace-time.[87]

Yet, in contrast to the American view, many on the Chinese side thought positively of planning at the time. For example, those who were responsible for industries that were experiencing hardship or outright extinction due to foreign competition and home overproduction, tended to look favourably on the Soviet system. This was precisely the case for the cement industry, where the whole industry acted collectively through their trade association and lobbied for government intervention in the post-war period.[88] From the point of view of the cement industry, the situation was hopeless. Yu Guocheng who had responsibility for the cement industry at the NRC reported in September 1949:

> The situation is confused: It is necessary for a planned economy to have planned production, and more importantly it needs a planned sales regime. Sales must be planned first and then production tailored to the planned sales. However, within an economically liberal country that is raising "support of competition" as its popularity banner, a planned sales regime is unacceptable. Hence, it has led to over-equipping, overproduction, rivalry and chaos, and the cement industry is no exception... After the victory over Japan, cement production capacity in our country suddenly doubled and the uncontrollable anarchy must not be allowed to continue.[89]

The People's Republic of China was founded just one month after this report when Chiang Kai-shek and his Nationalist government retreated to Taiwan after wrecking the economy through financial meltdown, losing industrialised Manchuria to the Communists and suffering defeat in the civil war.[90] This "anarchy" would eventually come to an end in this the upcoming "socialist transformation". It is worth noting that, the Republican government via the NRC attempted to use the commercial corporate form to achieve nationalisation and consolidate state economic power instead of destroying corporate persons and corporate personality.

In August 1948, the NRC issued the General Principles of Cooperation Between the NRC and Provincial (Municipal) Governments (*Ziyuan weiyuanhui yu ge sheng (shi) zhengfu heban shiye tongze*) which stipulated that all cooperative enterprises (*heban qiye*) should use "limited companies" (i.e., the corporate form) as the principle of operation and that the NRC should be the larger shareholder with at least 60 % of the issued shares. Moreover, this document also had detailed guidelines regarding the composition of the board of directors of these NRC-invested enterprises.[91] Thus, the NRC was a halfway house, somewhere between a holding company and state ministry. It favoured Soviet planning but did *not* have the constitutional power to *eliminate* corporate personalities; thus it chose to *accommodate* and use them to its advantage within the power consolidation nationalisation schema.[92]

Corporations: An Ephemeral Existence, 1904–1954

This unique method of using a government statutory body as a holding company to industrialise a country simply did not, for whatever reason, work, and with the combined disaster of a financial meltdown and war, China suffered economic collapse. Here, in the very last moments before the final defeat of the Nationalists in the civil war, it could be seen that the Republican state attempted to capture economic power by capturing some of the incorporate companies in society. This was the exact reverse of the process that took power away from the Qing imperial government because it attempted to reverse a trend of state power dissipation that began in 1904. This is in sharp contrast to Yuan Shikai's local economic build-up of incorporated companies in Zhili before the empire fell (1904–1911), or the economic autonomy that Sun Yat-sen and his followers had under the shelter of the incorporated Guangzhou City (1926–1936).

Unfortunately for Chiang Kai-shek and the Republican regime in 1948, time was not on their side and they were driven off the mainland to Taiwan. The Communist government that succeeded the nationalists from 1949 completely recaptured all economic power when they constitutionally eliminated corporate or legal personality in China. Similar to the Qing absolutist imperial industrial system where it was unable to accommodate incorporated entities, the state created by the 1954 "Constitution of the People's Republic of China" absorbed all corporate entities back into the state. By Article 4 of the 1954 Constitution, the Communist government set out the general principle of nationalising all commercial businesses:

Article 4 The People's Republic of China, by relying on the organs of state and the social forces, and through socialist industrialisation and socialist transformation, ensures the gradual abolition of systems of exploitation and the building of a socialist society.[93]

This principle was pronounced as policy by the *People's Daily* on 25 November 1955 in the editorial: "A well prepared and methodologically organised establishment of state-private cooperative ventures for private industries in all industrial sectors."[94] Finally, the dissipation of state economic power that had started with the introduction of legal personality in the 1904 Company Law came to an abrupt stop. Instead, economic power reversed back absolutely into the Central Government in Beijing. China was being transformed into a large modern state with an industrial economy controlled by a few people at the top. In this way, the ancient empire under a modern, albeit an "Eastern" Leninist, government regained its central economic power and reasserted itself both at home and in the world. Unity was achieved. Yet, as a result of a tripartite concentration of political power, military power and new industrial economic powers in the capital city, a highly unstable balance was created in the 1950s. Henceforth, a new uncharted era of explosive Chinese politics begins with Mao Zedong at the helm.

Notes

1. See Kai Yiu Chan, *Business Expansion and Structural Change in Pre-War China*, pp. 77–98.
2. Parks M. Coble, *The Shanghai Capitalists and the Nationalist Government.*
3. Frederick Hallis, *Corporate Personality*, p. xiii.
4. Albert Feuerwerker, *China's Early Industrialization*, p. 1.
5. Railways caused strain in the imperial system: David Faure, *China and Capitalism*, p. 61; Zhang Jian incorporated his regional enterprise in Nantong, the Dasheng Cotton Mill, in 1907; see Elisabeth Köll, *From Cotton Mill to Business Empire*, p. 126; and Sheng Xuanhuai incorporated the Hanyeping in 1908; see Albert Feuerwerker, "China's Nineteenth-Century Industrialization: The Case of Hanyehping Coal and Iron Company, Limited"; also the enterprises under Yuan Shikai and Zhou Xuexi discussed in Chap. 3 are examples of this.

6. Li Yu, *Beiyang zhengfu shiqi qiye zhidu jiegou shilun*, pp. 107–166.
7. William L. Tung, *The Political Institutions of Modern China*, p. 23; Yang Hongnian and Ouyang Xin, *Zhongguo zhengzhi shi*, p. 387.
8. Kenneth Pomeranz: the government as the promoter of industrialism; Kenneth Pomeranz, *The Making of a Hinterland*; Rawski and Marie-Claire Bergère: government initiatives led to failure: Marie-Claire Bergère, *The Golden Age of the Chinese Bourgeoisie*, p. 140; and Feuerwerker: traditional Chinese practices, nepotism and bureaucracy caused industrial failure; see Albert Feuerwerker, *China's Early Industrialization*.
9. Parks M. Coble, *The Shanghai Capitalists and the Nationalist Government*, p. 259.
10. John Fairbank and Edwin Reischauer, *China: Tradition and Transformation*, pp. 32, 52 and 60.
11. The Provisional Constitution of the Republic of China promulgated 11 March 1912; see Xia Xinhua et al. *Jindai Zhongguo xianzheng licheng*, pp. 156–161.
12. See Chap. 5.
13. Yang Hongnian and Ouyang Xin, *Zhongguo zhengzhi shi*, pp. 387–432.
14. Colin Arthur Cooke, *Corporation, Trust and Company*, p. 15.
15. Colin Arthur Cooke, *Corporation, Trust and Company*, p. 15.
16. Yang Hongnian and Ouyang Xin, *Zhongguo zhengzhi shi*, p. 516; see Chaps. 5 and 6.
17. Li Yu, *Beiyang zhengfu shiqi qiye zhidu jiegou shilun*, pp. 130–131.
18. Kai Yiu Chan, *Business Expansion and Structural Change in Pre-War China*.
19. See Introduction Chapter.
20. Kai Yiu Chan, *Business Expansion and Structural Change in Pre-War China*.
21. Information supplied by the Shanghai Portland Cement Works in *LHS* v. 1, p. 157.
22. See L. C. B. Gower, et al., *Gower's Principles of Modern Company Law*, p. 140.
23. Information supplied by the Port Authority of Shanghai in *LHS* v. 1, p. 49.
24. The oral testimony of the ex-assistant manager of the Shanghai Portland Cement Works Company Limited Xi Anzhai September

1963 *LHS* v. 1, p. 49 and Philip A. Alsop & James W. Post, *Cement Plant Operations Handbook*, pp. 29 and 38–42.

25. The talk, "the Cement Industry established by Chinese Nationals", by manager of the Shanghai Portland Cement Works Company Limited Wu Qingtai on 23 August 1936 in *LHS* v. 1, p. 157; the oral testimony of the ex-assistant manager of the Shanghai Portland Cement Works Company Limited Xi Anzhai September 1963 in *LHS* v. 1, p. 158.
26. "Establishing the Shanghai Portland Cement Works, Limited", in *LHS* v. 1, p. 158.
27. Hundred tons of limestone can manufacture 75 tons of cement: "Files from the archives of the Shanghai Portland Cement Works, Limited" in *LHS* v. 1, p. 158.
28. Raising capital to finish construction of the factory and Liu Hongsheng assuming the post of General Manager in *LHS* v. 1, p. 158.
29. The Minutes of the 11th Director's Meeting at the Shanghai Portland Cement Works, Limited on 14 September 1922 in *LHS* v. 1, p. 164.
30. The oral testimony of Xi Anzhai of April 1960 in *LHS* v. 1, p. 165.
31. "The investment ratios of Liu Hongsheng and Liu Jiesheng in the Shanghai Portland Cement Works Company Limited" and the oral testimony of Xie Peide of February 1959 in *LHS* v. 1, p. 163 and p. 165.
32. Minutes of the 14th Meeting of the Board of Directors of the Shanghai Portland Cement Works Company Limited on 8th May 1923 in *LHS* v. 1, p. 165.
33. The oral testimony of Xie Peide of February 1959 in *LHS* v. 1, p. 165.
34. Minutes of the 17th Meeting of the Board of Directors of the Shanghai Portland Cement Works Company Limited on 8 November 1923 in *LHS* v. 1, p. 168.
35. Albert Feuerwerker, "Industrial Enterprise in Twentieth-Century China: The Chee Hsin Cement Co.".
36. The cement market was flooded with Japanese-produced cement at this time. Cement from the Japanese Asano Cement Company's branch facility was selling very well because of it low price: letter from the southern sales office manager of the Shanghai Portland Cement Works Company Limited to Liu Hongsheng, 16 February

1925; the Japanese company Onoda Cement were also producing in Dalian, which was contributing to the oversupply: Albert Feuerwerker, "Industrial Enterprise in Twentieth-Century China: The Chee Hsin Cement Co."; and the oral testimony of Xi Anzhai in April 1960 in *LHS* v. 1, p. 184.

37. Li Yu, *Beiyang zhengfu shiqi qiye zhidu jiegou shilun*, p. 333.
38. Albert Feuerwerker, "Industrial Enterprise in Twentieth-Century China: The Chee Hsin Cement Co.".
39. Letter from Liu Hongsheng to Mr. Zu Weiyong of the Hankou Zhongfu Company dated 22 August 1924 in *LHS* v. 1, p. 188.
40. Letter from Liu Hongsheng to Yu Shouyi dated 13 April 1925 in *LHS* v. 1, p. 188.
41. Letter from Yu Shouyi to Liu Hongsheng dated February 1925 in *LHS* v. 1, p. 189.
42. Minutes of the 4th Shareholders Meeting of the Shanghai Portland Cement Works Company Limited on 30th August1925 in *LHS* v. 1, p. 189.
43. Minutes of the 23rd Meeting of the Board of Directors of the Shanghai Portland Cement Works Company Limited on 8th and 13th May 1925 in *LHS* v. 1, p. 189.
44. The contract between Shanghai Portland Cement Works Company Limited with Qixin Cement Company Limited dated and executed on 30 June 1925 in *LHS* v. 1, p. 190.
45. Letter from Liu Hongsheng to Hankou Fuzhong gongsi on 24 June 1925 in *LHS* v. 1, p. 193.
46. Letter from Liu Hongsheng to the general manager of the Qixin cement company in *LHS* v. 1, p. 194.
47. The oral testimony of Xi Anyyu in *LHS* v. 1, p. 194.
48. Letter from the acting general manager Hua Runquan to the Shanghai Cement Works manager Wu Qingtai 4 February 1926 in *LHS* v. 1, p. 199.
49. Minutes of the 39th Meeting of the Board of Directors of the Shanghai Portland Cement Works Company Limited on 12 April 1949 in *LHS* v. 1, p. 218.
50. This conforms to Frederick Hallis' descripton of the effects of corporate personality on modern society (see Chapter 1)
51. See Parks M. Coble, *The Shanghai Capitalists and the Nationalist Government,* p. 320 n72; this was meticulously analysed in this note.

52. Parks M. Coble, *The Shanghai Capitalists and the Nationalist Government,* p. 161.
53. Parks M. Coble, *The Shanghai Capitalists and the Nationalist Government,* p. 209.
54. Parks M. Coble, *The Shanghai Capitalists and the Nationalist Government,* p. 214.
55. Parks M. Coble, *The Shanghai Capitalists and the Nationalist Government,* p. 260.
56. William L. Tung, *The Political Institutions of Modern China*, pp. 115–119.
57. Officially as the President of the Executive Yuan.
58. Zhang Houquan, *Zhaoshangju shi: Jindai bufen*, pp. 260–361.
59. Yang Tianshi, *Jiang Jieshi yu Nanjing guomin zhengfu*, p. 483.
60. Lloyd E. Eastman, "Nationalists China during the Sino-Japanese War 1937–1945," in *The Cambridge History of China*, p. 569.
61. Yang Tianshi, *Jiang Jieshi yu Nanjing guomin zhengfu*, p. 482.
62. Parks M. Coble, *The Shanghai Capitalists and the Nationalist Government,* pp. 257–258.
63. Yang Tianshi, *Jiang Jieshi yu Nanjing guomin zhengfu*, p. 483.
64. Yang Tianshi, *Jiang Jieshi yu Nanjing guomin zhengfu*, p. 485; for a recent reassessment of the Nationalist government policy between the occupation of Manchuria in 1931 and the full invasion in 1937, see Peng Dunwen, *Guomin zhengfu dui Ri zhengce ji qi bianhua: cong jiu-yiba shibian dao qi-qi shibian.*
65. Xue Yi, *Guomin zhengfu ziyuan weiyuanhui yanjiu*, pp. 55–56.
66. Zhao Xingsheng, *Chuantong jingyan yu xiandai lixiang.*
67. Xue Yi, *Guomin zhengfu ziyuan weiyuanhui yanjiu*, p. 59.
68. Parks M. Coble, *The Shanghai Capitalists and the Nationalist Government,* p. 320.
69. See Chap. 6.
70. William L. Tung, *The Political Institutions of Modern China*, p. 387; Yang Hongnian and Ouyang Xin, *Zhongguo zhengzhi shi*, p. 436.
71. Zhao Xingsheng, *Chuantong jingyan yu xiandai lixiang*, pp. 201–202.
72. William L. Tung, *The Political Institutions of Modern China*, p. 176.
73. The *Industrial Policy Implementation (Outline) Procedure* was passed by the Congress on 31 March 1938; see Zhao Xingsheng, *Chuantong jingyan yu xiandai lixiang*, p. 204.

74. Zhao Xingsheng, *Chuantong jingyan yu xiandai lixiang*, p. 205.
75. The table categories are: electric power, coal mining, petroleum, metal mining, iron and steel, machinery, electric manufacturing, chemical works, sugar, cement and paper.
76. Wen Wenhao, "NRC Steps Up Chinese Industrialization".
77. Zhonghua Minguo shuini gongye tongye gonghui, "Guanyu jiejue shuini ye kunnan an".
78. S. Trone, "Letter to his Excellency, Dr. T. V. Soong, Minister of Foreign Affairs, Chongqing, Feb 9th, 1944".
79. See Li Xuetong, *Shusheng congzheng*.
80. See generally Zhao Xingsheng, *Chuantong jingyan yu xiandai lixiang* and Xue Yi, *Guomin zhengfu ziyuan weiyuanhui yanjiu*.
81. Henry C. Cassell, 2nd ed., *Guide to the Industrialization of China*.
82. Weng Wenhao, "Jing Jian fangxiang yu gongtong zeren" in *Ziyuan weiyuanhui gongbao*, pp. 79–84; G. M. Malenkov, "The gaijin zhong de Sulian gongye guanli.
83. G. M. Malenkov, "The "Gaijin zhong de Sulilan gongye guanli".
84. Weng Wenhao, "Jing Jian fangxiang yu gongtong zeren".
85. Henry C. Cassell, 2nd ed., *Guide to the Industrialization of China*.
86. Zhao Xingsheng, *Chuantong jingyan yu xiandai lixiang*, p. 441.
87. S. Trone, "Industrialization of China".
88. Zhonghua Minguo shuini gongye tongye gonghui, "Guanyu jiejue shuini ye kunnan an".
89. Yu Guocheng, "Quanguo shuini fenqu xiaoshou yijian".
90. Immanuel C. Y. Hsü, *The Rise of Modern China*.
91. NRC, "Ziyuan weiyuanhui yu ge sheng shi zhengfu heban shiye tongze", pp. 19–20.
92. A new *Revised Company Act* was issued on 12 April 1946, Xue Yi, *Guomin zhengfu ziyuan weiyuanhui yanjiu*, pp. 452–453.
93. The 1954 Constitution of the People's Republic of China.
94. "You zhunbei, you buzhou di tuidong siying gongye shixing quan hangye gongsi heying"; Chen Yun, "Shehui zhuyi gaizhao jiben wancheng yihou de xin wenti".

CHAPTER 8

Conclusion: State Power, Corporations and the Cement Industry

At the end of the Republican era in 1949, China's brush with corporations had almost gone full circle. It was introduced in 1904 by law and was removed in 1954 by law. China did not enact another company law until 1995 but formal reintroduction of the commercial corporations did begin in 1982 in the form of the Joint Venture Law of the People's Republic of China (PRC) under the reforms instigated by Deng Xiaoping. Much of the earlier history of China's initial embrace of corporations lay concealed to contemporary Chinese scholars endeavouring to understand the present-day Chinese privatisation possibilities that are poised to transform the huge state-owned concerns into modern corporations. These range from the enormous national monopolies of banks and electricity firms to present-day minor provincial and municipal cement plants in the PRC.

This study reveals that China has been at this dilemmatic point before. In 1906, state economic power was dissipated to the militarily powerful Yuan Shikai when he incorporated the only functioning imperial cement monopoly in China for his own benefits. The very large independent industrial income from these corporations buttressed and fortified his influence and power. He was able to withstand ousting as a minister of the imperial court after the Empress Cixi's death in 1908 and was invited to return as Prime Minister in the last days of the imperial dynasty to put down the rebellion in Wuhan. Instead, he negotiated Emperor Puyi's abdication. With this knowledge of the late Qing and early Republican history of corporations, the privatisation of present-day state-owned enterprises

H. Ko, *The Making of the Modern Chinese State*,
DOI 10.1007/978-981-10-2660-7_8

becomes easier to understand. Thus, it is not surprising that after 1995, Premier Zhu Rongji's government introduced the first Company Law of the PRC, reintroducing commercial corporations to China. The privatisation of state-owned enterprises took the form that the state remained as the majority shareholders in most "privatised" state-owned firms through elaborate cross-holding schemes.[1] In this way, the anomaly of why the Chinese Communist Party is still healthily in power can be understood: over two decades after the collapse of communism in Europe and more than 60 years after the CCP formed the first government in 1949. This can be explained from the way the state retains a hold on economic power. This is achieved by denying the opportunity for popular associations and large organisations with fully autonomous corporate personality to ubiquitously proliferate in modern China.

What made the present study of corporations via the cement industry possible was an event in history triggered by the Boxer Uprising of 1900. This is because the only cement monopoly in China since 1889, the Tangshan Cement Works, became the first imperial industry to be wrestled out of the old imperial enterprise monopoly system. This happened after the Qing imperial state's wrangle with a British company that occupied the neighbouring Kaiping coal mines during the Boxer Uprising. The fiasco ended with the British company seizing the imperial coal mines together with the imperial cement works from the state in 1900. Then, it was an incident in history that Yuan Shikai confiscated the cement works in late 1905 on the advice of his economic adviser Zhou Xuexi and incorporated it as the Qixin Cement Company Limited in early 1906 under the new company law. This created the first legally independent Chinese industrial corporation that originated from an imperial monopoly.

Moreover, it was also an important event in history that the second cement monopoly granted in 1906 by the Empress Cixi to Yuan Shikai's court rival Cen Chunxuan was used from 1917 by Sun Yat-sen, the revolutionary leader and "father of modern China", as his revolutionary headquarters. The Guangdong Cement Works located in the southern city of Guangzhou was used by Sun to challenge Yuan Shikai's Beijing government in the new Republic. Thus, the history of the Chinese cement industry and its intertwined relationship with the revolutionaries' activities in this southern city added further insights and intrigue into China's Republican history.

Finally, it was the commercial ambitions of Liu Hongsheng, a private ordinary Chinese citizen from the city of Shanghai, together with the third operational cement works in China which he established, the

Shanghai Portland Cement Works Limited, which provided this study with a clear view of three different manifestations of corporate personality and corporations: the top-down incorporated company, the bottom-up incorporated company and the incorporated government. These cement works made observable the corporate concept's previously illusive historical development in the Chinese setting and unveiled its previously concealed destructive and constructive effects on the Chinese state structure.

These historical crossovers provided examples for showing the effects of the corporate concept's influence on industrial business developments and on the Chinese state's structural alterations which would otherwise be difficult to show. Yuan Shikai's Qixin Cement Company Limited was shown to be a top-down incorporated company that broke away from the imperial structure. Sun Yat-sen's Guangdong Cement Works was an unincorporated firm sheltered under an incorporated government which empowered a renegade province. Finally, there were bottom-up incorporated companies built up with private capital diligently accumulated and gathered by entrepreneurs from Chinese investors in the early 1920s.

These historical examples of real corporations correspond to what Frederick Hallis described as the "reality of corporate persons" in his 1927 pioneering theoretical inquiry of corporate personality conducted at the University of Oxford. He detected and recognised by the end of World War I that these "living realities" implied a new conception of the state. Such "associations with legal personalities", he incisively observed, "will no longer require a benevolent concession of the state". Indeed, the early history of the incorporated and unincorporated cement industry of China illustrates faithfully the phenomenon that Hallis explained. These early industrial firms from the north, east and south of China reflected Hallis' insight that their rights were "inherent in them by reason of the place they occupy, the social function they perform, in the entire body politic".[2] The idea of a corporation or corporate/legal personality may be abstract but in reality it continues inconspicuously to form the backbone of both modern governments and modern non-governmental associations such as commercial corporations.

The Chinese Cement Industry

Political and economic power in the imperial Chinese state concentrated in the imperial system and its structure. This study also shows how the development of national industries along with the introduction of corporate bodies allowed industrial economic power to split away from the political hold and develop separately and independently. The cement industry lies at the centre of the history of this unusual process in the late nineteenth and early twentieth centuries because of the very special logistics of this industrial business. This industry empowered the political ambitions of Yuan Shikai who was in a political struggle with his Manchu imperial master. It also suited the political and military necessity of Sun Yat-sen and his revolutionary followers who subsequently controlled civil administration of Guangzhou. Local politics and geography may differ, but the fundamentals of this industry's relationship with local despotic powers remained the same.

This study shows that the cement industry began its life in one of the most intricate period of Chinese history. The formation of the Republic of China in 1911 was a result of a struggle between new and old ideals and ideas. Behind this grandiose frontage, legal personality and corporations was introduced covertly from the West without fanfare or notice. Yet, the study shows clearly that it directly contributed to the collapse of the imperial system. Cement was an important modern industrial material which was also introduced from the West, the manufacturing of which developed into a major national industry that played a part in the modernisation struggle of China. Consequently, the industrial and material history of cement in the Chinese setting must not only draw analytical concepts from economics and business history but also from the broad spectrum of Chinese history as a whole. Furthermore, this study has shown that in the Republican period it was nurtured by and developed within the corporate framework. This demonstrates that China, similar to England in medieval times, had to legally recognise both commercial and governmental forms of corporate or legal personality in its metamorphosis from an ancient to a modern state.

The cement industry is a local industry for a local market. Scholars correctly saw that cement is a "highly standardised product for which the required raw material is widespread and the manufacturing technology relatively simple and generally accessible" and that "even the relatively inexperienced management characteristics of an early stage of industrialisation is capable of producing at a profit cement generally free of major technical defects." Furthermore, "the technology employed, in the form of plans and machinery, was almost entirely imported". Better still, "the supply and quality of its raw materials were not dependent upon agricultural output".[3] They, however, saw nothing special in the northern China

Qixin Cement Company Limited, attributing its profitability to a close relationship with the Beijing government even after the death of its initial patron Yuan Shikai. Previous scholarships located the analysis within the ambit of the general argument of the necessity for official supervision - merchant management (*guandu shangban*) enterprises and lumped this unique business in with "the fortunes of industrial enterprise as a whole in the first half of the twentieth century in China".[4] So, were Western technology, finance and management innovations or local politics and logistics not crucial in the development of the Chinese cement industry?

It has been shown in this study that what was not previously identified was the true reason for the growth of this industry in the Republican period. It was not the "first mover advantage" or government patronage which Feuerwerker placed as the prime explanations. Neither was it completely Adam Smith's "invisible hand" of the market, nor the "visible hand" of Alfred Chandler's "Management Revolution".[5] The true reason for the growth of the industry is local geographical control, because the cases show that once the production process itself had been solved by the acquisition of Western equipment, the industry became a monopolistic creature which fell in line with the *modus operandi* of local powerbrokers such as Yuan Shikai in Zhili Province and Sun Yat-sen in Guangdong Province, as well as the powerful local business and industrial capitalist Liu Hongsheng. This was further assisted by legal protection from government intervention by either incorporated companies (e.g., Qixin Cement and Shanghai Portland Cement) or incorporated governments (e.g., Guangdong Cement and Xicun Cement). Local heavy industry, locally available raw materials and local protected markets suited the characteristics of a perishable, bulky, low-value and high-volume business that was not so susceptible to foreign or inter-provincial competition in line with G. William Skinner's analysis of China from a macro-regional angle.[6]

The difficulty that any cement industry management faced was not the production process but control of the logistics of raw material and fuel supply, as well as the logistics of supplying to customers. Thus, as expected, in the cases studied, the market was not free but was controlled and manipulated by state leaders, revolutionaries, warlords or powerful capitalists. Yuan Shikai and his band of cohorts had control of the railways in northern China. Sun Yat-sen and his followers tamed the wholesalers of Guangzhou with local government power. Finally, Liu Hongsheng enforced a Shanghai monopoly through a cartel arrangement. Therefore, the key to a successful cement-manufacturing business lies not in the techniques and management of production but in the control of the market, and therefore, for an underdeveloped market such as China in the early twentieth century, success lies fundamentally in politics. This *modus operandi* is the same despite physical, geographical and environmental variations across continental-size China.

Throughout Republican China, it could be expected that demand was, on the one hand, spurred by population growth and urbanisation. Hence, it was the natural market demand of cement that led the industry to huge profits for the importers. On the other hand, it was the management of the logistics of the market and not the production (which had been fully automated since the turn of the century) which the local administration or local power-holder could perform well. They could muster enough protection because they controlled local armies and administration. For example, they controlled the mining of raw materials and could offer protection to facilitate the transportation of raw materials from mines to factory, then from factory to markets and then any subsequent debt collection. In sum, they could brutally protect the industry and hence their revenue for the local military and local administration which in turn consolidated their rule and enhanced their power projection capabilities across other provinces.

Moreover, this authoritarian-friendly market control model for the cement industry could be found in the behaviour of the KMT government in Taiwan after they were driven to the island after losing the civil war in 1949. More interestingly, the new People's Republic in the 1950s also exploited the cement industry in the same manner as discussed. Lacking a big agricultural surplus, the minerals and metals industries became major drivers of the economy and export trades.[7] With relatively advanced equipment left over from the Republican period, the nationalised cement industry basically added value to a very low-value raw material, limestone, and hence contributed to improving the revenue stream to the Central People's Government in its early days. The early Communist economic regime essentially was a monopolistic model with the PRC state effectively becoming the only corporation.

As such, the pan-China state cement industry so formed after 1954 was subsumed within the corporate or legal personality of the entire state. This, of course, was in many ways very similar, but not entirely analogous, to the operation of the cement industry in Sun Yat-sen's Guangzhou. Here, his Nationalist or Guomindang regime had also subsumed the cement industry into this mini-state that they controlled. In this case, the cement industry was unincorporated in its own right but incorporated within that wider municipal or city corporation. Thus, the PRC exhibited a similar development pattern to that of the provincial or warlord model of the Republican period.

Finally, after recounting the history of corporations relating to cement, we arrive at the essence of the story and it is this: immediately after the Chinese Revolution in 1911, the Organic Law of the Provisional Government established the Provincial Government of the Republic of China in Nanjing on 1 January 1912. This short constitutional document established, firstly, a new Republican state, and secondly, a legally recognised state government from which the corporate personality implicitly arises. This *state corporate person*, the Republic of China, grew in power despite political infighting, war and invasion until taking its final shape as defined by the Constitution of the Republic of China which came into effect on Christmas Day of 1946. Yet throughout the reign of the Republic of China, incorporated companies in the commercial form of corporations were tolerated (or even encouraged) by the state. This was a policy of accommodation. However, the new socialist state created on 20 September 1954 by the Constitution of the People's Republic of China. With its ideal of "socialist transformation" explicitly written into the constitution itself, the policy of elimination of commercial corporations was adopted. In this way, the central state recaptured state powers which it had lost since 1911 in three short years between 1954 and 1957. In the end, the result was dramatic because by 1957 there was only one form of corporate or legal personality left in China: the governmental form, and there was only one corporate or legal person that remained: the state in the form of the People's Republic of China.

Notes

1. See Stephen Green and Guy S. Liu. eds., *Exit the Dragon? Privatization and State Control in China*.
2. Frederick Hallis, *Corporate Personality: A Study in Jurisprudence*, p. 244.
3. Albert Feuerwerker, "Industrial Enterprise in Twentieth Century China: The Chee Hsin Cement Co.".
4. Albert Feuerwerker, "Industrial Enterprise in Twentieth-Century China: The Chee Hsin Cement Co.," in *Studies in the Economic History of Late Imperial China*, p. 273.
5. Alfred D. Chandler, Jr., *The Visible Hand*.

6. G. William Skinner, "Presidential Address: The Structure of Chinese History," Skinner correlated long-term regional cycles of growth and decline to macro-regions and his approach is generally acceptable here but this study will stop at the borders of Guangdong Province instead of a larger region.
7. China was the largest producer of tungsten and antimony; Tim Wright, "The Nationalist state and regulation of Chinese industry during the Nanjing decade: Competition and Control in Coal mining".

Appendix

Glossary

Romanisation	*Chinese/Japanese*	*English*
(Pinyin/Hepburn)	*(中文/日本語)*	
Anxing gongsi	安兴公司	Anxing Company
Aomen	澳门	Macao
Asano semento	浅野セメント	Asano Cement of Japan
Asano Shoichiro	浅野総一郎	
bairi weixin	百日维新	The Hundred Days' Reform
Beijing	北京	
Beiping	北平	
Beiyang	北洋	
Beiyang dachen	北洋大臣	Minister of Beiyang
Beiyang jun	北洋军	Beiyang Army
Cao Yutang	曹雨塘	
Caofangwei	草方围	
Cai Shoukang	蔡守康	
Cen Chunxuan	岑春煊	
changjiandu	厂监督	factory supervisor
chaotian	潮田	marine paddies
Chen Jiongming	陈炯明	
Chen Jitang	陈济棠	
Chen Mingshu	陈铭枢	
Chen Youren	陈友人	Eugene Chen
Cheng Tiangu	程天固	

(*continued*)

H. Ko, *The Making of the Modern Chinese State*,
DOI 10.1007/978-981-10-2660-7

(continued)

Romanisation	*Chinese/Japanese*	*English*
(Pinyin/Hepburn)	*(中文/日本語)*	
Cheng Weidu	程韦度	
Chengde	承德	Jahor
Cixi Taihou	慈禧太后	Empress Dowager Cixi
Dabeimen	大北门	Great Northern Gate of Guangzhou
Dalonghao	大隆号	Dalong Company
Daotai	道台	
Dasheng	大生	Dasheng Cotton Mill
Da Qing Lüli	大清律例	Great Qing Code
De Cuilin	德璀琳	Detring, Gustav von
Deng Yanhua	邓彦华	
Dianbao zhongchu	电报总处	Imperial Telegraph Administration
Doudu	都督	Governor-General
Fan Shisheng	范石生	
Feichang shiqi jingji fangan	非常时期经济方案	Economic Programme for the Emergency Period
Feishuyan	飞鼠岩	
Feng Guozhang	馮國璋	
Feng Yuxiang	馮玉祥	
Fudan daxue	复旦大学	Fudan University
gailun	概论	A general survey/discussion
Gang'ao qiaoxian	港澳侨商	Hong Kong, Macao and overseas Chinese investors
Gaoxiong	高雄	Kaohsiung
Gongye zhengce shishi dayao an	工业政策实施大要案	Outline Procedures for the Implementation of Industrial Policy
Gongwuju	工务局	Public Works Bureau
Gongwu juzhang	工务局长	Director of Public Works
guanban	官办	Government-managed/ Government-operated / Official-management
Guangdong	广东	Guangdong Province
Guangdong Henan shimintu chang	广东河南士敏土厂	Guangdong Henan Cement Works
Guangdong Sheng sannian shizheng jihua	广东省三年施政计划	Guangdong Province Three Year Plan
Guangdong Sheng shiye yinhang	广东省实业银行	Guangdong Province Industrial Bank
Guangdong shengying wucan jinlichu	广东省营物产经理处	Guangdong Provincial Products Manager Office
Guangdong shengzhang	广东省长	Governor of Guangdong Province
Guangdong shengzhengfu	广东省政府	Guangdong Provincial Government

(continued)

Romanisation	*Chinese/Japanese*	*English*
(Pinyin/Hepburn)	*(中文/日本語)*	
Guangdong shengzhengfu gongbao	广东省政府公报	Guangdong Provincial Government Gazette
Guangdong Shimintu Chang	广东士敏土厂	Guangdong Cement Works
Guangdong Xicun Shimintu Chang	广东西村士敏土厂	Guangdong Xicun Cement Works
gongsi	公司	company
gongsifa	公司法	Company Law
gongsi zhangcheng	公司章程	Articles of Association
guandu shangban	官督商办	Offical supervision-merchant management
Guangzhou	广州	Canton
Guangzhou Minguo Ribao	广州民国日报	Guangzhou Republican Daily
Guangzhou Shi gongwu zhi shishi jihua	广州市工务之实施计划	City Public Works Execution Plan
Guangzhou Shi gongwu liangnian jihua	广州市工务两年计划	Guangzhou City Public Works Two Year Plan
Guangzhou Shi zhengfu	广州市政府	Guangzhou City Government
Guangzhou shizheng gongbao	广州市政公报	Guangzhou City Government Gazette
Guangzhou shizhengting	广州市政厅	Guangzhou City Council
Guangzhou Shi shili yinhang	广州市市立银行	The Guangzhou Municipal Bank
Guangzhou Shi zhanlanhui	广州市展览会	Guangzhou City Exhibition
Guangxi	广西	Guangxi Province
Guangxu	光绪皇帝	Emperor Guangxu
Guangxue Hui	广学会	The Society for the Diffusion of Christian and General Knowledge
guanli	官利	guaranteed dividend
Guanyinshan	观音山	
Guizhou	贵州	Guizhou Province
guohuo	国货	National Product
Guohuo tuixiao chu	国货推销处	National Product Sales Office
Guojia zongdongyuan weiyuanhui	国家总动员设计委员会	National Mobilisation Planning Commission
Guoli Guangdong daxue	国立广东大学	National Guangdong University

(*continued*)

(continued)

Romanisation	*Chinese/Japanese*	*English*
(Pinyin/Hepburn)	*(中文/日本語)*	
Guomindang	国民党	Nationalist Party
Guomin zhengfu	国民政府	Nationalist Government
Gu Yingfen	古应芬	
Haizhu qiao	海珠桥	Pearl River Bridge
Hankou	汉口	
Han Jiang	漢江	Han River
Hanyang	汉阳	
Hanyeping	汉冶萍	
Hanzu	汉族	Han Nationality
heban qiye	合办企业	cooperative enterprise
Hebei Pingyuan	河北平原	North China Plain
Henan	河南	
He Qi	何启	Sir Kai Ho Kai
Hongmian Yanluo	红面阎罗	Red-faced Pluto
Hu Hanmin	胡汉民	
Hua Runquan	华润泉	
Huadong meikuang gongsi	华东煤矿公司	East China Coal Mining Company
Huang Chengyu	黄成玉	
Huangpu Junxiao	黄埔军校	Whampoa Military Academy
Huaxian	花县	
Hu Jixian	胡继贤	
Hubei	湖北	Hubei Province
Huigong yintuan	惠工银团	Huigong Capital Syndicate
Huiqun Gonsi	惠群公司	Huiqun Company
Huizhou	惠州	
Jiang Jieshi	蒋介石	Chiang Kai-shek
Jiang Shanshou	江山寿	
Jianguo fanglüe: shiye jihua	建国方略:实业计划	The International Development of China
Jiansheting	建设厅	Provincial Construction Department
Jiawang meikuang	贾汪煤矿	Jiawang Coal Mining Company
ju	局	bureaus/offices
Junji dachen	军机大臣	Grand Councillor
Kailuan Kuangwu ju	开滦矿务局	Kailuan Coal Administration
Kailuan meikuang	开滦煤矿	Kailuan coal mines
Kaiping	开平	
Kaiping meikuang	开平煤矿	Kaiping coal mines
Kaiping kuangwuju youxian gongsi	开平矿务局有限公司	Chinese Engineering and Mining Company Limited
Kang Youwei	康有为	

(continued)

Romanisation	Chinese/Japanese	English
(Pinyin/Hepburn)	(中文/日本語)	
Kong Xiangxi	孔祥熙	H. H. Kung
Kunde	昆德	Hans Günther
Luanzhou	滦州	
Li Bake	李拔可	
Li Desan	李德三	
Li Hongzhang	李鸿章	
Li Timotai	李提摩太	Timothy Richard
Li Ximing	李希明	
Li Zhongren	李宗仁	
Liang Qichao	梁启超	
Liang Shiyi	梁士诒	
Liangguang	两广	The provinces of Guangdong-Guangxi
Liangguang Yanyun Shishu	两广盐运使署	Guangdong-Guangxi Salt Administration
Lijin	厘金	Likin
Lin Yuezhi	林乐知	Young John Allen
Lin Yungai	林云陔	
Liu Hongsheng	刘鸿生	Liu Ong Sung
Liu Jiesheng	刘吉生	Lieu Kyih Sung
Liu Jiwen	刘纪文	
Liu Juke	刘鞠可	
Liu Ping	刘平	
Liu Ruilin	刘瑞麟	
Liu Yanhua	刘彦华	
Long mai	龙唛	Dragon brand
Lu Yinfu	陆荫孚	
Luanzhou	滦州	
Lunchuan Zhaoshangju	轮船招商局/招商局	China Merchants' Steam Navigation Company
Lujun junzhang	陆军军长	Army Commander
Lujun zhongzhang	陆军总长	Commander of the Infantry
Luo Songfan	罗嵩藩	
lunshuo	论说	discourse essay
Ma Chaojun	马超俊	
Manzhou	满洲	Manchuria
Manzu	满族	Manchu
Mingzhi weixin/Meiji Ishin	明治維新	Meiji Restoration
Mo Lin	墨林	Charles Algernon Moreing
Nantong	南通	

(*continued*)

(continued)

Romanisation	*Chinese/Japanese*	*English*
(Pinyin/Hepburn)	*(中文/日本語)*	
Nanjing	南京	
Nandi	南堤	
Neizheng zhongzhang	内政总长	Interior Minister
Nonggongshang bu	农工商部	Ministry of Agriculture, Industry and Commerce
Peng Hui	彭回	
Puyi	溥仪	Emperor Puyi
Puyi gongsi	普益公司	Puyi Company
Qian Jinghui	钱镜辉	
Qianzhuang	钱庄	
Qing huangchao	清皇朝	Qing Dynasty
Qinghua daxue	请华大学	Tsinghua University
Qixin	启新	(Chee Hsin Cement Company)
Qu Hongji	瞿鸿禨	
Rong Lu	荣禄	
Sa Zhenbing	薩鎮冰	
shamian dao	沙面岛	Shamian Island
Shandong	山东	Shandong Province
shangban	商办	merchant-managed/merchant-operated
shangban gongyong shiye	商办公用事业	privately managed public enterprises
Shangbu	商部	Bureau of Commerce
Shanghai	上海	Shanghai
Shanghai Huashang Shuini Gufen Youxian Gongsi	上海华商水泥股份有限公司	Shanghai Portland Cement Works Company Limited
Shanhou ju	善后局	Reconstruction Bureau
Shanxi bu yong dao	山西补用道	Shanxi Assistant *Daotai*
Shehuizhuyi gaizao	社会主义改造	Socialist transformation
Shen Hongying	沈鸿英	
Shenbao	申报	The Shenbao Newspaper
shengli	省例	Provincial statutes
Shengying gongye shenhe weiyuanhui	省营工业审核委员会	Provincial Industrial Audit Committee
Sheng Xuanhuai	盛宣怀	
shiban	市办	city-operated/city-managed
Sichuan Sheng	四川省	Sichuan Province
shilipai	实力派	military faction
Shimintu yingye chu	士敏土营业处	Cement sales office
Shiye ting	实业厅	Enterprise Department
Shiqiu pai	狮球牌	Lion & Globe brand

(continued)

Romanisation	*Chinese/Japanese*	*English*
(Pinyin/Hepburn)	*(中文/日本語)*	
Shiying shiye gailun	市营事业概论	A General Survey of Municipal Enterprises
Shizheng gongbao	市政公报	City Government Gazette
Shizheng ting	市政厅	City council
Shi zizhifa	市自治法	Municipal Organisation Law
Shi zizhi zhi	市自治制	Municipal Autonomy System
shougui guoyou	收归国有	nationalisation
Si jing pin tang	四京品堂	Court of Sacrificial Worship
Song Ziwen	宋子文	T. V. Soong
Sun Ke	孙科	
Sun Zhongshan	孙中山(孙逸仙)	Sun Yat-sen
Tangxu tielu	唐胥铁路	Tangxu Railway
Taiping tianguo	太平天国	Taiping Heavenly Kingdom
Tangshan	唐山	Tangshan City
Tangshan	汤山	
Tan Sitong	谭嗣同	
Tang Shaoyi	唐绍仪	
Tang Tingshu	唐廷枢	
taizipai	太子派	Princeling faction
Ti	体	substance, essence
Tianjin	天津	
Tiaozheng zhongyang xingzheng jigou ling	调整中央行政机构令	Central Administrative Organs Reorganisation Order
Tieliang	铁良	Tie-lang
Tielu zhonggongsi	铁路总公司	National Railway Company
Tongmenghui	同盟会	The Chinese League
Tongzhi	同治	
Tongzhi Zhongxing	同治中兴	Tongzhi Restoration
Yu Ruiyun	余瑞云	
Wanzai	灣仔	Wanchai
Wang Jianxun	王建训	
Wang Jingwei	汪精卫	
Wang Wenzhao	王文韶	
Wanguo Gongbao	万国公报	The Review of the Times
Wei Ying	威英	T. R. Wynne
weitian	围田	inland paddies
Weng Wenhao	翁文灏	
Wenlan shuyuan	文澜书院	Wenlan College
Wenyuan jiujia	文园酒家	Wenyuan Restaurant
Wu Chaoshu	伍朝枢	

(continued)

(continued)

Romanisation	*Chinese/Japanese*	*English*
(Pinyin/Hepburn)	*(中文/日本語)*	
Wu Tingfang	伍廷芳	
Wuchang	武昌	
Wuhan	武漢	
Wuyangpai	五羊牌	Five Rams brand
Xianfeng	咸丰皇帝	Emperor Xianfeng
Xiangxiajiu	上下九	
Xie Peide	谢培德	
Xing'an huilan	刑案汇览	The Conspectus of Penal Cases
Xinjun	新军/新建陆军	New Army
Xiangshan	香山	
Xicun	西村	Xicun area of Guangzhou
Xicun shimintu chang	西村士敏土厂	Xicun Cement Works
Xiguan	西关	Western Suburbs
Xingzhonghui	兴中会	Revive China Society
Xinchou tiaoyue	辛丑条约	Boxer Protocol
Xinzheng	新政	New Policy
Xu Chongzhi	许崇智	
Xu Jing'an	徐静安	
Xu Run	徐润	
Yan Xishan	閻錫山	
Yang Tianshi	杨天石	
yanli	盐厘	Salt tax
Yanghuihang tongye lianjutang	洋灰行同业连聚堂	Cement Merchants Trade Association
Yangwu	洋务	Overseas affairs
Yangzi Jiang	扬子江	Yangtze River
Yangwu yundong	洋务运动	Self-Strengthening Movement
Yihetuan	义和团	Boxer
Yihetuan zhiluan	义和团之乱	Boxer Rebellion
Yikuang	庆亲王奕劻	Prince Qing
yong	用	function, utility
Yu Guocheng	郁国城	
Yu Shouyi	于守一	
Yuan Keding	袁克定	
Yuan Shikai	袁世凱	
yuanlao pai	元老派	elders' faction
Yue Haiguan Shu	粤海关署	Guangdong Customs
Yue Haiguan Sifu	粤海关司库	Guangdong Customs Office
Yuejun zongsiling	粤军总司令	Commander-in-chief of the Guangdong Military Forces
Yungui	云贵	The provinces of Yunan and Guizhou

(continued)

Romanisation	Chinese/Japanese	English
(Pinyin/Hepburn)	*(中文/日本語)*	
Yunnan	云南	Yunnan Province
Yuexiu Shan	越秀山	
Zai Zhen	载振	
zeli	则例	regulations
Zeng Guofan	曾国藩	
Zhang Cha	张察	
Zhang Jian	张謇	
Zhang Renjun	张人骏	
Zhang Xun	張勛	
Zhang Yi	张翼	
Zhang Zhidong	张之洞	
Zhang Zhuyin	张祖荫	
zhaoshang chengban	招商承办	merchant-operated
Zhaoshang chu	招商处	Offices for the recruitment of merchants
Zhaoshanju	招商局/轮船招商局	China Merchants' Steam Navigation Company
Zhenxing gongsi	振兴公司	Zhenxing Company
Zhiqiang yundong	自强运动	Self-Strengthening Movement
Zhili	直隶	Zhili Province
Zhili zongdu	直隶总督	Viceroy of Zhili
Zhiyuan weiyuanhui yu ge sheng (shi) zhengfu heban shiye tongze	资源委员会与各省（市）政府合办事业通则	General Principles of Cooperation between the NRC and Provincial (Municipal) Governments
Zhonghua Minguo Linshi Zhengfu Zuzhi Dagang	中华民国临时政府组织大纲	Organic Law of the Provisional Government of the Republic of China
Zhonghua Minguo Xianfa	中华民国宪法	Constitution of the Republic of China
Zhonghua Minguo Linshi Yuefa	中华民国临时约法	Provisional Constitution of the Republic of China or the Organic Law of the Provisional Government
Zhonghua Minguo Xunzheng Shiqi Yuefa	中华民国训政时期约法	Provisional Constitution of the Republic of China for the Period of Political Tutelage
Zhonghua Renmin Gongheguo Xianfa	中华人民共和国宪法	Constitution of the People's Republic of China

(*continued*)

(continued)

Romanisation	*Chinese/Japanese*	*English*
(Pinyin/Hepburn)	*(中文/日本語)*	
Zhongshan dianying yuan	中山电影院	Sun Yat-sen Cinema
Zhou Dongsheng	周东生	
Zhou Enlai	周恩来	
Zhou Fu	周馥	
Zhou Xuexi	周学熙	
Zhu Qinglan	朱庆澜	

Abbreviations

CCWJ	He Ping and Li Ludian. *Cen Chunxuan wenji* (The Collected Writings of Cen Chunxuan). Nanning: Guangxi renmin chubanshe, 1998
CPC-GZM	*Zhongyang zhengzhi huiyi Guangzhou fen hui yuekan* (The Central Political Conference Guangzhou Branch Conference monthly)
GDGB	*Guangdong Sheng zhengfu gongbao* (The Provincial Government Gazette)
GDQXX	Guangdong Sheng qingxinxi ku (Guangdong Province Information Bank)
GXGZ	*Gongshang xingzheng guanlizhi* (The Industrial and Commercial Administrative Management Gazette)
GZCA	*Guangzhou Shi dang'an guan* (Guangzhou City Archive)
GZGB	*Guangzhou Shizheng Gongbao* (The Guangzhou City Government Gazette)
GZSZ	*Guangzhou Shi Zhi* (Guangzhou City Gazetteer)
KMS	Xiong Xingmei and Yan Guanghua, comp. *Kailuan Meikuang Kuangquan Shiliao* (Historical Materials on the Mining Rights of the Kailuan Coal Mines). Tianjin: Nankai Daxue Chunbanshe, 2004
LHS	Shanghai shehui kexueyuan jingji yanjiusuo (The Institute of Economics of the Shanghai Chinese Academy of Social Science), comp. *Liu Hongsheng*

H. Ko, *The Making of the Modern Chinese State*,
DOI 10.1007/978-981-10-2660-7

	qiye shiliao (Historical Materials of Liu Hongsheng's Industrial Enterprises) Shanghai, Shanghai renmin chubanshe, 1981
Nanjing Archive	The Second Historical Archives of China, Nanjing
QXGS	Nankai daxue jingji yanjiusuo, Jinji xi (The department of economic research of the faculty of economics, Nakai University), comp. *Qixin Yanghui Gongsi shiliao* (Historical Materials of the Qixin Cement Company). Beijing: Shenghuo, dushu, xinzhi sanlian shudian, 1963
RCC4	Zhongguo di er lishi dang'an guan (The Second Historical Archives of China), Zhonghua minguo shi dang'an ziliao hui bian di si ji: Cong Guangzhou jun zhengfu zhi Wuhan guomin zhengfu (Republican China: A Collection of Archival Documents. v. 4: From the Guangzhou Military Government to the Wuhan National Government). Nanjing: Jiangsu guji chubanshe 1986
SZWBB	Hao Shengchao and Wang Gengxiong, eds. *Sun Zhongshan ji wai ji bu bian* (The Supplementary Text Collection to Sun Yat-sen's Extra-Collection). Shanghai: Shanghai renmin chubanshe, 1994
WQJB	Li Yunjun. *Wan Qing Jingji Shishi Bian Nian* (The Late Qing Economic Chronicle). Shanghai: Shanghai guji chubanshe, 2000
ZJGS3	Chen Zhen ed., *Zhongguo jindai gongye shi ziliao: di san ji* (Historical Materials on Modern Chinese Industrial History Part 3). Beijing: Shenghuo, Dushu, Xinzhi Sanlian shudian, 1957–1961, 1957–1961
ZXJ	Yu Heping and Xia Liangcai, comps. *Zhou Xuexi ji* (Collected Works of Zhou Xuexi). Wuhan: Huazhong shifan daxue chubanshe, 1999

Bibliography

Primary Sources

Articles 4–6, the constitution of the People's Republic of China of 1954, see Liu Shao-chi. 1962. *Report on the Draft Constitution of the People's Republic of China*. Peking: Foreign Language Press.

Beiyang dachen Li Hongzhang gei Kaiping Kuangwuju Tang Tingshu de zha chi (Short order issued by Viceroy Li Hongzhang, Commissioner of the Northern Ports to Tang Tingshu). *QXGS*, p. 19.

Bing Zhi du Yuan Tangshan yanghui gongsi gufen zhao qi gengming ni zhang qing zi bu li'an wen (Submission to the Viceroy of Zhili concerning opening a case file concerning the drafting of the Articles of Association of the Tangshan Cement Joint Stock Company upon full subscription of issue shares) 26th August, 1907. *ZXJ*, pp. 228–236.

Cai zheng weiyuanhui han (Letter from the Finance Committee), 8th July 1924. In *Zhonghua minguo shi dang'an ziliao hui bian di si ji cong Guangzhou jun zhengfu zhi Wuhan guomin zhengfu* (Republican China: A collection of archival documents. Vol. 4, from the Guangzhou Military Government to the Wuhan National Government, hereafter *Zhonghua minguo shi dang'an ziliao*), ed. Zhongguo di er lishi dang'an guan, 1509–1511. Nanjing: Jiangsu guji chubanshe 1986.

Campbell, F. A. 1904 nian 1 yue 18 ri Ying waiwu ciguan Kang Baier zhidian Kaiping gonsi mishu han (Letter from the Under-Secretary of Foreign Affairs F. A. Campbell to the Chinese Engineering and Mining Company Limited 18th January 1904). *KMS*, p. 254.

Cassell, Henry C. *Guide to the industrialization of China*, 2nd edn. Nanjing Archive NRC 28(13) 113.

H. Ko, *The Making of the Modern Chinese State*,
DOI 10.1007/978-981-10-2660-7

Chen Jitang and Lin Yungai. 2002. "The Guangdong Three Year Plan" reprinted in Xiao Zili, *Chen Jitang*, 529. Guangzhou: Guangdong renmin chubanshe.

Chen Yun. Shehui zhuyi gaizhao jiben wancheng yihou de xin wenti (New problems after the near completion of socialist transformation). *Renmin ribao* (People's Daily), 21st September 1956, reprinted in *Zhongguo Ziben zhuyi gong-shangye de shehui zhuyi gaizao: Zhongyang juan* (The socialist transformation of capitalist industrial and commercial sector of China: Central government volume), p. 1199.

Chen Zhen, ed. 1957–1961. *Zhongguo jindai gongye shi ziliao: di san ji* (Historical materials on modern Chinese industrial history Part 3). Beijing: Shenghuo, Dushu, Xinzhi Sanlian shudian.

Cheng Tiangu. 1993. *Cheng Tiangu huiyilu* (The Memoir of Cheng Tiangu). Taipei: Longwen chubanshe.

Chinese Engineering and Mining Company Limited. Kaiping Kuangwu youxian gongsi sheli zhangcheng, 1900 nian 12 yue 20 ri (The Memorandum and Articles of Association of the Chinese Engineering and Mining Company Limited, 20th December 1900). *KMS*, pp. 140–144.

Detring, Gustav. 1898 nian 8 yue 14 ri De Cuilin zhi Mo Lin han (Letter from Gustav Detring to Charles Moreing, 14th August 1898). *KMS*, pp. 54–55.

Editor. 1993. You zhunbei, you buzhou di tuidong siying gongye shixing quan hangye gongsi heying (A well prepared and methodologically organised establishment of state-private cooperative ventures for private industries in all industrial sectors). *Renmin ribao* (People's Daily), 25th November 1955 reprinted in Li Qing et al. eds., *Zhongguo Ziben zhuyi gong-shangye de shehui zhuyi gaizao: Zhongyang juan* (The socialist transformation of capitalist industrial and commercial sector of China: Central government volume). Beijing: Zhongguo dangshi chubanshe, p. 97.

Fan Shisheng. 1986. Fan Shisheng zhi Dayuanshuai han (Letter from Fan Shisheng to the Generalissimo) (1st July 1924). *Zhonghua minguo shi dang'an ziliao hui bian di si ji cong Guangzhou jun zhengfu zhi Wuhan guomin zhengfu* (Republican China: a collection of archival documents. Vol. 4, from the Guangzhou Military Government to the Wuhan National Government), ed. Zhongguo di er lishi dang'an guan, 1509–1511. Nanjing: Jiangsu guji chubanshe.

GDPG. Guangdong Xicun shimintu chang dongshi hui zushi zhangcheng (The articles of association for the Guangdong & Xicun Cement Works board of directors), Guangdong Xicun shimintu chang zu zhi zhang cheng (The articles of organisation for the Guangdong Xicun shimintu chang), Guangdong Xicun shimintu chang, Henan fen chang zhuzhi zhangcheng, jianli banshi guize (The articles of organisation, and the rules of responsibility and powers for the supervisor at the Guangdong Xicun Cement Works Henan branch factory). *GDGB*, GZCA *zhi/zheng* 134:264, pp. 26–35.

GDPG. Biantong shou yong xinshi shimintu chang changzhi tudi banfa an (The flexible methods for the requistion of land at the decided location for the modern cement works). *GDGB* July 1929. GZCA *zhi/zheng* 114:6, pp. 18–19.

GDPG. Chexiao Guangdong shimintu chang Puyi gongsi cheng an (The case of relinguishing of the contract to operate the Guangdong Cement Work awarded to the Puyi Company). *GDGB* 20 June 1931, GZCA *zhi/zheng* 123:167, p. 137.

GDPG. Chi shu caimai shiqiupai shimintu an (Ordering all departments to purchase Lion & Globe brand cement). *GDGB* 19 August 1930, GZCA *zhi/zheng* 118:121, p. 14.

GDPG. Cheng ban shimitu fu jia daxue jingfei (The collection agreement for the university funding surcharge on cement). *GDGB* 23 September 1937, GZCA *zhi/zheng* 617, p. 206.

GDPG. Cheng Sheng fu cheng fu guanyu Xicun shimintu chang shou yong nanbian shangang (Letter to the Provincial Government in reply to the matter concerning the requistioning of the hills on the southside of the Xicun cement works). *GDGB* 19 April 1933, GZCA *zhi/zheng* 593:425, p. 48.

GDPG. Guangdong shimintu chang chupin mian sui (Exemption from tax for Guangdong manufactured cement). *GDGB* 20 June 1931, GZCA *zhi/zheng* 123:157, p. 87.

GDPG. Guangdong shimintu chang jiang gong fuwu daiyu tiaoli (The Guangdong Cement Works conditions for service for technicians ordinance). *GDGB* 14 November 1931, GZCA *zhi/zheng* 124:172, p. 62.

GDPG. Guangdong shimintu chang yingye chu zuzhi zhangcheng ban shi xize (Detailed rules to the Guangdong cement works sales office articles of organisation). *GDGB* 29 August 1932, GZCA *zhi/zheng* 127:198, pp. 4–5, 86.

GDPG. Guangdong shimintu chang zushi zhangcheng (The Guangdong Cement Works articles of organisation). *GDGB* 19 December 1931, GZCA *zhi/zheng* 125:175, p. 2.

GDPG. Guangdong shimintu yingye chu banli zhuanying shiwu zhangcheng (The Guangdong Cement sales & marketing office monopoly charter). *GDGB* 21 June 1933, GZCA *zhi/zheng* 130:227, p. 6.

GDPG. Guangdong shimintu yingye chu bo lai shimintu bao ling xuke zheng ji daxue fujia fei zhengshou xiji (The Guangdong cement sales & marketing office regulations on the applications for a permit for importing cement and the university funding surcharge on imported cement) and Zhuanying yu dai zheng daxue fujia fei banshi xiji (The regulations for the collection monopoly and collection agency for the university funding surcharge on imported cement). *GDGB* 21 June 1933, GZCA *zhi/zheng* 130:227, pp. 7–13.

GDPG. Guangdong Xicun Henan shimintu chang jianli banshi guize (The rules of responsibility and powers for the Supervisor at the Guangdong & Xicun Cement Works). *GDGB* 17 May 1932, GZCA *zhi/zheng* 126:188, p. 38.

GDPG. Guangdong Xicun shimintu chang dongshihui zuzhi zhangcheng (The articles of association for the Guangdong & Xicun Cement Works board of directors). *GDGB* 10 June 1932, GZCA *zhi/zheng* 126:190, p. 10.

GDPG. Guangdong Xicun shimintu chang zuzhi zhangcheng (The memorandum & articles of association of the Guangdong Xicun shimintu chang). *GDGB* 9 May 1932, GZCA *zhi/zheng* 126:187, p. 36.

GDPG. Guifu Guangdong shimintu chang (Restoring the operation of the Guangdong Cement Work). *GDGB* 12 October 1931, GZCA *zhi/zheng* 124:168, p. 84.

GDPG. Guangzhou Shi zhengfu Guangdong Jiansheting heban Guangdong Henan shimintu chang zhangcheng (The memorandum and articles of association of the Guangzhou City Government & the Construction Department of Guangdong Provincial Government Cooperatively Managed Guangdong Henan Cement Works). *GDGB* 19 December 1931, GZCA *zhi/zheng* 125:175, p. 1.

GDPG. Henan shimintu chang you Jiansheting shou hui zi ban (The management of the Henan Cement Works shall be returned to Construction Department). *GDGB* 24 January 1933 GZCA *zhi/zheng* 129:212, p. 76.

GDPG. Henan Xicun shimintu chang yinye shiwu you jianting she chu banli (The Construction Department shall establish an office to takevoer the sales & marketing of the Henan and Xicun Cement Works). *GDGB* 12 August 1932, GZCA *zhi/zheng* 127:196, p. 116.

GDPG. Hezhun bensheng Xicun Henan liang shimintu yu Anxing gongsi dingli quanquan tuixiao heyue (Approval granted for both Xicun and Henan Cement Works to award complete sales & marketing rights to Anxing company). *GDGB* 19 May 1932, GZCA *zhi/zheng* 126:188, p. 122.

GDPG. Hezhun Guangdong shimintu chang yuangong fuwu guicheng (Approval for the staff employment directive for the Guangdong Cement Works). *GDGB* 18 April 1932, GZCA *zhi/zheng* 126:185, p. 159.

GDPG. Hezhun Guangdong Xicun shimintu chang yuangong fuwu guicheng (Approval for the employment by-law for the Guangdong & Xicun Cement Works). *GDGB* 6 June 1932, GZCA *zhi/zheng* 126:190, p. 100.

GDPG. Hezhun shou yong Xicun shimintu chang beibian diyu wei huaxue gongchang jianzhu dizhi (Approval granted for requistioning adjacent land on the northside of the Xicun cement works for the construction of a chemical plant). *GDGB* 21 October 1932, GZCA *zhi/zheng* 128:203, p. 105.

GDPG. Hezhun Xicun shimintu chang yuangong qingjia guize (Approval granted for by-laws of the Xicun cment works concerning staff vacation leaves). *GDGB* 19 May 1932, GZCA *zhi/zheng* 126:188, p. 122.

GDPG. Hezhun Xicun shimintu chang zeng shou tudi (Allowing the Xicun Cement Works to increase land requistion). *GDGB* 21 July 1930, GZCA *zhi/zheng* 118:113, pp. 34–35.

GDPG. Hezhun zhui jia xinshi shimintu chang buchong jixie fei. (Allowing the increase in machinery expenditure for the modern cement works). *GDGB* 13 December 1930, GZCA *zhi/zheng* 120:138, p. 82.

GDPG. Jia bei zhengshou bo lai shimintu fujia fei choulü (Doubling of the tax rate for the university funding surcharge on imported cement). *GDGB* December 1933 quoted in Xiao Zili, *Chen Jitang*. Guangzhou: Guangdong renmin chubanshe, 2002, p. 332.

GDPG. Ling caizheng ting she zai Xicun xuanze Xicun shimintu chang zhi an (Ordering the Finance Department to choose a site at Xicun for the construction of the Xicun Cement Works). *GDGB* July 1929, GZCA *zhi/zheng* 114:3, p. 41.

GDPG. Ling Jiansheting xuan shang cheng zhu xicun shimintu chang (Ordering the Construction Department to select contractors for the construction of the Xicun Cement Works). *GDGB* 5 June 1930, GZCA *zhi/zheng* 117:99, p. 21.

GDPG. Ling mian Guangdong shimintu chang chupin ge sui (An order to exempt products from the Guangdong Cement Works from all taxes). *GDGB* 4 March 1932, GZCA *zhi/zheng* 125:181, p. 83.

GDPG. Pai Li Luchao wei Guangdong shimintu chang dong shi (Sending Li Luchao to become the Director of the Guangdong Cement Works). *GDGB* 12 May 1932, GZCA *zhi/zheng* 126:187, p. 49.

GDPG. Renming Liu Juke wei Guangdong Xicun shimintu chang zhang (Appointing Liu Juke as the factory manager for the Guangdong Xicun Cement Works). *GDGB* 13 April 1932, GZCA *zhi/zheng* 126:184, p. 23.

GDPG. Shouyong Xicun shimintu chang ce shan di chou ban huaxue gong ye chang (The requistioning of the adjacent hills on the side of the Xicun cement works for the establishment of a chemical factory). *GDGB* 24 November 1932, GZCA *zhi/zheng* 128:207, p. 112.

GDPG. Shouzheng tongzhi shimintu zhangze (Genben banfa, Guangdong shimintu yingyun qudi guize, yinyun shang daili tuixiao shengying shimintu guize, yingyun shang daili tuixiao shengying shimintu jiangli guize, Guangdong Sheng guohuo tuixiao chu shimintu bu gong zuzhi zhangcheng, Guangdongsheng guohuo tuixiao chu shimintu bu fen banshichu zuzhi zhangcheng, Guangdongsheng guohuo tuixiao chun shimintu bu qi huo si shimintu bian jia ji geijiang zhangcheng, Guangdong Sheng guohou tuixiao chu shimintu bu chufa bo lai shimintu si yu zhangcheng, Guangdong Sheng guohuo tuixiao chu shimintu bu gonchang ji fen banshichu banshi xize (The Revised Cement Laws and Regulations under the Unified System (Basic Rules; Regulations banning the sales of cement)); Regulations for cement marketing of the Guangdong Province National Product Sales Office (hereafter GNPSO) Cement Department (hereafter GNPSO-CD); Regulations for agents in the selling of provincially produced cement; Regulations for rewarding agents in selling provincially produced cement; Articles of Association for the GNPSO warehouse; Articles of Association for the GNPSO-CD; GNPSO-CD Charter for pricing and re-selling of confiscated illegal cement and the conferrment of reward; GNPSO-CD Charter for imposing penalty on illegal cement imports; GNPSO-CD warehouse and branch office Rules). *GDGB* 4 October 1934, GZCA *zhi/zheng* 129:211, p. 141.

GDPG. Ting fa gou yun bo lai shimintu mian sui huzhao (The discontinuation of issuing Tax-free Passports for the purchase and transportation of imported cement). *GDGB* 23 September 1934, GZCA *zhi/zheng* 135:272, p. 94.

GDPG. Yijue heping Henan ji Xicun shimintu chang (Reslution for the merging of the Henan and Xicun cement works). *GDGB* 9 May 1933, GZCA *zhi/zheng* 130:223, p. 104.

GDPG. Zhun Dacheng gongsi yi qi xu ban quan sheng bo lai shimin tu fujia daxue jingfei (Renewal of collection rights of the university funding surcharge on imported cement for the Jindacheng company). *GDGB* 29 December 1931, GZCA *zhi/zheng* 125:177, p. 92.

GDQXX. http://www.gd-info.gov.cn:8080/was40/detail?record=2&channelid=58844 & searchword=%B3%CC%CC%EC%B9%CC. Last accessed 1 September 2007.

GDQXX. http://www.gzlib.gov.cn/shequ_info/ndgz/NDGZDetail.do?id=18460. Last accessed 1 November 2008.

GDQXX. http://www.gd-info.gov.cn:8080/was40/outline?page=3&channelid=12084. Last accessed 1 September 2007.

Green Island Cement Holdings Limited. Introduction: Company Profile. *The GIC Website*, http://www.gich.com.hk/Company_Profile/cp_main.htm; Last accessed 26 June 2016.

Guangdong dadoudu (The Governor-General of Guangdong). 1913. Ling heji yuan he ming shimintu chang dinggou dianji yi an wen, (The Order for the Audit Yuan to audit the purchase of eletrical machines by the cement factory). *GDGB* 3 Feb, 1913, GZCA *zhi/zheng* 93:159, pp. 6–7.

Guangdong Sheng jianshe hui bian (Guangdong Provincial Construction consolidated volume). Wu nian lai zhi guangdong jianshe (Construction in Guangdong in the last 5 years). In *Zhongguo jindai gongye shi ziliao: di san ji, Qing zhengfu, Beiyang zhengfu he Guomindang guanliao ziben chuangban he longduan de gongye* (Historical materials of industrial enterprises in China's modern history: Industries established and monopolised by bureaucratic capital of the Beijing Government and the Nationalist Party), ed. Chen Zhen, 1957–1961. Beijing: Shenghuo, Dushu, Xinzhi Sanlian Shudian.

Guangdong Sheng Jiansheting (The office of economic affairs of Guangdong province). 1957–1961. Wu nian lai zhi guangdong jianshe (Construction in Guangdong in the last 5 years). In *Zhongguo jindai gongye shi ziliao: di san ji, Qing zhengfu, Beiyang zhengfu he Guomindang guanliao ziben chuangban he longduan de gongye* (Historical materials of industrial enterprises in China's modern history: Industries established and monopolised by bureaucratic capital of the Beijing Government and the Nationalist Party), ed. Chen Zhen, 325–326. Beijing: Shenghuo, Dushu, Xinzhi Sanlian Shudian.

GZCG. Guangzhou Shi gongwuju qudi shimintu buchong banfa an" (The Guangzhou Government ublic Works Bureau Charter for the Banning of Cement Sales). *GZGB* 26 March 1928, GZCA *zhi/zheng* 585:353, p. 10.

GZCG. Buchong qudi shimintu banfa an Wenlan shuyuan qinghao kuan an (Supplementary Regulations for the Banning of Cement Sales; Drainage cleaning funds of the Wenlan College). *GZGB* 12 April 1928, GZCA *zhi/zheng* 620:15, p. 162.

GZCG. Chufa Dalong hao fanmai wei shimintu (Penalising Dalong company for the sale of counterfeit cement). *GZGB* 17 August 1929, GZCA *zhi/zheng* 584:338, p. 70.

GZCG. Chufa dayi dian weijin fanmai shimintu (Penalising Dayi company for contravening the sales prohibtion for cement). *GZGB* 19 June 1928, GZCA *zhi/zheng* 581:296, p. 61.

GZCG. Fan gong gong jianzhu yi lü gou yong Guangdong shimintu chang zhi tu bing tingzhi fa gei gou yun bo lai shimintu mian sui zhizhao (All public constructions must purchase cement manufactured by the Guangdong cement works and the discontinuation of issuing Tax-free Passports for the purchase and transportation of imported cement). *GDGB* September 1934, GZCA *zhi/zheng* 135:272, p. 102.

GZCG. Gongwuju shiyan shiqiupai shimintu zhi jieguo (Test results from the Public Works Bureau on the Lion & Globe brand cement). *GZGB* 12 August 1930, GZCA *zhi/zheng* 587:370, p. 49.

GZCG. Guangzhou Shi gongwuju qudi shimintu zhangcheng (The Guangzhou Government Public Works Bureau Charter for the Banning of Cement Sales). *GZGB* 26 March 1928, GZCA *zhi/zheng* 585:353, p. 10.

GZCG. Guangzhou Shi qudi fanmai shimintu guize (Guangzhou Municipal Regulations for the Banning of Cement Sales). *GZGB* 29 August 1925, GZCA *zhi/zheng* 576:194, p. 282; Guangzhou City Council, "Gongwuju qudi chan za shimintu guize an" (The case of the Public Works Bureau's regulations prohibiting the amixing of foreign materials in cement). 2 September 1925, GZCA 4-01/1 1:1, p. 117.

GZCG. Guanyu chufa Dade dian fanmai wei tu (Penalising Dalong company for the sale of counterfeit cement). *GZGB* 4 December 1929, GZCA *zhi/zheng* 585:349, p. 69.

GZCG. Guyanyu chufa shimintu shangren Tongde gongsi (Concerning penalisng cement merchant the Tongde Company). *GZGB* 13 November 1929, GZCA *zhi/zheng* 585:347, p. 134.

GZCG. Guanyu fanmai long mai shimintu (Regarding the sales of Dragon brand cement). *GZGB* 13 December 1929, GZCA *zhi/zheng* 585:350, p. 80.

GZCG. Guanyu jin shou long mai shimintu an (Regarding the case of the sales prohibition of the Dragon brand cement). *GZGB* 10 July 1928, GZCA *zhi/zheng* 581:298, pp. 44–46.

GZCG. Guanyu long mai shimintu an (The case concerning the Dragon brand cement). *GZGB* 17 June 1928, GZCA *zhi/zheng* 581:297, p. 37.

GZCG. Guanyu shiyan long mai shimintu an (The case concerning the testing of the Dragon brand cement). *GZGB* 16 November 1929, GZCA *zhi/zheng* 584:347, p. 135.

GZCG. Guanyu shiyan shiqiupai shimintu an (The case concerning the testing of the Lion & Globe brand of cement). *GZGB* 11 December 1930, GZCA *zhi/zheng* 587:374, pp. 57–59.

GZCG. Han fu Jiancha Yuan jiang cha ban fanmai wei lie tu diau qingying ji jiang ni fa ge dian shumu fenbie he qing shimintu dian (Letter in reply to the Control Yuan conerning the matter of investigating merchants selling low quality and counterfeit cement, and the matter of listing the number of merchant businesses to be penalised). *GZGB* 7 December 1925, GZCA *zhi/zheng* 576:280, p. 857.

GZCG. Jishi: Gongwuju shiyan shimintu lali zhi baogao (Record: The Guangzhou Government Public Works Bureau Charter for the Banning of Cement Sales). *GZGB* 20 May 1928, GZCA *zhi/zheng* 580:292, pp. 17–19.

GZCG. Juya si fan wei tu jianshang (Arresting counterfeit selling wicked merchants). *GZGB* May 1930, GZCA *zhi/zheng* 585:353, p. 22.

GZCG. Long mai shimintu zan zhun yunxiao an (The case concerning the temporary lifiting of the prohibition on the sale Dragon brand cement). *GDGB* 21 October 1929, GZCA *zhi/zheng* 584:345, p. 64.

GZCG. Lunshuo: shiying shiye gailun (An Essay: A General Survey of Municipal Enterprises). *GZGB* June 1928, GZCA *zhi/zheng* 581:297, pp. 1–4.

GZCG. Qudi shimintu buchong banfa an (The Supplementary Regulations for the Banning of Cement Sales). *GDGB* 13 March 1928, GZCA *zhi/zheng* 580:287, p. 40.

GZCG. Qudi shimintu buchong banfa an (The case of the Supplementary Regulations for the Banning of Cement Sales). *GZGB* 26 March 1928, GZCA *zhi/zheng* 580:288, p. 34.

GZCG. Shi Xingzheng Huiyi tiyi qudi fanmai shimintu buchong banfa yijian shu. Fu buchong qudi shimintu banfa (Opinon on the Executive Council proposed Supplementary Regulations for the Banning of Cement Sales). *GZGB* 2 March 1928, GZCA *zhi/zheng* 580:286, p. 14.

GZCG. Wenlan shuyuan qinghao kuan an (Drainage cleaning funds of the Wenlan College). *GZGB* 12 April 1928, GZCA *zhi/zheng* 620:15, p. 162.

GZCG. Xicun shimintu chang gengzheng shouyong Zhayougang deng chu diduan (The Xicun cement works made a correction modified the requistionion to that of the locality of Zhayougong and its surrounding land). *GDGB* 13 November 1934, GZCA *zhi/zheng* 600:482, pp. 73–75.

GZCG. Yancheng fanmai wei shimintu shangren (Heavily penalising the merchants for selling counterfeit cement). *GZGB* March 1930, GZCA *zhi/zheng* 585:347, p. 68.

GZCG. Yanfa Dadelong hao deng dian mai wei shimintu an (The case of seriously penalising Dalong company for the sale of counterfeit cement). *GZGB* 12 October 1929, GZCA *zhi/zheng* 584:344, p. 77.

GZCG. Yanjin fanmai wei shimintu (Banning the sale of counterfeit cement). *GZGB* 8 October 1929, GZCA *zhi/zheng* 584:340, p. 37.

GZSZ. 1 August 1929; GZCG, Guanyu jinshou long mai shimintu an (The case concerning the prohibition on the sale Dragon brand cement). *GDGB* 18 August 1929, GZCA *zhi/zheng* 584:339, p. 104.

GZSZ. http://www.gzsdfz.org.cn/gzsz/20/rw/gz20rw030201.htm; Last accessed 1 September 2007.

GZSZ. http://www.gzsdfz.org.cn/gzsz/02/dsj/sz02dsj0222.htm; Last accessed 1 September 2007.

GZSZ. http://www.gzsdfz.org.cn/gzsz/21/fl/sz21fl0301.htm; Last accessed 1 September 2007.

GZSZ. Xicun shimintu chang, di-yi ci jinxing kuojian touchan (Start of production after the first exapansion of the Xicun Cement Works). April 1935.

Hao Shengchao and Wang Gengxiong, eds. 1994. *Sun Zhongshan ji wai ji bu bian* (The supplementary text collection to Sun Zhongshang extra-collection). Shanghai: Shanghai renmin chubanshe.

Hebei juan bianshen weiyuanhui bian (Hebei juan editorial committee), ed. 1991. *Zhongguo zibenzhuyi gongshangye de shehuizhuyi gaizao: Hebei juan* (The socialist transformation of the capitalist industrial and commercial sector of China: vol. on Hebei province). Beijing: Zhonggong dang shi chubanshe.

Huashang Shanghai shuini chang chengli (Establishing the Shanghai Portland Cement Works, Limited). *LHS*, v. 1, p. 158.

Jiansheting, Chou ban xinshi shimintu chang jiekuan hetong (Loan agreement for the construction of a modern cement works). *GDGB* July 1929, GZCA *zhi/zheng* 114:9, pp. 18–21.

Jiemi 73 sui Mao Zedong zuihou yici changyou Changjiang guocheng (Lifting the veil: what happened to Mao Zedong's final swim across the Yangtze River at 73 years old) on *Xinliang dushu* (Sina Books), 23rd June 2008, http://book.sina.com.cn/Jiyizhongdeyingxiang/excerpt/sz/2008-06-23/1859239084.shtml. Last accessed 8th October, 2008.

Judgement of the Chancery Division, High Court of Justice delivered on 1st March 1905. *KMS*, pp. 275–284.

Kaiping kuangwu youxian gongsi shang Yuan gongbao bing (Chinese Engineering and Mining Company, Limited reporting to Yuan Shikai, Guardian of the Palace. *QXGS*, p. 27.

Kaiping kuangwu youxian gongsi shangbing gongbao (Report submitted to Yuan Skikai, Guardian of the Palace, by the Chinese Engineering and Mining Company, Limited), 12th June 1906. *QXGS*, p. 29.

Kaiping Lushi Meng Shen and Gan boshi de laixin (Letter from Kaiping's lawyers Meng Shen and Dr. Gan), 3rd September 1906. *QXGS*, p. 33.

Kuangwu ju fu zongli laixin (Letter from the Assistant general manager of the China Mining and Engineering Company), 23rd August 1906. *QXGS*, p. 32.

Letter from Detring to Zhou Xuexi, 24th September 1906. *QXGS*, p. 35.

Letter from Zhou Xuexi to Detring attached to the reply: "Wei yu De Cuilin wen se shi bing Yuan Shikai," 26th September 1906. *ZXJ*, p. 224.

Li Hongzhang gei Tang Tingshu de pishi (the opinion given by Li Hongzhang to Tang Tingshu) 1889. *QXGS*, p. 22.

Li Lushan. An Account of the Wenlan College of Xiguan. *GZSZ*; http://www.gzsdfz.org.cn/ycjg/shgc/shgc126.htm; Last accessed 1 September 2007.

Li Xuetong. 1996. *Shusheng congzheng: Weng Wenhao* (An Academic in Politics: Wen Wenhao). Lanzhou: Lanzhou daxue chubanshe.

Li Yu. 2007. *Beiyang zhengfu shiqi qiye zhidu jiegou shilun* (On the structure of the corporate system in modern China governed by the northern warlords), 107–147. Beijing: Shehui kexue wenxian chubanshe.

Lin Yungai. Baohu huaqiao hui guo yu ban shiye an (The protection of returning Overseas Chinese and their investment in industries). *GZGB* 16 November 1929, GZCA *zhi/zheng* 585:347, pp. 120–121.

Lin Yungai. Weichi zhengfu zhi shimintu chang yingye an (The case of the continution of the carrying on of the government cement business). *GZGB*, 14 April 1928, GZCA *zhi/zheng* 580:290, p. 39.

Lin Yungai. Zou ban Guangdong shimintu chang gongwen shimo jilüe, di er juan (A brief description of memorials to the imperial court for the establishing of the Guangdong Cement Works, hereafter Establishing the GCW) *Zhongguo jindai gongye shi ziliao: di san ji* (Historical materials on modern Chinese industrial history Part 3), pp. 332–333.

Lin Yungai. Establishing the GCW. In *Zhongguo jindai gongye shi ziliao: di san ji* (Historical materials on modern Chinese industrial history, Part 3), ed. Chen Zhen, 332.

Liu Linrui. 1957–1961b. Guangdong shimintu chang chongjian choukuan kaiban shimo jilüe di si juan (A brief account of the financing arrangement for the establishement of the Guangdong Cement Works). In *Zhongguo jindai gongye shi ziliao: di san ji, Qing zhengfu, Beiyang zhengfu he Guomindang guanliao ziben chuangban he longduan de gongye* (Historical materials of industrial enterprises in China's modern history: Industries established and monopolised by bureaucratic capital of the Beijing Government and the Nationalist Party), ed. Chen Zhen, 328. Beijing: Shenghuo, Dushu, Xinzhi Sanlian Shudian.

———. 1957–1961. Establishing the GCW. In *Zhongguo jindai gongye shi ziliao: di san ji, Qing zhengfu, Beiyang zhengfu he Guomindang guanliao ziben chuangban he longduan de gongye* (Historical materials of industrial enterprises in China's modern history: Industries established and monopolised by bureaucratic capital of the Beijing Government and the Nationalist Party), ed. Chen Zhen, 332–333. Beijing: Shenghuo, Dushu, Xinzhi Sanlian Shudian.

Ma Chaojun. Chou she xinshi shimintu chang (Preparation for establishing a modern cement works). *CPC-GZM*, 12 October 1928, GZCA *zhi/zheng* 620:15, p. 162.

Malenkov, G. M. Gaijin zhong de Sulian gongye guanli (The improving industrial management of the Soviet Union). In *Ziyuan weiyuanhui gongbao* (The Gazette of the National Resource Commission), 1:1 August 1941.

Minguo Ribao (The Daily Republic), 5th October 1924.

Mo Yinggui. 1987. Yinjin qiao zi suo yi (Fragmented recollections of measures in attracting overseas Chinese investments) collected in *Nan tian sui yue: Chen Jitang zhu yue shiqi jianwen shilu* (The days under the southern skies: eyewitness accounts during the rule of Chen Jitang), compiled by Guangzhou Shi zheng xie wenshi ziliao yanjiu weiyuanhui (Guangzhou CPPCC *wenshi ziliao* research committee). Guangzhou: Guangdong renmin chubanshe, Guangdong Sheng Xinhua shudian.

Nankai daxue jingji yanjiusuo, Jinji xi (The department of economic research of the faculty of economics, Nakai University) comp. 1963. *Qixin Yanghui Gongsi shiliao* (Historical materials of the Qixin Cement Company). Beijing: Shenghuo, dushu, xinzhi sanlian shudian.

NRC. Ziyuan weiyuanhui yu ge sheng shi zhengfu heban shiye tongze (The general principle of cooperation between the NRC and provincial and city governments). In *Ziyuan weiyuanhui gongbao* (The Gazette of the National Resource Commission), 15:2 August 1948, pp. 19–20.

Quanguo wenhua xinxi ziyuan gongxiang gongcheng (National cultural information resources sharing project); http://www.ndcnc.gov.cn/datalib/2003/Character/DL/DL20031227130316. Last accessed 28 August 2008.

Trone, S. Industrialization of China. Nanjing Archive NRC 28 v. 4 No.18382.

Trone S. Letter to his Excellency, Dr. T. V. Soong, Minister of Foreign Affairs, Chongqing, Feb 9th 1944. Nanjing Archive NRC 28 v. 4 No.18382.

Shanghai Shi gangwu guanliju diyi zhuangxie qu tigong ziliao (Information supplied by the Port Authority of Shanghai). *LHS*, v. 1, p. 49.

Shanghai shuini chang tigong ziliao (Information supplied by the Shanghai Portland Cement Works). *LHS*, v. 1, p. 157.

Shanghai shuini chang yange (The development of the Shanghai Cement Works, Limited). *LHS*, pp. 76–77.

Shanghai shuini gonsi dan'an (Files from the archives of the Shanghai Portland Cement Works, Limited). *LHS*, v. 1, p. 158.

Shen Minte and Fang Guorong. 1999. *Jiangnan weidao*. Nanfang chubanshe: Haikou.

Statement of claim filed at the High Court of Justice, Chancery Division: His Excellency Chang Yen-mao and the Chinese Engineering and Mining Company of Tientsin (plaintiffs) and Chales Algernon Moreing, Bewick Moreing & Company, and the Chinese Engineering and Mining Company, Limited (defendants). *KMS*, pp. 239–246.

Sun Ke. Shun ling Gongwu Ju zhun shimintu song lai xin tu yang shiyan you (Ordering the Public Works Bureau to test the new cement). *GDGB* March 1924, GZCA *zhi/zheng* 573:124, pp. 29–30.

Sun Zhongshan. 1930. *Jian guo fang lüe* (The International Development of China). 10th ed. Shanghai: Shangwu yinshu guan.

———. 1993. Dayuanshuai chanjun chu zhi shimintu chang Sun zong ban han (A letter from the Generalissimo military office to the General Manager Mr. Sun of the cement works). In Ruixiang Tang, *Sun Zhongshan yu hufa haijun lunji* (Collected essays on Sun Yat-sen and the Constitution Protection Navy). Guangzhou: Guangdong gaodeng jiaoyu chubanshe.

———. 1994a. She chou liangxiang zongju tongling (General order to establish the command bureau for military food supply). In *Sun Zhongshan ji wai ji bu bian* (The Supplement to the Extra Collection of the Sun Yat-sen Collection), ed. Hao Shengchao and Wang Gengxiong, 377. Shanghai: Shanghai renmin chubanshe.

———. 1994b. Tongyi caizheng de tongling (The General Unified Financial Order) 3rd February 1924. In *Sun Zhongshan ji wai ji bu bian* (The supplementary text collection to Sun Zhongshang extra-colletction), compiled by Hao Shengchao and Wang Gengxiong. Shanghai: Shanghai renmin chubanshe.

Tang Tingshu gei Li Hongzhang de bingtie (The report from Tang Tingshu to Li Hongzhang). *QXGS*, p. 22.

The 1948 Report of the Cement Business. Nanjing Archive: NRC 28 (2) No. 3269.

Tian. 1908 nian 5 yue 8 ri Zhili Zhongdu Yang Shixiang zha Luanzhou gongsi wen (The despatch from the Governor-General of Zhili Yan Shixiang to the Luanzhou company, 8th May 1908). *KMS*, pp. 323–326.

Tianjin dang'an wang (The Tianjin Archives Web), http://www.tjdag.gov.cn/daby/daby_lssdjt_xiangxi.asp?n_id=1604. Last accessed 21 March 2008.

Tianjin Shi dang'an guan. 1990. *Yuan Shikai Tianjin dang'an shiliao xuan bian* (The selected historical materials of Yuan Shikai at the Tianjin Archive). Tianjin: Tianjin guji chubanshe.

University of Kentucky. Tang, Ming and Qing Codes. *Journal of Asian History* web page. http://jalh.ku.edu/chinese_law_codes.htm. Last accessed 16 June 2009.

Wei choucuo zijin wancheng jianchang, Liu Hongsheng churen zongjingli (Raising capital to finish construction of the factory and Liu Hongsheng assuming the post of general manager). *LHS*, v. 1, p. 158.

Wei yu De Cuilin wen se shi bing Yuan Shikai, 26th September 1906. *ZXJ*, p. 224.

Wen Wenhao. NRC Steps Up Chinese Industrialization. *China Economist*, May 31, 1948, v. 1, No. 9. Nanjing Archive NRC 28(3)–28(18) No. 331.

Weng Wenhao. Jing Jian fangxiang yu gongtong zeren (The direction of the economic construction and collective responsibility). In *Ziyuan weiyuanhui gongbao* (The Gazette of the National Resource Commission), 2:1 August 1942, pp. 79–84.

Wo guo shuini gongye huifu jihua dagang chaoan (The draft outline plan for the reviving of our nation's cement industry) 1949. Nanjing Archive NRC 28 v. 3 No. 17433.

Xi Anzhai. The oral testimony of Xi Anzhai of April 1960. *LHS* v. 1.

Xian Zien. 1987. Ban tang chang jingguo ji qi zhen xiang (The experience and realities of operating the sugar factory) collected in *Nan tian sui yue: Chen Jitang zhu yue shiqi jianwen shilu* (The days under the southern skies: eyewitness accounts during the rule of Chen Jitang) compiled by Guangzhou Shi zhengxie wenshi ziliao yanjiu weiyuanhui (Guangzhou CPPCC *wenshi ziliao* research committee), 245. Guangzhou: Guangdong renmin chubanshe, Guangdong Sheng Xinhua shudian.

Xie Peide. Xie Peide koushou (The oral testimony of Xie Peide) of February 1959. *LHS* v. 1.

Xie Yingming. 1987. Shengying gongye gaikuang ji yishu (A general account of provincial operated industries) collected in *Nan tian sui yue: Chen Jitang zhu yue shiqi jianwen shilu* (The days of southern skies: eyewitness accounts during the rule of Chen Jitang), compiled by Guangzhou Shi zhengxie wenshi ziliao yanjiu weiyuanhui (Guangzhou CPPCC *wenshi ziliao* Historical Materials research committee). Guangzhou: Guangdong renmin chubanshe, Guangdong Sheng Xinhua shudian.

Xiong Xingmei and Yan Guanghua. 2004. *Kailuan Meikuang Kuangquan shiliao* (Historical materials of the Kailuan coal-mines mining rights). Tianjin: Nankai daxue chubanshe.

Xu Chongde. 2003. *Zhonghua Renmin Gongheguo xianfa shi*. Fuzhou: Fujian renmin chubanshe.

Yi jiu er er nian jiu yue shisi ri Huashang Shanghai Shuini Gongsi di shiyi ci dongshihui huiyi jilu (The Minutes of the 11th Director's Meeting at the Shanghai Portland Cement Works, Limited on 14th September 1922). *LHS*, v. 1, p. 164.

Yi jiu er jiu nian si yue shier ri Huashang Shanghai shuini gongsi di sanshijiu ci dongshihui huiyi jilu (Minutes of the 39th Meeting of the Board of Directors of the Shanghai Portland Cement Works, Limited on 12th April 1949). *LHS*, v. 1, p. 218.

Yi jiu er liu nian er yue si ri Huashang Shanghai shuini gongsi dai zong jingli Hua Runquan zhi chang jingli Wu Qingtai han (Letter from the acting general manager Hua Runquan to the Shanghai Cement Works manager Wu Qingtai 4th February 1926). *LHS*, v. 1, p. 199.

Yi jiu er san nian shi yi yue ba ri Huashang Shanghai Shuini Gongsi di shiqi ci dongshihui huiyi jilu (Minutes of the 17th Meeting of the Board of Directors of the Shanghai Portland Cement Works Limited on 8th Novemeber 1923). *LHS*, v. 1, p. 168.

Yi jiu er san nian wu yue ba ri Huashang Shanghai Shuini Gongsi di shisi ci dongshihui huiyi jilu (Minutes of the 14th Meeting of the Board of Directors of the Shanghai Portland Cement Works Limited on 8th May 1923). *LHS*, v. 1, p. 165.

Yi jiu er si nian ba yue ershier ri Liu Hongsheng zhi Hankou Zhongfu gongsi Xu Weiyong han (Letter from Liu Hongsheng to Mr. Zu Weiyong of the Hankou Zhongfu Company dated 22nd August 1924). *LHS*, v. 1, p. 188.

Yi jiu er wu nian ba yue sanshi ri Huashang Shanghai shuini gongsi di si jie gudong hui huiyi jilu (Minutes of the 4th Shareholders Meeting of the Shanghai Portland Cement Works, Limited on 30th August 1925). *LHS*, v. 1, p. 189.

Yi jiu er wu nian er yue si ri Yu Shouyi zhi Huashang Shanghai Shuini gongsi han (Letter from Yu Shouyi to Liu Hongsheng dated 4th February 1925). *LHS*, v. 1, p. 189.

Yi jiu er wu nian lu yue ershisi ri Liu Hongsheng zhi Hankou Fuzhong Gongsi han (Letter from Liu Hongsheng to Hankou Fuzhong gongsi 24th June 1925). *LHS*, v. 1, p. 193.

Yi jiu er wu nian qi yue shiwu ri Liu Hongsheng zhi Qixin yanghui gongsi jinli Chen Yipu han (Letter from Liu Hongsheng to the general manager of the Qixin Cement Company on 15th July 1925). *LHS*, v. 1, p. 194.

Yi jiu er wu nian si yue shisan ri Liu Hongsheng zhi Yu Shouyi han (Letter from Liu Hongsheng to Yu Shouyi dated 13th April 1925). *LHS*, v. 1, p. 188.

Yi jiu er wu nian wu yue shisan ri Huangshang Shanghai shuini gongsi di ershi san ci (Minutes of the 23rd Meeting of the Board of Directors of the Shanghai Portland Cement Works Limited on 8th and 13th May 1925). *LHS*, v. 1, p. 189.

Yi jiu er wu nian wu yue shisan ri Huangshang Shanghai shuini gongsi yu Qixin yanghui gonsi (The contract between Shanghai Cement Works Limited with

Qixin Cement Company Limited dated and executed on 13th May 1925). *LHS*, v. 1, p. 190.

Yi jiu san liu nian ba yue ershisan ri Huashang Shanghai shuini gongsi chang jinli Wu Qingtai zai Shanghai yihang gonghui jiyi shetan "Guomin jinri suo ban de shuini gongye" (The talk: "The Cement Industry established by Chinese Nationals" by manager of the Shanghai Portland Cement Works Limited Wu Qingtai on 23rd August 1936). *LHS*, v. 1, p. 157.

Yu Guocheng. Quanguo shuini fenqu xiaoshou yijian (An Opinion on National Sales of Cement by Regional Division), September 1949. Nanjing Archive NRC 28 v. 4 No. 18627.

Yu Guocheng. Ribenren zai dongbei zhi shuini shiye (Japanese cement enterprises in the Northeast), June 1946. Nanjing Archive NRC 28 (2) No. 2957.

Yu Heping and Xia Liangcai, eds. 1999. *Zhou Xuexi ji* (Zhou Xuexi Collection). Wuhan: Huazhong shifan daxue chubanshe.

Yu Lu. Yu Lu gei Zhou Xuexi de zhawen (A brief order to Zhou Xuexi from Yu Lu). *QXGS*, p. 27.

Yuan Hua Shang Shanghai shuini chang gonsi xiangli Xi Anzhai koushu (The oral testimony of the ex-assistant manager of the Shanghai Portland Cement Works, Limited Xi Anzhai) September 1963. *LHS*, v. 1, p. 49.

Yuan Shikai. 1903 nian 3 yue 13 ri Yuan Shikai zhi Wei Ying han (Letter from Yuan Shikai to the General Manager of the Chinese Engineering and Mining Company Limited in China to T. R. Wynne, 13th March 1903). *KMS*, p. 235.

Yuan Shikai. Mian jiao Li Ximing, Kunde shuntiao (Order by hand to Li Ximing and Kunde) 25th May, 1906. *ZXJ*, p. 217.

Yuan Shikai. Yuan Shikai's first memorial to the throne 13th March 1903. *KMS*, pp. 235–237.

Yuan Shikai. Yuan Shikai's second memorial to the throne November 1903. *KMS*, pp. 248–250.

Yuan Shikai. Yuan Shikai's third memorial to the throne, 31st March 1904. *KMS*, pp. 261–262.

Yuan Shikai. Yuan Shikai gei Zhou Xuexi de pishi (Yuan's approval order to Zhou Xuexi) 3rd, October 1906. *QXGS*, p. 35.

Zhiyuan weiyuanhui shuini huiyi ji shencha yijia (The opinion of the NRC meeting and survey), 1947. Nanjing Archive NRC 28 v. 2 No. 8003.

Zhongguo di er lishi dang'an guan (The Second Historical Archives of China), comp. 1986. *Zhonghua Minguo shi dang'an ziliao hui bian: di 4 ji, cong Guangzhou jun zhengfu zhi Wuhan guomin zhengfu* (Republican China: a collection of archival documents, Part 4, From the Guangzhou Military Government to the Wuhan National Government). Nanjing: Jiangsu gu ji chubanshe.

———. 1997. *Zhonghua Minguo shi dangan ziliao hui bian. di 5 ji, di 2 bian. Caizheng jingji* (Republican China: a collection of archival documents, Part 5 v.2, Economic and Finance). Nanjing: Jiangsu guji chubanshe.

Zhongguo Renmin Zhengzhi Xieshang Huiyi quanguo weiyuanhui, Guangdong Sheng weiyuanhui, Guangzhou Shi weiyuanhui wenshi ziliao yanjiu weiyuanhui (The *wenshi zhiliao* research committee of the National Committee, Guangdong Committee & Guangzhou City Committee of the CPPCC). 1986. *Nan tian sui yue: Chen Jitang zhu yue shiqi jianwen shilu* (The days under the southern skies: eyewitness accounts during the rule of Chen Jitang). Beijing: Zhongguo wenshi chubanshe.

Zhongguo shuini gongye tongyehui chensong huiyi jilu ji lijianshi ming ce (The submission of the minutes and officer register of the China Cement Industrial Business Union), April-October 1948. Nanjing Archive NRC 28 v. 2 No. 8003.

Zhonghua Minguo shuini gongye tongye gonghui (The Cement Association of the Republic of China). Guanyu jiejue shuini ye kunnan an (Re: Relieving the difficulties of the cement industry), 30 August 1948. GZCA *zhi/zheng* 32 15:32, pp. 1–7.

Zhou Xuexi. Qixin gongsi chuangban jingguo (What happened in the initial founding of the Qixin company). *QXGS*, p. 27.

Zhou Xuexi. Wei kuangchong yanghui gongsi shi cheng Yuan Shikai wen (Submission to Yuan Shikai concerning matters for the expansion of the cement company), 3rd May 1906. *ZXJ*, p. 215.

Zhou Xuexi. Zhi De Cuilin han (The second letter from Zhou Xuexi to Detring), 15th May 1906. *ZXJ*, p. 217.

Zhou Xuexi. Zhi De Cuilin han (The third letter from Zhou Xuexi to Detring), 28th May 1906. *ZXJ*, p. 218.

Zhou Xuexi. Zhou Xuexi gei Kaiping kuangwu ju de fu xin (The reply from Zhou Xuexi to the Kaiping Coal Mining Company Limited), 15th September 1906. *QXGS*, p. 34.

Zhou Xuexi. 1988. *Zhou Zhi'an Xiansheng Zixu Nianpu* (The Autobiographic Chronicle of Zhuo Xuexi). Taipei: Wenhai.

Zhou Xuexi and Sun Duosen. Chen Yuan Shikai wen (Report to Yuan Shikai), 24th May 1906. *ZXJ*, p. 219.

Zhou Xuexi, Sun Duoxin, Xu Liyang. Bin zhi du Yuan Tangshan yanghui gongsi gufen zhao qi geng ming ni zhang qing zibu lian wen (Reporting to His Highness The Viceroy Yuan Shikai following the full subscription of the share issued pleading the Zhibu to compose draft documents). *QXGS*, p. 228.

Secondary Sources

Alsop, Philip, and James Post. 1995. *Cement Plant Operations Handbook*. Portsmouth: Tradeship Publications Limited.

Bergère, Marie-Claire. 1989. *The Golden Age of the Chinese Bourgeoisie, 1911–1937*. Cambridge: Cambridge University Press.

Berle, Adolf A. Jr. 1928. *Studies in the Law of Corporation Finance*. Chicago: Callaghan and Company.

Berle, Adolf A. Jr., and Gardiner C. Means. 1932. *The Modern Corporation and Private Property*. New York: Macmillan.

Berle, A.A., and G.C. Means. 1968. *The Modern Corporation and Private Property*. New York: Harcourt, Brace & World.

Carlson, Ellsworth C. 1971. *The Kaiping Mines, 1877–1912*. Cambridge, MA: East Asian Research Center, Harvard University; distributed by Harvard University Press.

Chan, Wellington. 1977. *Merchants, Mandarins, and Modern Enterprise in Late Ch'ing China*. Cambridge, MA: East Asian Research Center, Harvard University; distributed by Harvard University Press.

Chandler, Alfred D. Jr.; with the assistance of Takashi Hikino. 1962. *Strategy and Structure: Chapters in the History of the Industrial Enterprise*. Cambridge: M.I.T. Press.

———. 1977. *The Visible Hand: The Managerial Revolution in American Business*. Cambridge, MA; London: Harvard University Press.

———. 1994. *Scale and Scope: The Dynamics of Industrial Capitalism*. Cambridge, MA; London: Belknap Press of Harvard University Press.

Ch'en, Jerome. 1961. *Yuan Shih-kai, 1859–1916: Brutus Assumes the Purple*. London: George Allen & Unwin.

———. 1972. *Yuan Shih-k'ai*. 2nd ed. Stanford, CA: Stanford University Press.

Coble, Parks M. 1980. *The Shanghai Capitalists and the Nationalist Government, 1927–1937*. Cambridge, MA: Council on East Asian Studies, Harvard University Press.

———. 1996. The Kuomintang Regime and the Shanghai Capitalists, 1927–29. In *Chinese Business Enterprise*, ed. R. Ampalavanar Brown. New York: Routledge.

Cochran, Sherman. 1966. Chinese Mediation on the Eve of Modernization. *California Law Review* 54 : 1212–1215.

———. 2000. *Encountering Chinese Networks: Western, Japanese, and Chinese Corporations in China, 1880–1937*. Berkeley, CA: University of California Press.

Cohen, Paul A. 1974. *Between Tradition and Modernity: Wang T'ao and Reform in Late Ch'ing China*. Cambridge, MA: Harvard University Press.

———. 1984. *Discovering History in China: American Historical Writing on the Recent Chinese Past*. New York: Columbia University Press.
Cooke, Colin Arthur. 1950. *Corporation, Trust and Company: An Essay in Legal History*. Manchester: Manchester University Press.
Davies, Paul L. 2003a. *Gower & Davies' Principles of Modern Company Law*. 7th ed. London: Sweet & Maxwell.
Davies, Stephen. 2003b. *Empiricism and History*. Basingstoke: Palgrave Macmillan.
Day, Richard B. June 1976. Dialectical Method in the Political Writings of Lenin and Bukharin. *Canadian Journal of Political Science* 9 (2): 255.
Dicey, Albert Venn. 1902. *Introduction to the Study of the Law of the Constitution*. 6th ed. London: Macmillan and Co.
Ding Shenzun, and Xia Zhuoqiong, eds. 2004. *Guangdong Minguo shi* (The History of Republican Guangdong). Guangzhou: Guangdong renmin chubanshe.
Duan Yunzhang, and Shen Xiaomin. 2003. *Sun Wen yu Chen Jiongming shishi bian nian* (The Historical Chronical of Sun Yat-sen and Chen Jiongming). Guangzhou: Guangdong renmin chubanshe.
Eastman, Lloyd E. 1986. Nationalist China During the Sino-Japanese War 1937–1945. In *The Cambridge History of China*, ed. John K. Fairbank and Albert Feuerwerker. Cambridge: Cambridge University Press.
Esherick, Joseph W. 1987. *The Origins of the Boxer Uprising*. Berkeley: University of California Press.
Fairbank, John K., and Albert Feuerwerker, ed. 1986. *The Cambridge History of China*. Vol. 14. Cambridge: Cambridge University Press.
Fairbank, John K., and Edwin O. Reischauer. 1989. *China: Tradition & Transformation*. Boston: Houghton Mifflin Company.
Faure, David. 2006. *China and Capitalism: A History of Business Enterprise in Modern China*. Hong Kong: Hong Kong University Press.
Feuerwerker, Albert. 1958. *China's Early Industrialization: Sheng Hsuan-huai (1844–1916) and Mandarin Enterprise*. Cambridge, MA: Harvard University Press.
———. 1964. China's Nineteenth-Century Industrialization: The Case of the Hanyehping Coal and Iron Company, Limited. In *The Economic Development of China and Japan*, ed. C. S. Cowan, 79–110. London: Allen & Unwin; reprinted in *Studies in the Economic History of Late Imperial China*. Centre for Chinese Studies, Ann Arbor: The University of Michigan 1995, pp. 165–199.
———. 1967. Industrial Enterprise in Twentieth-Century China: The Chee Hsin Cement Co. In *Approaches to Modern Chinese History*, ed. Albert Feuerwerker, Rhoads Murphy, and M. C. Wright, 304–341. Berkeley: University of California Press; reprinted in *Studies in the Economic History of late Imperial China*. Centre for Chinese Studies, Ann Arbor: The University of Michigan 1995, pp. 273–308.

Francis, A.J. 1978. *The Cement Industry 1796–1914: A history.* Newton Abbot: David and Charles.

Frazier, Mark W. 2002. *The Making of the Chinese Industrial Workplace: State, Revolution, and Labor Management.* Cambridge: Cambridge University Press.

Frederick, Hallis. 1927. An Examination of Some Modern Theories of the Relation of Law and State with Special Reference to the Juristic Doctrine of Corporate Personality: A Study in Jurisprudence. D.Phil. thesis, University of Oxford.

———. 1930. *Corporate Personality: A Study in Jurisprudence.* London: Oxford University Press, H. Milford.

Gang, Jin-a. 2005. 20 shiji 30 niandai Guangdong Sheng de huobi tongyi zhengce de bengkui guocheng (The process of the collapse of the Guangdong provincial unified currency policy). In *Shijie jingji tizhi xia de Minguo shiqi jingji* (The Chinese economy winthin the global economic framework), ed. Zhang Donggang et al., Beijing: Zhongguo caizheng jingji chubanshe.

Gani, Mary S.J. 1997. *Cement and Concrete.* London: Chapman & Hall.

Gerth, Karl. 2003. *China Made: Consumer Culture and the Creation of the Nation.* Cambridge, MA; London: Harvard University Asia Center: Dist. by Harvard University Press.

Gower, L. C. B., J. B. Cronin, A. J. Easson, and Lord Wedderburn of Charlton. June 1956. Some Contrasts between British and American Corporation Law. *Harvard Law Review* 69 (8): 1369–1402.

———. 1979. *Gower's Principles of Modern Company Law.* 4th ed. London: Stevens & Sons.

Green, Stephen, and Guy S. Liu (eds). 2005. *Exit the Dragon? Privatization and State Control in China.* London: Chatham House; Malden, MA: Blackwell.

Guo, Xuyin. 1993. *Guomindang paixi douzheng shi* (The history of factional squabble within the Nationalist Party). Taipei: Guiguan tushu gufen youxian gongsi.

Hao, Qingyuan. 1991. *Zhou Xuexi zhuan* (The story of Zhou Xuexi). Tianjin: Tianjin renmin chubanshe.

He, Ping, and Li Ludian. 1998. *Cen Chunxuan wenji* (The collected writings of Cen Chunxuan). Nanning: Guangxi renmin chubanshe.

Hill, Emily M. 2010. *Smokeless Sugar: The Death of a Provincial Bureaucrat and the Construction of China's National Economy.* Vancouver: UBC Press.

Horowitz, Richard S. 2003. Breaking the Bonds of Precedent: The 1905–6 Government Reform Commission and the Remaking of the Qing Central State. *Modern Asian Studies* 37 : 775–797.

Hou, Chi-ming. 1965. *Foreign Investment and Economic Development in China, 1840–1937.* Cambridge, MA: Harvard University Press.

Hsü, Immanuel C.Y. 2000. *The Rise of Modern China.* 6th ed. New York: Oxford University Press.

Huang, Philip C.C. 1994. Codified Law and Magisterial Adjudication in the Qing. In *Civil Law in Qing and Republican China*, ed. Kathryn Bernhardt and Philip C.C. Huang, 142–186. Stanford, CA: Stanford University Press.

———. 1996. *Civil Justice in China: Representation and Practice in the Qing*. Stanford: Stanford University Press.

———. 2001. *Code, Custom, and Legal Practice in China: The Qing and the Republic Compared*. Stanford: Stanford University Press.

Huang, Ray Renyu. 2008. *Cong da lishi de jiaodu du Jiang Jieshi riji* (Reading the diary of Chiang Kai-shek from a macro history angle). Beijing: Jiuzhou chubanshe.

Huang, Philip C.C., and Kathryn Bernhardt. 1994. *Civil Law in Qing and Republican China*. Stanford, CA: Stanford University Press.

Kirby, William C. Feb. 1995. China Unincorporated: Company Law and Business Enterprise in Twentieth-Century China. *The Journal of Asian Studies* 54 (1): 43–63.

Köll, Elisabeth. 2003. *From Cotton Mill to Business Empire: The Emergence of Regional Enterprises in Modern China*. Cambridge, MA: Harvard University Asia Center; Distributed by Harvard University Press.

Kwong, Luke S.K. 1984. *A Mosaic of the Hundred Days: Personalities, Politics, and Ideas of 1898*. Cambridge, MA: Harvard University Press.

Lai Chi-Kong. June 1994a. China's First Modern Corporation and the State: Officials, Merchants, and Resource Allocation in the China Merchants' Steam Navigation Company, 1872–1902: Papers Presented at the Fifty-Third Annual Meeting of the Economic History Association. *The Journal of Economic History* 54 (2): 432–434.

———. 1994b. Li Hung–chang and Modern Enterprise: The China Merchants Company, 1872–1885. In *Li Hung-chang and China's Early Modernization*, ed. Samuel C. Chu and Kwang-ching Liu, 216–247. New York: M. E. Sharpe Inc.

———. 1996. The Qing State & Merchant Enterprise: The China Merchants' Company, 1872–1902. In *Chinese Business Enterprise*, ed. Raj Ampalavanar Brown. New York: Routledge.

Leonard, Jane Kate, and John R. Watt, ed. 1992. *To Achieve Security and Wealth: The Qing Imperial State and the Economy, 1644–1911*. Ithaca: East Asia Program, Cornell University.

Li Yongsheng. 2005. *Qing Mo Zhong Wai Xiuding Shangye Jiaoshe Yanjiu* (A study of the late Qing Sino-foreign revision of commercial treaties). Tianjin: Nankai daxue chubanshe.

Li Yu. 2007. *Beiyang zhengfu shiqi qiye zhidu jiegou shilun* (On the structure of the corporate system in modern China governed by the northern warlords). Beijing: Shehui kexue wenxian chubanshe.

Li Yumin. 2005. *Zhongguo Fei Yue Shi* (The history of abolishing the Unequal Treaties of China). Beijing: Zhonghua shuju.

Lin Keming. 1987. Guangzhou shizheng jianshe ji xiang zhong dian gongcheng yishu (Several major construction in Guangzhou city's urban development). In *Nan tian sui yue: Chen Jitang zhu yue shiqi jianwen shilu* (The days under the southern skies: eyewitness accounts during the rule of Chen Jitang), ed. Guangzhou Shi zheng xie wenshi ziliao yanjiu weiyuanhui. Guangzhou CPPCC *wenshi ziliao* research committee). Guangzhou: Guangdong renmin chubanshe, Guangdong Sheng Xinhua shudian.

Liu Kunyi, and Zhang Zhidong. 1979. The Joint Proposals of Liu Kunyi and Zhang Zhidong 1901. In *China's Response to the West: A Documentary Survey, 1839–1923*, ed. Ssu-yu Teng and John K. Fairbank, 197–204. Cambridge, MA: Harvard University Press.

Liu Ping. 4 December 2002. Wu Xu bianfa: Shuang shi xiangyu – Zai chuantong he xiandai xing zhi jian: Zhongguo zhishi fenzhi yu xifang chuan jiao shi (The Hundred Day's Reform: The Meeting of Two Men of Letters – Chinese Intellectuals and Western Missionaries in Between Tradition and Modernity). *Xueshuo lianxian* (Academic Discussion Online). http://www.xslx.com/htm/zlsh/zjyj/2002-4-11605.htm. Last accessed 6 April 2007.

Luo Zhaoqian. 2004. *Wang Qing guandu shangban yanjiu* (A study of the late Qing guandu shangban system). Xiamen: Xiamen daxue chubanshe.

MacKinnon, Stephen R. 1980. *Power and Politics in Late Imperial China: Yuan Shi-kai in Beijing and Tianjin, 1901–1908*. Berkeley: University of California Press.

McCraw, Thomas K., ed. 1988. *The Essential Alfred Chandler: Essays toward a Historical Theory of Big Business*. Boston, MA: Harvard Business School Press.

Miller, Arthur S. 1959. Private Governments and the Constitution. In *An Occasional Paper on the Role of the Corporation in the Free Society*. Santa Barbara, CA: Center for the Study of Democratic Institutions.

Ocko, Jonathan K. 1983. *Bureaucratic Reform in Provincial China: Ting Jih-Ch'ang in Restoration Kiangsu, 1867–1870*. Cambridge, MA: Council on East Asian Studies. Harvard University Press.

Paine, S.C.M. 2003. *The Sino-Japanese War of 1894–1895: Perceptions, Power, and Primacy*. Cambridge: Cambridge University Press.

Paton, George Whitecross. 1972. *A Textbook of Jurisprudence*. 4th ed. Oxford: Clarendon Press.

Peng Dunwen. 2007. *Guomin zhengfu dui Ri zhengce ji qi bianhua: cong jiu-yiba shibian dao qi-qi shibian* (The Nationalist government's policy towards Japan and its policy modification. Beijing: Shehui kexue wenxian chubanshe.

Pomerantz-Zhang, Linda. 1992. *Wu Tingfang 1842–1922: Reform and Modernization in Modern Chinese History*. Hong Kong: Hong Kong University Press.

Pomeranz, Kenneth. 1993. *The Making of a Hinterland: State Society and Economy in Inland North China, 1853–1937.* Berkeley: University of California Press.

Pong, David. 1994. *Shen Pao-chen and China's Modernization in the Nineteenth Century.* Cambridge: Cambridge University Press.

Purcell, Victor. 1963. *The Boxer Uprising: a Background Study.* Cambridge: University Press.

Quan Hansheng. 1972. *Hanyeping gongsi shilue* (A brief history of the Hanyeping Company). Hong Kong: Chinese University Press.

Rawlinson, John L. 1967. *China's Struggle for Naval Development, 1839–1895.* Cambridge, MA: Harvard University Press.

Reilly, Thomas H. 2004. *The Taiping Heavenly Kingdom: Rebellion and the Blasphemy of Empire.* Seattle and London: University of Washington Press.

Rhoads, Edward J.M. 1975. *China's Republican Revolution: The Case of Kwangtung, 1895–1913.* Cambridge, MA: Harvard University Press.

———. 2000. *Manchus & Han: Ethnic Relations and Political Power in Late Qing and Early Republican China, 1861–1928.* Seattle; London: University of Washington Press.

Roberts, J.A.G. 2003. *The Complete History of China.* Stroud: Sutton.

Rungta, Shyam Radhe. 1970. *The Rise of Business Corporations in India, 1851–1900.* Cambridge: Cambridge University Press.

Sandler, Todd. 2001. *Economic Concepts for the Social Sciences.* Cambridge: Cambridge University Press.

Sharp, David W. 2003. *A. The Penguin Dictionary of Chemistry.* 3rd ed. London: Penguin.

Shi Changjun. (2003). Qingzhou, Qixin: shui shi zhongguo shuini gongye de faxiang di? (Which plant is the oldest in China's cement industry? Green Island Cement or Chee Hsin Cement?) *Zhongguo Shuini* (China Cement) 11.

Skinner, G. William. Feb 1985. Presidential Address: The Structure of Chinese History. *Journal of Asian Studies* 44 (2): 271–292.

Soule, Mason H., Jeffrey S. Logan, and Todd A. Stewart. March 2002. Toward a Sustainable Cement Industry: Trends, Challenges, and Opportunities in China's Cement Industry. *World Business Council for Sustainable Development.* http://www.wbcsd.org/DocRoot/QnoY08cZaWF2bRC8m4rv/sub_china.pdf; Last accessed 16 June 2009.

Tang Degang. 1998. *Yuan Shi Dang Guo* (Yuan Shikai managing the country). Taipei: Yuanliu chuban shiye gufen youxian gongsi.

Tang Ruixiang. 1993. Dayuanshuai chanjun chu zhi shimintu chang Sun zong ban han (A letter from the Generalissimo military office to the General Manager Mr Sun of the Cement Works). In *Sun Zhongshan yu hufa haijun lunji* (Collected discussions of Sun Yat-sen and the navy for the protection of the Constitution). Guangzhou: Guangdong gaodeng jiaoyu chubanshe.

Teng, Ssu-yü, John K. Fairbank, E-tu Zen Sun, Chaoying Fang, et al. 1954. *China's Response to the West: A Documentary Survey, 1839–1923.* Cambridge: Harvard University Press.

Thomas, Stephen C. 1984. *Foreign Intervention and China's Industrial Development, 1870–1911.* Boulder, Colorado: Westview.

Tsin, Michael. 1999. *Nation, Governance, and Modernity: Canton, 1900–1927.* Stanford, CA: Stanford University Press.

Tung, William L. 1968. *The Political Institutions of Modern China.* 2nd ed. The Hague: M. Nijhoff.

Wakeman, Frederick Jr. 1997. *Strangers at the Gate: Social Disorder in South China, 1839–1861.* Berkeley: University of California Press.

Wang Zhaogang. 2004. *Guomindang xunzheng tizhi yanjiu* (A study of the political tutelage system of the KMT). Beijing: Zhongguo shehui kexue chubanshe.

Wei, Betty Peh Ti. 2005. *Liu Chi-Wen: Biography of a Revolutionary Leader.* Hong Kong: The Liu Chi-Wen Family.

Wong Young-tsu. 2001. *A Paradise Lost: The Imperial Garden Yuanming Yuan.* Honolulu: University of Hawai'i Press.

Wright, Mary C. 1962. *The Last Stand of Chinese Conservatism: The T'ung-Chih Restoration, 1862–1874.* Stanford, CA: Stanford University Press.

Wright, Tim. 1985. The Nationalist State and Regulation of Chinese Industry During the Nanjing Decade: Competition and Control in Coal mining. In *Ideal and Reality: Social and Political Change in Modern China, 1860–1949*, ed. David Pong and Edmund S.K. Fund, 127–152. Lanham: University Press of America.

Xia Dongyuan. 1992. *Yangwu yundong shi* (History of the Self-Strengthening Movement). Shanghai: Huadong shifan daxue chubanshe.

———. 2007. *Sheng Xuanhuai Zhuan* (The biography of Sheng Xuanhuai). Shanghai: Shanghai Jiaotong daxue chubanshe.

Xia Xinhua et al. 2004. *Jindai Zhongguo Xianzheng Licheng: Shiliao Huicui* (Modern Chinese constitutional developments: A selection of historical documents). Beijing: Zhongguo zhengfa daxue chubanshe.

Xiao Zili. 2002. *Chen Jitang.* Guangzhou: Guangdong renmin chubanshe.

Xue Yi. 2005. *Guomin zhengfu ziyuan weiyuanhui yanjiu* (A study of the Resource Committee of the National Government). Beijing: Shehui kexue wenxian chubanshe.

Yang Hongnian, and Ouyang Xin. 2005. *Zhongguo zhengzhi shi* (History of the Chinese political system). Wuchang: Wuhan daxue chubanshe.

Yang Tianshi. 2007. *Jiang Jieshi yu Nanjing guomin zhengfu* (Chiang Kai-shek and the Nanjing Nationalist Government). Beijing: Zhongguo renmin daxue chubanshe.

———. 2008. *Zhaoxun zhenshi de Jiang Jieshi: Jiang Jieshi riji jiedu* (The search for the real Chinag Kai-shek: making sense of Chinag Kai-shek's diary). Hong Kong: Joint Publishing (Hong Kong) Company Limited.

Yang Zaijun. 2006. *Wanqing Gongsi yu Gongsi Zhili* (Company and company management in the late Qing period). Beijing: Shangwu yinshuguan.

Yin Shouhua, Liang Fuliu, and Yang Tinggang. 1986. *Haijun nan xia hufa shimo* (Explaining the southward sailing by the Chinese navy in the movement to protect the constitution). In *Sun Zhongshan sanci zai Guangdong jianli zhengquan* (Sun Yat-sen's three attempts in establishing political authority in Guangdong province), ed. Zhongguo renmin zhengzhi xieshang huiyi quanguo weiyuanhui, Guangdong Sheng weiyuanhui (the Chinese People's Political Consultative Conference), Guangzhou Shi weiyuanhui wenshi ziliao yanjiu weiyuanhui. Beijing: Zhongguo wenshi chubanshe.

Yu Yan'guang, and Chen Fulin. 1989. *Nanyue geju: Cong Long Jiguang dao Chen Jitang* (Establishing a separatist regime in the southern province of Guangdong: from Long Jiguan to Chen Jitang). Guangzhou: Guangdong renmin chubanshe.

Zelin, Madeleine. 2004. A Critique of Rights of Property in Prewar China. In *Contract and Property in Early Modern China*, ed. M. Zelin, J. Ocko, and R. Gardella. Stanford, CA: Stanford University Press.

Zelin, Madeleine, Johnathan Ocko, and Robert Gardella, ed. 2004. *Contract and Property in Early Modern China*. Stanford, CA: Stanford University Press.

Zeng Qingliu. 2003. *Guangzhou guomin zhengfu.* (The Nationalist Government of Guangzhou). Guangzhou: Guangdong renmin chubanshe.

Zhang Houquan. 1988. *Zhaoshang Ju Shi: Jindai Bufen* (The history of China Merchants' Company: the modern period). Beijing: Renmin jiaotong chubanshe.

Zhang Jinfan. 2003. *Zhongguo jindai shehui yu fazhi wenming* (The legal system and modern Chinese society). Beijing: Zhongguo zhengfa daxue chubanshe.

Zhang Xiaohui. 2005. *Minguo shiqi Guangdong shehui jingji shi* (The economic history of Guangdong in the Republican period). Guangzhou: Guangdong renmin chubanshe.

Zhang Xueji. 2005. *Yuan Shikai Mufu* (Yuan Shikai's administrative advisers). Beijing: Zhongguo guangbo dianshi chubanshe.

Zhang Yufa. 2001. *Zhongguo xiandai shi* (Modern history of China). 9th ed. Taipei: Taiwan dong hua shuju gufen youxian gongsi.

Zhang Zhongmin. 2002. *Jiannan de bianqian: jindai Zhongguo gongsi zhidu yanjiu* (The difficult transition and transformation: a study of the modern corporate system in China). Shanghai: Shanghai shehui kexueyuan chubanshe.

Zhao Xingsheng. 2004. *Chuantong jingyan yu xiandai lixiang: Nanjing guomin zhengfu shiqi de guoying gongye yanjiu* (Traditional experience & modern ideals:

A research on the Nanjing Nationalist Government's state enterprises). Jinan: Qilu shushe.

Zhemeisen, *Yingguo gongsi dingli* (Regulations on Companies in England). In *Huangchao jingshiwen sanbian* (State Craft Essays of the Dynasty, third compilation, n.p., preface of 1898), ed. Chen Zhongyi. 39/3b-5b.

Zhong Zhuo'an. 1999. *Chen Jitang* (The warlord Chen Jitang). Guangzhou: Guangdong Sheng ditu chubanshe.

Zhongguo jindai jingji shi ziliao congkan bianji weiyuanhui. 1994. *Xinchou heyue dingli yihou di shangyue tanpan* (The commercial negotiations after the signing of the Boxer Protocol). Beijing: Zhonghua shuju.

Zhu Congbing. 2006. *Li Hongzhang yu Zhongguo tielu: Zhongguo jindai tielu jianshe shiye de jiannan qibu* (Li Hongzhang and Chinese railways: the difficult first step of modern Chinese railway building). Beijing: Qun yan chubanshe.

Index

Note: Page numbers followed by 'n' denote notes

H. Ko, *The Making of the Modern Chinese State*,
DOI 10.1007/978-981-10-2660-7

Q

R

The manufacturer's authorised representative in the EU is Springer Nature Customer Service Centre GmbH, Europaplatz 3, 69115 Heidelberg, Germany. If you have any concerns regarding our products, please contact ProductSafety@springernature.com

Printed and bound by CPI Group (UK) Ltd, Croydon, CR0 4YY

30/09/2026

02225451-0008